AMERICA'S ECONOMIC MORALISTS

AMERICA'S ECONOMIC MORALISTS

A History of Rival Ethics and Economics

Donald E. Frey

STATE UNIVERSITY OF NEW YORK PRESS

Published by
STATE UNIVERSITY OF NEW YORK PRESS, ALBANY

© 2009 State University of New York

For information, contact
State University of New York Press, Albany, NY
www.sunypress.edu

Production by Laurie Searl
Marketing by Michael Campochiaro

Library of Congress Cataloging-in-Publication Data

Frey, Donald E., 1941–
  America's economic moralists : a history of rival ethics and economics / Donald E. Frey.
    p. cm.
  Includes bibliographical references and index.
  ISBN 978-0-7914-9351-9 (hardcover : alk. paper)
  ISBN 978-0-7914-9352-6 (pbk. :alk.paper)
1. Economists—United States—History. 2. Economics—Moral and ethical aspects—
United States. 3. Economics—Sociological aspects—United States. 4. Social ethics—
United States—History. 5. Economics—United States—History. I. Title.
  HB119.A3F73 2009
  174.092'27—dc22

                                                                    2008042320

            10   9   8   7   6   5   4   3   2   1

Contents

Acknowledgments

My thanks are due to the Archives of the Moravian Church in America, Southern Province, for permission to cite their unpublished document, *Brotherly Agreement and Contract of the Evangelische Brüder-Gemeine at Salem in North Carolina*, 1773.

In addition, I thank Wake Forest University for providing two research leaves—one that launched this project several years ago and another that helped to conclude it. I also appreciate the fact that the university and my department have allowed me the freedom to design and teach courses on economics and ethics. Exploring alternative economic moralities with students has helped to clarify my ideas and to find ways to present them succinctly.

ONE

Introduction

TWO MAJOR ECONOMIC moralities have existed as rivals in America since the colonial era. They have a family resemblance, for each is an individualistic ethic. But the two interpretations of economic individualism started with different emphases and have increasingly diverged. One has ordered its vision of economic good around the autonomy of the individual—for example, holding economic self-reliance to be a major virtue. The other has defined the economic good in terms of its contribution to right relations among individuals— for example, holding that property rights exist to serve the wider human community in addition to serving the owner.

Two colonial Americans illustrate these alternatives. Benjamin Franklin worried that his fellow colonials were not self-reliant enough and far too ready to become parasites on others, or government. His Poor Richard maxims advocated virtues that would contribute to long-term economic independence. The economic welfare of the self was the goal of his value system. At about the same time, the Quaker John Woolman invoked the biblical notion of human kinship to think about economic morality. Woolman held that humans so valued the respect of others that living in intentionally dependent ways would never prove attractive. He attributed poverty to unjust relations among people rather than innate dependency. The poor, he held, if given the chance, would work even more than their creator intended.

These rival economic moralities have not stood alone, but have drawn support from rival economic theories. For example, in the early nineteenth century, major economic thinkers widely accepted that resources were scarce (despite America's abundant natural resources). Not surprisingly, self-reliance, competitiveness, and thrift—the virtues of autonomy—were favorites among people whose attention was captured by scarcity. For their part, relational moralists drew support from different economic theory and trends that emphasized potential abundance. The story of economic morality presented in

1

this volume will show how economic moralities have partnered with compatible economic theories.

The ideas of moralists are the subject of this volume. Religious and economic writers are prominent. However, as seen in the case of Franklin, many other professions are represented as well. It is not the case that all the moralists from one profession favor one of the rival moralities, while all from another profession favor the other morality. Autonomy and relational morality have drawn support from all professions. Not all the moralists have been *systematic* moralists in the sense of fully elaborating an economic ethic; many have contributed a part or two to one or the other of the two major moralities. Among these have been a few inconsistent moralists, who failed to see the illogic of attempting simultaneously to affirm parts of the two rival moralities. Some, particularly economists, have been *unintentional* moralists; yet, when a piece of economic theory aligns with certain moral values, while implying other values to be inconsistent with what is economically possible, such a theory becomes relevant to economic morality.

This is a story, predominantly, of American moralists; when others are represented, it is because they add a crucial bit to the story and were influential among Americans. When the focus occasionally shifts to a school of thought, or the values of a group, I have used secondary interpreters more than when dealing with individual moralists, whose own words I normally favor. It has been impossible to survey the work of every moralist or school. Those who have had a great impact in the wider culture, or who have been especially significant in stating a particular case, have been preferred over others. Given the richness of the subject, it would have been a miracle if every economic moralist fit into the framework I propose—autonomy morality and relational morality, with their partner economic theories. However, even granting exceptions, I believe the proposed framework is robust; indeed, some apparent exceptions are moralists who were simply inconsistent. A few of these hard-to-fit-in moralists are treated in chapter appendices, in footnotes, or as commentators assessing the major figures.

As this broad selection of authors suggests, this volume understands economic morality to be a society's articulated values—not narrow codes of professional ethics, formal philosophical ethics, or the even highly formal "normative" statements of neoclassical welfare economics. In other nations, socialist ethics often would deserve significant coverage. In the United States, however, socialism has served mainly as a critique of the more viable ethical contenders, which are both individualistic, and so socialism is the focus of but one chapter.

References to particular economic events, actors, or institutions are subordinate to the explanation of moral ideas. That said, the book recognizes the significant impacts of abolitionism, Darwinism, and the 1930s Depression on economic morality. However, even in these cases, the emphasis remains on how these events influenced moral and economic ideas.

THE MAJOR THEMES

The alternative moralities have spun out alternative versions of key ethical constructs such as: the proper role of self-interest in economic life; the nature of economic rights, obligations, and government; the nature of economic virtues; the moral status of economic inequality; the mandate for human dignity; and the moral boundaries to economic activity. Taken together, these constructs imply alternative notions of the economic good. Before turning to these issues, we first consider how the two major moralities partner with economic theories.

ECONOMIC ETHICS AND ECONOMIC THEORY

Any economic morality must make sense in terms of some economic theory if for no other reason than that no one can be morally obliged to do that which is believed impossible in terms of existing knowledge. Classical political economy, for example, defined economics in terms of self-interested humans operating in a world characterized by the law of diminishing returns and other manifestations of scarcity. Belief in pervasive natural scarcity made poverty seem inevitable and so minimized any obligation for individuals or society to alleviate or cure it. Thus, in this view, advocates of poor relief not only proposed infringing individual freedoms by imposing (tax) obligations to care for others, but they were ignorant of economic laws. Social Darwinism later reiterated the same outlook using the new terminology of evolution. By the twentieth century, economics kept scarcity front and center, by shifting from an absolute to relative scale: resources were always short relative to the insatiable wants of individuals. This theory strongly complemented the values of autonomy ethics.

Relational moralists, including some economists, resisted from the start the notion of natural scarcity and of economic laws as expressions of rational responses to scarcity. They thought the evidence for such laws was weak and rejected the very idea of a stingy nature. These moralists have been more impressed with trends in mass production, invention, and technical innovation. Relational moralists have tended to view economics as a study of relatively free human choices, not of economic behavior tightly constrained by facts of nature and by the logic of scarcity. Scarcity, they argued, originated with imperfect human institutions, and they understood self-interested behavior as the response to insecurity created by such faulty institutions. A related theme of these economists has been that self-interested actions can disrupt the *systemic* operations of the economy. Alexander Hamilton, a man of wide experience, insisted that economic institutions are human inventions that can always be improved for the social good. In more recent times, John Kenneth Galbraith attacked the "conventional wisdom" of scarcity, which put high value on private production, no matter the cost to society.

Moralities, then, partner with compatible economic doctrines or economic worldviews. A morality that defines right and wrong with respect to
the autonomy, or unrestricted freedom, of the individual also tends to see self-
interest as a rational reaction to natural scarcity. In this view, moral values that
fail to respect harsh economic realities may be dismissed as unscientific sentimentality. Conversely, a morality that affirms obligation and rights in a wider
community tends to understand economic life in terms of human institutions
and relationships. Relational moralists see faulty human institutions, not natural scarcity, as the fundamental economic constraint. We turn next to several
persistent differences between the rival moralities.

CONFLICTING INTERPRETATIONS OF SELF

A positive interpretation of self-interest, owing much to the secular European Enlightenment, achieved a secure place in nineteenth-century America. Enlightenment ideas of individual autonomy built on the individualism
already present in colonial religion, which had emphasized work, success,
and private property—and viewed government as a potential usurper of
individual rights. This colonial code was secularized and sharpened by early
economists.

As individualistic as colonial Puritans were, however, they were always
suspicious of the unbridled self. Their doctrine of sin held that the individual is always tempted to exalt the self to the exclusion of God and others.
Unlike the Enlightenment economist Adam Smith, who optimistically
fused self-interest and the public good, the Puritan ethic always saw self and
neighbor as potentially at odds. This difference in outlooks continued, and
erupted in the debate over slavery prior to the Civil War: abolitionists consistently advanced a Protestant moral psychology that feared the slave
owner's power would lead invariably to abuses as he tried to satisfy an ego
that in principle was insatiable. Conversely, anti-abolitionists often portrayed the slave owner as rationally pursuing economic interests to which
abuse was counterproductive.

The major American economic moralities are both individualistic. Relational morality understands the individual self to exist within a web of relationships, which defines the self and confers social rights and obligations. Further, in this view, human kinship also implies an ability of people to
comprehend each other and conduct meaningful moral discourse. Because
relationships persist, this morality has a historical perspective. Conversely,
autonomy morality makes freedom to advance one's interests the linchpin of
ethics. As this morality has matured, it has heightened the importance of individual differences so much that moral dialogue and consensus have been portrayed as almost impossible; thus the maximization of individual freedom
appears the only viable social choice. Nor surprisingly, the economic theories

favored by autonomy moralists have emphasized how individuals maximize their welfare by their choices in market contexts. Such theories tend to emphasize logic over historical components.

ECONOMIC OBLIGATIONS, RIGHTS, AND GOVERNMENT

Any economic morality must ultimately decide how the individual ought to relate to the community and cooperate for the common good. Government is a major agent of cooperation; it enforces (or defines) rights and obligations. Autonomy morality paradoxically has seen government simultaneously as necessary protector of individual economic rights and potential infringer of those very rights. Autonomy moralists sometimes propose the market as an alternative mechanism for organizing society, minimizing the technical or moral problems of markets while questioning the efficacy of governmental alternatives. Further, what appear to some to be deficiencies of market economies—such as large inequalities of income or of wealth—may not be failures at all when viewed through the lens of autonomy ethics. Inequality may be the crucial incentive that provokes individual effort and social progress.

Relational economic moralists, on the other hand, infer economic obligations and rights from human interrelatedness. The premise of a deep human kinship also implies the possibility of moral dialogue and agreement on what constitutes the economic good. As an instrument to act on moral consensus, government plays a positive role. Even in an era when governments typically served the king's private interests, and made no pretense to serve the greater good, William Penn's *Frame of Government* criticized governmental minimalists "that think there is no other use for government than correction," holding that in reality "affairs more soft and daily necessary make up much the greater part of government" (in Penn 1957, 110).

ECONOMIC VIRTUES

Benjamin Franklin's Poor Richard maxims provide a good example of the virtues of autonomy morality: self-reliance was at the center, surrounded by a host of minor virtues, such as thrift, honoring one's debts, and careful management. These virtues had utilitarian value in a world of scarcity, as did competitive and entrepreneurial behaviors. Such autonomy morality had a strong utilitarian bent, for virtue is what leads to the higher welfare of the individual. Thus, Franklin could argue for honesty in commerce because it led to success. Autonomy ethics makes tolerance a virtue: with people focused on their own economic welfare, they have little or no concern for the economic choices of others provided these do not impinge on someone else.

Stated abstractly, virtue in relational ethics is that which affirms the common dignity of members of a community. The virtues of relational moralists tend to have a familiar ring, because they echo traditional religious values:

respect for the "image of God" in others, love of neighbor, compassion for the weak. A recurring virtue in the writing of relational moralists, starting with figures such as William Penn, is self-restraint—knowing when too much injures relationships—whether in pressing one's advantage in competition, or in consuming luxuries, or exploiting nature. Relational morality also has seen virtue in historical processes, such as democratic discourse and consensus, from which common values have emerged.

INEQUALITY AND POVERTY

Economic inequality and poverty are intertwined issues that well illuminate the nature of a value system. Early autonomy moralists attributed most poverty to the choices of the poor themselves; their allies, early economists, argued that pervasive scarcity made poverty inevitable. Either interpretation minimized the ethical responsibility of others toward those poor. Later in the nineteenth century, Social Darwinists used evolutionary terminology to restate much the same argument. In the twentieth century, welfare economists rejected any scientific case for greater income equality because, they said, any sense of gain by the poor from more income was merely subjective, not measurable fact. Economic science could not pierce the veil of subjectivity because individuals were too different from each other. Autonomy morality consistently held that inequality has a positive role, as an incentive for economic effort.

If—as early Quakers, abolitionists, and others held—the metaphor of kinship was central to moral thought, then great inequality would not be tolerated: members of a family share the same standard of living. And kin can understand each other; thus the benefits of higher incomes for the poor can be known. Further, poverty simultaneously blights individual human dignity and the relationships binding poor members of the community to others. Similarly, work is understood to be a powerful form of participation in, and connection to, the community; thus, the insecurity threatened by poverty is not needed to induce people to work.

HUMAN DIGNITY

Human dignity—and the impact of economics on human dignity—is as morally significant as inequality. Indeed, the two issues are closely related since vast inequalities may demean human dignity and deny kinship. The roots of the ideal of human dignity lie in the biblical tradition, which asserts that humans are made in the image of God; however, this ideal has been affirmed for other, nonreligious reasons. Harriet Beecher Stowe's abolitionist novel attacked the slave system because its callous disregard of slaves' family relationships demeaned their human dignity. A later economist, Arthur Okun, held that membership in a human community, as such, should bestow certain economic rights that need not be earned. This is a consistent position of relational moralists.

Autonomy moralists have resisted the notion of innate human dignity, for a social acknowledgment of dignity implies rights that some people might exercise. Such rights inevitably imply economic obligations on government. To meet its obligations, government might extract taxes from citizens; such levies infringe the autonomy of those asked to pay. Instead, autonomy ethicists see dignity as something to be earned by individuals through their personal efforts. Autonomy moralists seek independence from imposed obligations to others; dignity exists in respecting the individual's independence, one's autonomy.

The doctrine of innate human dignity raises the issue of material incentives. If dignity confers rights, say, to a minimum standard of living, such rights harm the incentive to work and save. Such negative incentives are often cited by autonomy moralists opposed to expansive definitions of human dignity. Conversely, relational moralists tend to discount material incentives. People work to contribute to the human community of which they are an integral part; participation in the community is essential to individuals, apart from incentives.

THE MORAL BOUNDARIES TO ECONOMICS

An economic morality must decide where to locate the boundaries of economic behavior, or whether economic behavior should be bounded at all. Moral boundaries appear in various forms as the following questions illustrate. What kinds of markets are consistent with a society's values, and which are out-of-bounds? Should society permit markets for vice, or sales of children, or of slaves? What are the boundaries of individual, self-interested economic behavior—does anything go, or may a person be prevented from demeaning himself or herself for profit? Should income inequality in principle be unlimited, or are there moral limits?

Autonomy moralists have long answered the question of limits with one principle: that no person's self-interested action may impinge on another's self-interest. Without reciprocal respect for others' rights, a system of self-interest breaks down. However, as logically true as this is, the moral *psychology* of the autonomous person may resist it. The truly autonomous person might not curb self-seeking behavior simply because such behavior might harm the system that permits it to take place. In this sense, autonomy morality is not self-constraining. Even Adam Smith believed that his proposed system of "natural liberty," motivated by economic self-interest, lacked internal restraint and needed externally imposed "laws of justice." Autonomy morality historically has demanded the improbable: asking the free self to restrain the self.

Conversely, boundaries to economic behavior are intrinsic to relational morality. In the most fundamental sense, excesses tend to harm human relationships, which are crucial to both the individual and community. The abolitionists made the case against slavery on the grounds that it destroyed the normal human relationships of the slaves and so denied their moral stature (which they exhibited in heroic efforts to save those very relationships).

THE NATURE OF THE GOOD ECONOMY

If the freedom, or autonomy, of the individual is the highest good, then individuals are left to define their notions of the good economy, based on personal preferences. Looked at this way, there is no single good economy, but a host of personal answers as to what economy is best for self. Autonomy morality may transcend what appears to be moral relativism by focusing on the whole economic system: the good economy would be designed to allow the greatest economic autonomy to individuals. The good economy would place the fewest constraints on individual economic freedom; as much as possible would be accomplished through voluntary market transactions. These moralists recently have added that such an unconstrained environment will free human creativity, increase efficiency, and so produce abundance, which will benefit all.

Relational morality makes human dignity, as perfected in community, its highest good. Individuals live in a reciprocal relationship with the larger community, contributing to the economic life but also receiving guarantees against want and insecurity. Because human dignity exists in more dimensions than just the economic, the good economy may tolerate some inefficient economic arrangements if such arrangements support other values, such as those found in traditional ways of life or in the history of a community. That is, the multiple dimensions of human life warn against measuring an economy's goodness only by its efficiency. The good economy would affirm the equal value of each member with rights and obligations. It also would reflect common, consensus values that emerge because people, as human kin, engage in meaningful dialogue. Finally, members of the good economy will know when "enough is enough," because the meaning of their lives is defined with regard to others.

AN OVERVIEW OF CHAPTERS

Chapter 2 details how individualism in faith and economic life grew from the soil of Calvinistic colonial religion. Nevertheless, this religious individualism never could be reduced to pure self-interest, which ignored God and neighbor. The Protestant work ethic always related economic activity to what was understood as its proper end: the glory of God and the welfare of others, not exclusively the betterment of the self. Both colonial Puritan and Quaker moralists saw the economic life as part of a set of fuller human relationships. During the eighteenth century, however, the emphasis on the relational aspects of economic life dissolved. Chapter 3 relates how Cotton Mather and Benjamin Franklin, in different ways, emphasized more strongly self-interested, utilitarian motives. By 1800, many American colleges were teaching the "theological utilitarianism" of William Paley, which treated ethics as an economic exercise, a spiritual cost-benefit calculation.

Chapter 4 outlines laissez-faire in the early nineteenth century as a comprehensive, interlocking set of economic and moral ideas that clashed with the evangelical ethic of American Protestantism. Yet, Francis Wayland of Brown University managed to wed laissez-faire with the evangelical ethic. This unlikely union combined self-interested moral autonomy with post-Puritan Protestantism, which at its core feared the sinful potential of self-interest.

The next two chapters tell of some early critics of laissez-faire theory and ethics. Chapter 5 sketches individual opponents of laissez-faire: Alexander Hamilton, perhaps because he had too much actual experience in finance and economics, was skeptical of the economics of laissez-faire; Daniel Raymond, a post-Puritan intellectual, rejected Adam Smith's optimistic view of self-interest as an economic motive; and Horace Mann, who pioneered universal public education, expressed the vision of a moral commonwealth relating all persons in mutual obligation. The obligation of society, Mann said, was to foster a child's full human potential through education; the implied alternative was a stunting of human potential as children labored in factories and fields. Chapter 6 examines the colonial and federal-period Moravians, who conducted a decades-long struggle to maintain their religious-socialist values and practices against the encroaching values of individualism and private enterprise.

Chapter 7 turns to the abolition movement, which insisted that moral boundaries must be set around markets, that some things must *never* be bought and sold. Abolitionists made innate human dignity a moral norm that economic institutions must respect, never violate. Harriet Beecher Stowe's famous novel portrayed the moral stature of slaves struggling to preserve family relationships within a system that systematically destroyed those relationships for economic reasons. Though many autonomy moralists also condemned slavery, they did not do so on the pathbreaking ground that the impact of economic arrangements on human dignity should become a moral standard by which to measure those arrangements.

Chapter 8 tells, first, how early Social Darwinists restated earlier laissez-faire values in a new vocabulary. In passing, they taught that the only dignity a person deserved was what he or she could earn. However, Andrew Carnegie, a self-proclaimed Social Darwinist, harbored the suspicion that the winners of the economic struggle didn't really do it all alone—and owed something to their community. He advocated philanthropy, which he believed could be consistent with Social Darwinism, but in so doing may have created an incompatible mixture. Finally, iconoclastic Thorstein Veblen argued that the American business class was an evolutionary dead end, not the embodiment of economic fitness. The values of that class, he said, did not represent contemporary realities.

Chapter 9 turns to those around the end of the nineteenth century who attempted to turn economic ethics in a new direction. Henry George rejected the premise that poverty was inevitable, instead attributing it to perverse forms of land ownership. Richard Ely, a founder of the American Economic Association, worked to show that laissez-faire doctrines lacked empirical evidence; as a religious liberal, he noted that laissez-faire economics resembled in many ways the rigid doctrines of religion he rejected. John Bates Clark had a vision of dynamic economic change that provided hope for a better life to workers. Ironically, Clark's vision rendered irrelevant one of his own proposals about the nature of wage justice.

Chapter 10 traces the convergence of Protestant Social Gospel and Catholic social thought toward the close of the nineteenth century and start of the twentieth. The Social Gospel had roots in German liberal religion and argued that *individual* morality was inadequate in large economic systems, which created their own moral cultures. It proposed that economics should be judged by its impact on human dignity. Drawing from Pope Leo XIII's encyclical *On the Condition of Labor*, the American Monsignor John Augustine Ryan used human-dignity arguments to endorse a minimum living wage, which he lived to see legislated in the 1930s. Both Protestant and Catholic social thought converged on the status of workers, with special concern for the impact of wage rates and working conditions on the weakest members of the labor force.

Chapter 11 recounts how the 1920s witnessed the popular revival of economic individualism, and the early expressions of prosperity theology. After 1929 and the Depression, the ethics of self and success lost popular credibility as millions found individual virtue rewarded only with economic insecurity; people confronted the possibility that they had much in common. New Deal programs, for the first time, acknowledged a social responsibility to counteract wide-scale economic insecurity. Paul Samuelson, American interpreter of a new macroeconomic theory forged in the Depression, emphasized that the economy was a system prone to systemic ills, whose cures were now understood. With the ability to direct the economic system, new importance was assigned to the social values that might guide the direction taken.

Chapter 12 examines what happened as some economists sought to make economics more scientific and value-free. Welfare economists tried to rank economic improvements by observing only changes in the welfare reported by highly autonomous individuals. In the end, they decided that such observations could rank an efficient economy better than an inefficient one. Otherwise, they failed to answer most significant moral questions about economic goodness. Their effort to be scientific led to an excessive agnosticism about people: desiring to assume as little as possible, they ruled out-of-bounds much knowledge that (many would assert) *can* be known about people. About this time, University of Chicago economists made a virtue of the welfare economists' limited method, declaring that self-interested rationality of the autonomous individual provided the only necessary premise for defining the economic good. The chapter ends with results from experimental economics that seriously challenge this premise.

Post–World War apologists for capitalist values are the subjects of chapter 13. Friedrich Hayek's *Road to Serfdom* attacked central planning, which served as his foil for capitalism. He argued that highly individualistic people could never reach consensus on any common action; any central plan, therefore, could be imposed only against the will of most people. Libertarian Milton Friedman stretched the doctrine of autonomy, applying it to businesses, which, he said, should reject calls for socially responsible actions other than efficiently earning a profit. Michael Novak, a self-described lay theologian, portrayed capitalism as congruent with his interpretation of Christianity within a democratic society.

Chapter 14 turns to recent critics of neoclassical economics, the partner of autonomy ethics. John Kenneth Galbraith argued that American economics was biased by the continued existence of nineteenth-century "conventional wisdom," which kept the realm of purely private activity too large. Arthur Okun argued that some economic efficiency must be traded away in order to enhance human dignity with economic rights and greater income equality. The philosopher John Rawls showed that the self-interested utilitarianism, favored by economists, could produce far more egalitarian norms than traditional economists typically endorsed. This cast serious doubt on how well economists had interpreted their own preferred moral frame of reference. Nobel-winner in economics Amartya Sen argued that the self-interested "economic man" was a one-dimensional character, unworthy to be used as a representative human when thinking morally.

Chapter 15 presents an ecumenical array of late twentieth-century religious thinkers on economic morality. Most found modern autonomy morality to present an impoverished understanding of humanity and to undermine both human and natural environments. And all placed high moral importance on ideas and institutions undergirding the values of community.

In chapter 16 the responses of the rival ethics to the major questions of economic morality are restated. The chapter also reprises the work of those moralists who tried, in one way or another, to mediate between the rival moralities—usually creating more problems than they solved. On analysis, one sees that relational individualism is already a coherent middle position between autonomous individualism and nonindividualistic ethics, such as socialism. This chapter closes with an assessment of the prospects for the two rival moralities. Autonomy morality has appealed in pluralistic America because it is inherently tolerant of individual behavior, and it has been associated with a productive economic system. Yet, in recent decades, such tolerance has permitted excesses to develop in economic life; these excesses threaten only to increase. Conversely, relational morality provides the rationale for social constraints on practices that produce such excesses. At the same time, environmental and ecological concerns have created a new awareness of the relatedness of humans with each other and nature itself.

TWO

Colonial Faith

Work, Wealth, and the Wider Welfare

THE AMERICAN COLONIAL period largely overlapped the English Enlightenment, during which British thinkers puzzled over the role of self-interest in ethics and society. Over the course of a century, self-interest was transformed from a being viewed as a social problem into the driving force behind economic welfare (Myers 1983). Prior to the English Enlightenment, Puritan thinkers had confronted self-interest as a moral and religious problem. Self-interest was of acute interest for Puritans, because their faith was highly individualistic and even contained a component of economic individualism. Self-interest of some degree is inherent in individualism.

Max Weber's well-known *The Protestant Ethic and the Spirit of Capitalism* (1930) has been interpreted by some to say that Puritanism was little more than a religious prologue to Adam Smith's proclamation in 1776 that self-interest was the great source of private and social good.[1] However, this ignores that the Calvinist Puritan divines saw a sinful dimension to self-interest to which the more secular Enlightenment thinkers were blind. Puritans believed that even morally acceptable self-interest was always on the brink of transforming itself, within the human soul, into an evil twin, self-centeredness that crowded out God and neighbor. Of course, the boundary between morally acceptable self-interest and sinful self-centeredness was bound to shift. And so, the descendants of the early Puritans were to increase greatly the realm of acceptable self-interest in economics (see chapters 3, 4). This chapter, however, deals with those early colonials who worried about the moral status of self-interest.

Quakers of the middle colonies shared the intense religious individualism, dissenting spirit, and capitalistic orientation of the New England Puritans (and some scholars include them on the Puritan spectrum). And they, too, wrestled with self-interest. Puritans used the common good as a counterweight to run-away self-interest. The Friends refined the common good to portray it as the good of the human family. The metaphor of human kinship meant that the self was not autonomous—one was always part of a family.

Puritan and Quaker versions of the Protestant ethic influenced a relatively large proportion of Americans. As late as 1776, three-fourths of Americans were of a Puritan heritage and perhaps another fifteen percent shared Calvinist views (Ahlstrom 1972, 124). The articulated values of the South were no exception. Virginians were "so thoroughly Protestant as to be virtually indistinguishable from the Puritan" (Miller 1956, 106).

THE PURITAN ETHIC AND MODERN INDIVIDUALISM

Puritans had a distinct biblical and theological frame of reference, and they did not easily tolerate those who would not conform to that frame. This well-known intolerance tends to obscure the fact that Puritan thought, *within* its frame of reference, was highly individualistic. Despite its own authoritarian tendencies, Puritanism justified freedom of individuals from old authority and traditional constraints. At the same time, Puritan moralists insisted that individualism did not amount to autonomy, lack of obligation to God and neighbor.

As Calvinists, Puritans believed that God graciously elected persons to the salvation gained by Christ, and that no human or institution—not church, clergy, sacraments, or a system of good deeds—could alter the divine election. In short, humans truly faced God's mercy or justice as *individuals*. No longer subordinate to religious intermediaries, the person was truly an individual before God. The rejection of human authority in religion easily extended itself in other directions. Among Puritans, empirical science, which was practiced by individuals doing self-designed experiments, replaced the rationalistic and deductive approaches of church-approved medieval natural philosophy (see Merton 1938, 71). Freed of such authority, the mind could examine God's work in the world for itself—just as the individual could interpret God's word in scripture for itself. Despite this love of empiricism, the earliest Puritans still inhabited a prescientific world: they were sure the infant science would simply confirm the outlook of holy scripture; events in the world (e.g., famine or abundance) were attributed to God.

Individualism in faith and science was complemented by economic individualism. Whether among the elect or not, each person, according to Puritan belief, was called by God to an individual vocation. Just as the individual mind could see God's work in science, or God's word in scripture, it could seek his will for one's own vocation. A vocation served to glorify God by serving others in worldly activity. Worldly activity was the only valid way to serve others, for religious vocations with an intermediary church, which in Catholicism had been preferred, had lost their significance as a way to salvation. And a personally assigned vocation raised the significance of both the individual receiving the assignment from God and the work itself.

That one might earn for oneself and also glorify God and serve others in a vocation tended to give divine warrant to self-interest. Yet, Puritans believed self-love that went so far as to shut out God and neighbor was the fundamental sin. Ideally, one would serve the neighbor and glorify God as well as serve one's own legitimate needs with a productive vocation. This was a relational individualism, in which one's vocation was service to the community, not purely service of the self.

Moral character and personal discipline were exceptionally important within this theological framework. While good character could never win salvation, good character was thought to come naturally to the elect. And one's vocation provided a channel to manifest good character. Many of the minor virtues, such as diligence, thrift, careful management, sobriety—what Max Weber called the ascetic virtues—advanced one in a calling. The emphasis on inner character marked by the ascetic virtues left little room for frivolous diversions or external adornment—which gave the traditional view of very serious Puritans.

Puritan relational morality was stated in terms of *obligation*, or duty to obey God's moral law, which was revealed and recorded in scripture and spelled out details of proper relational behavior. Ideally, the Puritan was motivated by duty to the will of God, not the selfish hope for reward—temporal or spiritual. While it might be true, as Benjamin Franklin would later note, that certain virtues enhance one's business prospect, that consideration was not supposed to be the motive for virtuous living. That upright character was required to glorify God and serve fellow humans was reason enough. Obligation extended to both the elect and others. And obligations might be enforced on recalcitrants.

Puritanism was an activist and reforming faith. This was inherent in the Puritan's Calvinist understanding of God's will as the truly sovereign reality; all else was conditional and relative. And, what was conditional and relative was always subject to change and reform. Puritans, as well known, believed they discerned God's will (often in the Old Testament), and did not hesitate on that basis to purify an old society—or establish a holy commonwealth in the New World. While this proved to be a formula for self-righteousness and intolerance, the Puritans, at their best, acknowledged that their own commonwealths also stood under the judgment of God.

Finally, from their familiarity with scripture and from their discerning God's will for society, Puritans developed a profound sense of God's action in history. And they sensed their role in God's history, which was "a drama in which they were the actors" (Bainton 1952, 252). Thus one's economic role was always projected against a history of people that gave it meaning that transcended merely private needs and wants.

THE INNER LOGIC OF THE PURITAN ETHIC

The Puritan calling produced an economic individualism in parallel to its theological individualism.[2] Personal responsibility to God was the root of Puritan economic ethics as well as of faith. The English Puritan William Perkins (1558–1602), in a work published between 1626 and 1631, admonished that each person should understand the calling "in which God hath placed him, to be best of all callings for him" (Perkins, in Morgan 1965, 54). That is, God—not tradition, ancestry, or even personal desire—placed one in a vocation. This singled the individual out by God in a way that paralleled God's election of individuals to salvation. It also put a divine endorsement on all productive callings, and implied individual responsibility to perceive and fulfill the calling. Indeed, with the loss of an intermediary church as a way to salvation, religious callings lost any special significance; among Protestants, for example, mendicant monks were actually viewed as following an unproductive, even antisocial, calling.

Perkins's statement was hardly an unambiguous endorsement of individualism in the modern sense. In Perkins's view, God did the "placing" of someone in a calling—the individual was not the chooser. Perkins also said that God assigned vocations on the basis of what was best for the individual. Yet, this quote from Perkins could be read in a more socially conservative way, as requiring one to assume that one's work *must* be for the best if God assigned it. This would stifle vocational restlessness based on self-improvement motives. Perkins indeed may have exerted such a conservative influence on Puritan thought (Bernstein 1997, 84). Nevertheless, that Perkins had conservative instincts makes his statements all the more compelling: in speaking of vocation, he addressed the individual and did not invoke human authority. While the individual was obediently to accept God's choice, the perceiving of God's will was the job of the individual. Perkins also cited the diversity of individuals' gifts, and implied a fit between personal calling and personal gifts—again, an individualistic emphasis. For its era, this was an exceptionally individualistic approach.

Puritans looked favorably on economic success, another characteristic of individualistic values. Max Weber, in his classic work on the Protestant ethic, even argued (somewhat controversially) that Puritans looked to vocational success as a sign that one was among the elect. At a minimum, many Puritans held that success was a sign that one had read God's calling aright. The seedbed for self-interested, capitalist values clearly existed in Puritan thought.

The Puritan clergy, however, tempered this with relational ethics. Puritan divines balanced the goodness of a calling for the self with warnings about its potential to serve selfishness—a turning away from the true purpose of a vocation to serve the common good. Theologian William Ames (1576–1633) enjoined his readers to have in the soul "moderation in the desire of gaine" (Ames 1643, 250). Ames balanced his endorsements of economic activism with a call for moderation, or restraint of selfishness. William Perkins, too, subordinated the vocational calling to the *general* calling to the gospel (Bernstein 1997, 83–84). And the gospel emphasized relationships: love of God and love of neighbor. While endorsing habits that tended to economic success, the Puritan divines always tied those habits to obligation to others. For example, thrift, which denied self to find the excess resources to serve others, was a virtue, but thrift spurred by a miserly spirit was condemned (Ames 1643, 254–55). One's own prosperity was never the sole goal.

Puritan individualism was other-oriented, beginning with one's own family. Governor John Winthrop in 1630 declared a person "worse than an Infidell [*sic*]" who neglected his family (Winthrop, in Morgan 1965, 79). Puritan morality started with responsibility for one's immediate family and radiated outward. Individualism was thus rooted in a relational context. One commentator cites Perkins and Ames to the effect that moral responsibilities are determined by relationships and extend outward from closer to further relationships (Wright 1992, 25–26). The Puritan vision of responsible relationships had limits; relationships with others did not necessarily extend outward indefinitely. After all, there were political and theological boundaries to the Puritans' holy commonwealths. Yet, in principle, the individual should have perceived extensive responsibilities for others, even if limited to the Puritan domain. Those who did not honor such responsibilities were condemned by the moralist Perkins (in Morgan 1965, 39) and the moralist Cotton (1641, 447).

The danger of self-interest was fundamental because it resulted directly from the fall of Adam. Governor Winthrop stated the orthodox position by noting that Adam's fall resulted directly in humans acquiring the sinful principle of exclusive self-love—that is, the principle of selfishness, which tears apart the human community (in Morgan 1965, 86). Self-love, selfishness, was sin itself. Here, then, was an individualism that inherently valued the self. However, the Puritan notion of sin always warned against self-absorption, which destroyed one's relationship to God and neighbor—a classic, religious statement of relational individualism.

PURITAN ECONOMIC PRACTICES AND INSTITUTIONS

Economic life is complex, requiring all kinds of arrangements (such as private property) and raising all kinds of problems (such as economic inequality) that the Puritan economic ethic had to address. Puritan moralists always kept the central principle in view: economic arrangements that served individual interests existed in the divine economy also to preserve the common good. That is, given the reality of sin, God made concessions, such as private property, to restrain some kinds of social disorder; but the divine reason for property was to serve a larger good—not to grant absolute rights to individuals (Frey 1998, 1577). The Puritans knew their Old Testament too well: God ultimately

owned all things; humans held only temporary rights, subject to God's purposes. This core principle also defined the Puritan position on questions such
as boundaries on economic behavior: permissible economic behavior always
was contingent on its being used in a manner that served a common good as
well as the self.

Elsewhere (Frey 1998, 1577–78), I have outlined the Puritan perspective
on several economic practices and attitudes associated in the modern mind
with individualistic economics. Beside a right to property, these included the
legitimacy of wealth, modern—rather than medieval—attitudes toward the
poor, modern notions of contracts among individuals, acceptance of market-
pricing of goods and modern attitudes toward interest on loans. In each
instance, the key point was that an economic freedom or institution that could
enhance the individual was never considered an absolute right. Giving a sinful human such absolute rights would invariably lead to the wrong outcome—
the denial of the rightful claims of God and neighbor on the self.

Puritans, for example, affirmed private wealth as legitimate, but worried
that great wealth might set some apart from the human fellowship. Thus, it
followed that "adherents of the notion of the calling were uneasy with anything more than moderate economic success" (Crowley 1974, 61). Puritan
ethics could justify only those differences of wealth that tended to glorify God
and build the human community, thereby ruling out wealth that amplified differences among people.

Assuming wealth was of a morally acceptable amount, it could still be
dangerous if it tempted the wealthy to think in terms of their autonomy from
others. The great moral risk of wealth was the temptation to believe oneself
different from the rest of humanity, self-sufficient and insulated from the
common existence of mankind. The temptation of riches is to place "idola-
trous trust in them" leading to the "contempt of God" (Ames 1643, 254). The
"contempt of God" is the illusion of self-sufficiency, which alienates one from
God and neighbor. The Puritan divines would accept individual wealth; yet
they worried that it carried with it the sinful temptation to set one's self apart
from God and others.

A discussion of wealth suggests a discussion of Puritan views of poverty.
In sharp contrast to medieval Catholicism, Puritans did not view the existence
of poverty as an opportunity for those of means to earn spiritual merit through
charity—for salvation was solely by God's free grace. Poverty, in fact, might
hint that a poor person had failed to respond to God's vocational calling.
Here, then, was a punitive consequence of Puritan individualism: assignment
of blame to at least some of the poor for individual moral failings. Some Puritan moralists even approved of state action against the nonworking poor (e.g.,
Perkins, in Morgan 1965, 52). (This punitive strand of Puritanism would ultimately merge with the Enlightenment idea that incentives were very important in guiding self-interested behavior. Thus, harsh treatment of the poor

must be used to deter behavior that led to poverty.) Yet, countering the punitive tendencies, Puritan moralists readily admitted that the poor were part of the human community. And, while charity could never earn spiritual merit, they insisted that those of means had a *moral obligation* to assist those poor whose poverty was no fault of their own. Even at its harshest, the Puritan ethic affirmed human relationships.

Some economists have considered a society's views on the legitimacy of market-pricing and the charging of interest on loans to be the main indicators of its friendliness to capitalism. As noted, these issues were relatively small compared to the much broader issues of economic morality. But on issues of pricing and interest, the Puritans hewed to their logic: individual freedom in pricing and interest-collecting was endorsed, but this freedom was never absolute. For example, extreme price increases in time of scarcity were viewed not as a morally neutral, technical process (i.e., the action of supply and demand), but as potential exploitation of others during hard times. Merchant Robert Keayne discovered this limit on market freedom when he was tried for excess profiting (see, e.g., Bernstein 1997, 89). As with the just price, the same logic applied to interest on loans. The lender should forgo his (legitimate) interest if a borrower could not repay. Things that were permissible at normal times became wrong at times when they could harm the greater community and so deny the greater importance of relationship.

The Puritan ethic of the early colonial period was already recognizable as typically American. It embraced religious and economic individualism; the latter was rooted fundamentally in God's calling of individuals to worldly work. It valued success, wealth, and property, and tended to favor freedom within the market. As relational moralists, Puritans understood government to be God's instrument for serving the common good. Yet, they were wary of government because all humans, including those who governed, were sinners. Puritans believed that human sin could result in the individual ego expanding to obliterate the common good in the economic sphere. Individuals' economic freedoms had to be bounded because they did not exist merely as instruments to serve the autonomous individual. As noted, property rights, wealth, and freedom to charge interest or set prices were never viewed as absolute rights of individuals, but were contingent on serving a common good as well. Puritans were individualistic, but it was a relational individualism that resisted tears in the human fabric—at least as far as the borders of the Puritan commonwealth. At the same time, Quakers developed a similar relational ethic that abolished any borders and implied the most expansive responsibility.

QUAKERS: WILLIAM PENN AND JOHN WOOLMAN

With their belief in the "direct revelation of Christ to the soul," Quakers in the religious sense were even more individualistic than the orthodox Puritans

(Ahlstrom 1972, 176–77). Quaker thinkers responded with a heavier moral counterweight to the sinful pressures of excessive individualism. They likened humanity to a family, and suggested that moral obligations among kin were thereby created. Furthermore, they held that moral actions were channels for God to transform the economic life. Therefore, to fail to act condemned society to an existence that did not have to be.

William Penn (1644–1718), like all Protestants, insisted that "true godliness don't [sic] turn men out of the world" to lives in monasteries and the like (Penn 1957, 48). And his writings admonished the well-off and common tradesmen to turn way from luxury and diversions, which, he believed, harmed society. Underlying his advice was the belief that that broad prosperity was the consequence of well-ordered lives and of diligence (see, e.g., Penn 1957, 57, 59). Like the Puritans, he made no sharp distinction between worldly work and the work of the gospel.

Quaker John Woolman (1720–1772) sold his profitable grocery business to become an itinerant Quaker minister of the eighteenth century. But this was not to turn away from the world; he began preaching against the evils of slavery, mistreatment of Indians, and excess wealth (McFague 2001, 188). He believed self-interest was close to the center of such evils because it warps one's very perception. He asserted that selfishness "being indulged clouds the understanding," making objectivity toward the self impossible (Woolman 1971, 225).

Human harmony for Woolman was defined by the metaphors of family and kinship. In fact, to relate to humans as "other than brethren," he said, supposes "darkness in the understanding" (Woolman 1971, 202). European settlers and American Indians were kin, said Woolman, and so he lived among them and experienced their straitened conditions (McFague 2001, 190). He advocated relative equality of wealth because great inequality denied kinship.

Penn saw government as an instrument for achieving a harmonious and humane society, a far cry from either the self-serving royalist states of his era or the minimal governments that the American revolutionaries would conceive. Penn rejected the idea that government's sole purpose was to correct evil and added that "affairs more soft and daily necessary make up much the greatest part of government" (Penn 1957, 110). Penn here portrayed government in an almost mothering role. He did not fear too large a government, because he was optimistic about the efficacy of Christianity as a remedy for sin. Penn worried little about the form of government, saying, "Let men be good and the government cannot be bad" (Penn 1957, 111).

Rather simply, Penn believed that the civil order should pursue obedience to the example of Jesus. If luxury and diversions were curbed, Penn wrote, there would be "no beggars in the land, the cry of the widow and orphan would cease" (59). For his part, Woolman inverted the belief that much poverty was due to idleness. To the contrary, the poor are often self-driven to work "harder than was intended by our gracious Creator" (Woolman 1971,

238). Optimism that the reformation of society was possible meant that sin and misery did not have the last word.

Property existed to serve the greater human family. However, mere legal possession of property was not the same as moral possession, as Woolman demonstrated with an example. Twenty men settled an empty island, each man possessing a twentieth of the island. Nineteen divided their shares equitably among their descendants; their successors continued to divide equitably. One, however, passed everything to a favored son, leaving his other children as tenants. This pattern continued for some generations. With thrift and industry the descendants of the original nineteen would, according to Woolman, be living in dignity still. (Woolman had no explicit economic theory, but implicitly, in making this claim, he advocated an economic science far different from the scarcity oriented political economy that later arose.) Woolman continued that the tenants on the last share would be overworked and poor. The tenth-generation landlord of that last share would hold a *legal title that was nevertheless morally untenable*. The impoverished tenants would have a moral right to a share "though they had no instruments to confirm their right" (Woolman 1971, 261–62). The tenants and the landlord literally were kin, and inequality was a perversion of the meaning of kinship. For Penn, too, property existed for the common good. Of private property, he affirmed that the "public may claim a share with us" (Penn 1957, 191).

The kinship of humans, as noted, was Woolman's starting metaphor from which morality flowed. He approached the issue of slavery through his understanding of human kinship. He asked readers to place themselves in the slave's position (Woolman 1971, 204). Asking a reader to mentally exchange positions with the slave was asking the reader to acknowledge a common humanity with the slave. Such common humanity implies that humans can understand one another at a moral level. Appealing directly to his reader's compassion for kin, Woolman compared the distress of the Africans to the suffering of the reader's own injured child. One's child's broken bone, bruise, or one's child's being lost—all "these move us with grief," he wrote. Then he added that the reader would experience similar grief if the "calamities" imposed on Africans by slavery were "transacted in our presence" (233). His appeal was to a shared humanity that transcended race and made a deep understanding of other humans possible.

Slave-owning was motivated by selfishness, that danger of any individualist morality. Self-interest, to have its way, might deny human kinship—and certainly denied it when rationalizing slavery. Woolman suggested that selfishness would drive one to take advantage of inferiors, and asked "what then shall we do when God riseth up" (207)? Woolman argued that self-love, given absolute power over others, would lead to every abuse: the slave-owner's "irregular appetites" run free when he exercises absolute power over others

(221–22). Thus, for Woolman, the profoundest moral peril lay in the self holding absolute power over others. Slavery was wrong because it denied the common humanity of slave and master and subordinated the fundamental human relationships among slaves to a master's will. Woolman clearly had a profound sense of sin, although he was unlike the conservative Protestants who believed that sin in this world would never be overcome.

Although Quaker individualism in faith was intense, moralists such as Woolman bound the individual closely to the rest of the entire human family. On the grounds of human kinship, John Woolman declared that vast wealth inequality and slavery were wrong. Perhaps Woolman's relational ethic was elastic enough to expand *beyond* the human family. He wrote early in his life that true religion is "to exercise true justice and goodness, not only toward all men but also toward the brute creatures" (28). Love of God included his creatures.

In important ways, the Quaker ethic overlapped that of the orthodox Puritans: religious and economic individualism, the understanding of excessive self-interest as sin, the emphasis on calling, sobriety, and simplicity, a respect for property combined with a countervailing concern for great inequality. Yet, there were differences. The Puritan commonwealths had their covenants with God and the horizons of their relational morality might end at the borders of their holy commonwealths. The Quakers recognized no such boundaries, and their relational morality was in principle universal. The Puritan, perhaps without instinctively sensing it, derived economic morality formally from a theological and scriptural framework that embedded relational ethics. The Quaker morality emerged from a sense of what should be the behavior among the kin; the meaning of Jesus' life was a model. There was another difference: the Puritan viewed the fallen world as always recalcitrant despite imposed reforms (which the Puritans were always willing to impose). Woolman and Penn taught that the moral structure of the universe was responsive to God (Tolles and Alderfer, in Penn 1957, xxiv–xxv). People could be brought into accord with the moral reality and restored "to primitive harmony" (Woolman 1971, 208). Sin was "discord" of relationships to be set right in the present. Failures in human existence could be restored, and nature presented no obstacle, for "God had so ordered the universe that the needs of all would be met insofar as each person was guided by universal love to seek only what he really required" (Moulton, in Woolman 1971, 9). In short, any Quaker economic theory would have been based on the premise of potential abundance, not scarcity. Woolman and Penn believed that despite the visible discord of the universe, it was structured benignly. Moral actions would reveal the fundamental reality, which was good. Despite differences between orthodox Puritans and Quakers, their moral vision in turn was vastly different from the outlook of laissez-faire economics, which was to come.

CONCLUSION

Consider what is missing from early Puritan and the Quaker economic moralities. While consequences were never wholly irrelevant, the material consequences for oneself of economic actions never dominated moral decision-making. While the Puritan divine John Cotton believed that economic virtues, exercised in a calling, tended to success, it was not the ability to produce success that defined virtues. This differed greatly from a much more utilitarian outlook that was to develop in the later colonial period (see chapter 3).

Both Puritans and Quakers built their ethic on a relational, rather than exclusively self-oriented, individualism. Their theology saw sin in a single-minded focus on self; their individualism was of a kind that understood self in relation to God and neighbor. The Quakers defined the good as the affirmation of human kinship, which flowed from all persons having a common creator and redeemer. Penn and Woolman were optimists—surely more optimistic than Puritans—about the efficacy of moral actions. But morality did not depend on efficacy. Morality resided in living consistently in a way that strengthened human kinship.

American economic morality has been profoundly shaped by its Protestant colonial origins, which established an individualistic faith and individualistic economics, and which invested the individual with a host of rights and responsibilities. Yet, this was a Christian individualism that warned against the self imagining itself autonomous, at the center of its own universe. Even radical Protestantism, which removed all human intermediaries that might come between a person and God, never thought in terms of autonomy, for no Protestant ever thought the individual *was* God. The individual was always a dependent creature among, and related to, other creatures. This implied a commonality with other humans. In fact, sin, in the words of Governor Winthrop, was the very kind of self-love that rends apart that human commonality. The slogan of the Reformation was grace alone, faith alone, scripture alone—but never the *self alone*. However, the temptation of "self alone" always existed among Protestants, for it was inherent in their religious and economic individualism.

Concerns about uncontrolled self-interest, leading to excess that would hurt the community, were manifest in Puritan teachings on property, wealth, price-setting, income inequality, and usury. In each case, the service to the individual that property (or other economic arrangements) could provide was recognized as part of a larger divine arrangement that also served a greater human good. Therefore moral constraints, for the sake of the human community, were raised against absolute freedom to use property, to price goods, to collect interest, or to pile up wealth. In effect, the Puritans and Quakers exercised a moral logic that knew when enough was enough. Although Puritanism freed the individual from numerous feudal constraints, it never went to the opposite extreme to define that freedom in absolute terms—as license for pure self-interest. It erected moral boundaries because it feared the sin of the unbounded ego.

The relational outlook provided the basis for building a consensus on issues of economic morality, for if humans were kin, they could understand each other and engage in moral dialogue. Although Puritans (still struggling to free themselves from feudal ways) understood moral dialogue as dialogue among elites, the principle was there. The Quaker metaphor of human kinship stated more forcefully than the Puritans that people could understand each other, thus allowing moral dialogue and persuasion.

Although these Protestants were open to empirical science, they came too early to mesh their ethics to a scientific outlook on the world. In their worldview, God's providence, not scientific laws, directed events. Thus, one was free to do what was right and rest assured that a just God was in charge of consequences. These were not utilitarians who defined the good solely by consequences.

This relational individualism, however, was inherently unstable. For unless obligations to others are constantly asserted, the claims of the self always loom larger from one's own perspective. The true relationship with God and others was constantly stretched by the gravitational pull of selfishness. A morality that insisted that the self face outward, toward God and neighbors, was asking people to undertake a difficult task. The task became even more difficult when a competing morality emerged, born of the Enlightenment; this ethic minimized what the early Protestant moralists saw as the moral threat inherent in self-interest. The transition to this new moral outlook is the subject of the next chapter.

THREE

Acting for Self's Sake

The Later Colonial Era

BY THE EARLY eighteenth century, self-interest was accepted with fewer qualifications than the first Puritans imposed—even among Puritan clergy, who no doubt lagged behind average people on this score. That this would happen is not surprising: Puritan individualism in faith and vocation implied the importance of the self. Keeping the self focused outward, on God and others, instead of inward on itself, would always require effort. By the eighteenth century, moralists were shifting to a much more positive view of self-interest.

The trend was noticeable in the thought of Puritan Cotton Mather early in the century. Later, secular moralist Benjamin Franklin advocated virtue because it would benefit the self. Leading to the American Revolution, preachers blended Puritan and Enlightenment ideas to question the legitimacy of the British monarchy, and in the process created a generalized suspicion of government as the enemy of the individual's interests. Following independence, American denominational colleges largely adopted the moral philosophy of Anglican William Paley, whose utilitarian ethics were explicitly based on religious self-interest. Thus, the eighteenth century saw the transition from a morality that emphasized the self's obligations to God and community to one that recast ethics in terms of self-interest.

COTTON MATHER

Cotton Mather (1663–1728), influential Puritan clergyman at the turn of the eighteenth century, reiterated the form of seventeenth-century ethical formulas even while interpreting them in new ways. Mather retained the orthodox position that salvation rested on God's grace alone, not good works. However, if good works could not *earn* salvation, he suggested that they might at least bring some worldly benefits. In his *Essays to Do Good* (1710), Mather wrote that doing good "brings its own recompense," citing "the incomparable pleasure" that comes from benevolent actions (Mather 1710, 11, 50). Although Mather referred only to a good feeling at being benevolent, his holding out this motivation to his readers represented a long step from the earlier Puritan preaching based on obligation. Mather sometimes moved beyond intangible rewards, implying unabashedly that tithing was *an investment* yielding a material return: "they who [tithe] have usually been remarkably blessed in their estates by the providence of God" (89). While not quite stating that tithing was an economic transaction with God, Mather certainly implied as much. Here the Puritan morality of obligation was being replaced with a morality that motivated behavior by means of promised rewards—of a more tangible sort at that. Service to the common good, instead of being a constraint on self-interest, was now recommended as a way to enhance one's self-interest.

Mather, moralizing on the raising of children, took pains to outline the responsibility of the Christian parent: "I wish that my children may, at a very early period, feel the principles of reason and honor working in them" (37). The Puritan emphasis on inner character remained, but it now reflected Enlightenment "reason and honor," rather than obedience to God. (Mather, however, expressed more traditional sentiments regarding the children's religious upbringing.) Mather did not see children's misbehavior as a serious sign of original sin, as his Puritan ancestors might have; he excused much misbehavior as childishness and recommended that parents only frown "a little for some real wickedness."

Mather reinterpreted the vocational calling with an Enlightenment flavor, wishing that "daughters as well as sons may have so much acquaintance with some profitable avocation . . . that they may be able to obtain for themselves a comfortable subsistence" (41). Mather's concern for daughters, as well as sons, is immediately noticeable to the modern reader. As morally significant, however, is his focus on *profit and comfort* as worthy considerations in choosing work preparation. Discerning the divine will in one's choice of a vocation was no longer highlighted in his few words on the vocational decision. Indeed, much of Mather's essay emphasized the layperson's Christian service to be in his or her volunteer efforts outside the work world.

A certain tone of utilitarianism and individualism had crept into this Puritan's outlook. It had profound implications for Mather's attitude toward the poor. Emphasizing the personal choice involved in choosing a vocation led to a harsh corollary: namely, that failure to find a successful vocation was also a choice, perhaps due to moral defect. Hence, Mather became intolerant of the idle, who presumably chose their condition: "take pains to cure them of their idleness: do not nourish and harden them in it, but find employment for them; set them to work, and keep them at work" (50).

The main theme of *Essays to Do Good* was that Christian laypersons should care for those about them. Following the lead of German Pietism, Mather urged young laymen to form groups for devotions and mutual spiritual encouragement; he also suggested they find ways to do service to their neighbors. Within a century and a quarter, voluntarism had become widespread among evangelical Protestants. Mather surely did not produce the rise of individualism, but he accommodated readily to it—voluntary societies fit perfectly with an age of increasing individualism and autonomous choice.

If one interpreter of American Puritanism is correct, Mather was a conservative reacting against the new age (Miller 1953 V. 2: 414). Nevertheless, his very revolt drew from much of the Enlightenment. In Mather's book, divine will was less important and self-inclination was proportionately more important than in the older theology. The Puritan ethic of obligation Mather amended with *inducements* for doing good—the promise of rewards, even if just good feelings. He could talk about a "comfortable subsistence" weighing in the balance when discussing life's work. Mather retained the forms of Puritan orthodoxy while filling them with more self-will than had been the norm. Mather's work also provided a preview of the harsher side of the age's growing emphasis on human freedom: he blamed economic losers for their own plight, which must have resulted from their free choices.

BENJAMIN FRANKLIN

Raised in Boston, Benjamin Franklin (1706–1790) personified the minor Puritan virtues and even credited Mather's *Essays to Do Good* with influencing his life. Franklin's life was long, and in later life he exemplified public service without desire for personal gain. However, there is a contrary theme running throughout Franklin's writings that anticipated the economic ethics of the nineteenth century. Franklin's writings show how readily the Puritan virtues could be stripped of their theological foundations and justified, instead, by an appeal to self-interest.

Benjamin Franklin's publications ever preached the virtues of industry, frugality, temperance and good order (Franklin 1987, 1384–85). The earlier Puritan, at least as an ideal, practiced these virtues to glorify God and serve others. In Franklin's "Rules Proper to be Observed in Trade," the motive shifted to self-interest, for business virtues were "natural means of acquiring wealth, honour [*sic*], and reputation" (Franklin 1987, 345). Poor Richard always kept the focus on personal gain as the reason for practicing virtue: "No man e'er was glorious, who was not laborious," or "Deny Self *for Self's sake*" (1191 and 1198).

For Franklin, *economic incentives* provided the contours of the terrain through which one pursued one's interest. In 1753, he stated that if incentives rewarded laziness, then laziness would abound. Despite his own philanthropic endeavors, Franklin argued that the English poor laws, "which compel the Rich to maintain the Poor," have trained the English to a state of dependency. He called relief "encouragement for Laziness and supports for Folly" (469). Incentives were integral to Franklin's philosophy, for he defined self-interest against a material incentive system of rewards and punishments. He worried that governmental care for the aged and ill would undermine the incentive to save when young and healthy. A materialistic view of human motivation appeared in Franklin's writings, anticipating political economy yet to come.

In the same letter of 1753, Franklin argued against government interference in the economy, for efforts to ameliorate social and economic ills would inevitably backfire. He recounted the story of a New England town that sought to end the damage blackbirds inflicted on the corn crop. But once the blackbirds were exterminated, "a kind of Worms . . . encreased prodigiously; [so] they wished again for the Black-birds" (469). This was not a parable about ecological imbalance, but about economic morality. Franklin was promoting a utilitarian ethic in which consequences, not intentions, establish the goodness of an action. Specifically, in a complex world, good intentions especially may be liable to produce bad consequences. By implication, governments should not interfere in economics—thus Franklin anticipated nineteenth-century laissez-faire.

Just as bird and worm populations interacted to produce bad outcomes, the interactions of social incentives and human propensities would also produce outcomes one might not want. For example, assistance to the poor would simply encourage idleness. In a strange passage, in which compassion struggles with hard-heartedness, Franklin admitted that compassion for others is "Godlike," but immediately reversed course, arguing that relief may actually be "fighting against the order of God and Nature, which perhaps has appointed Want and Misery as the proper Punishments for, and Cautions against . . . Idleness and Extravagancy" (469). In this passage, Franklin seemed at war with himself. Compassion apparently reflected God's expressed will. Unfortunately such kindness, if given out liberally, inevitably provided an incentive for idleness—a chief human propensity. In a world driven by self-interest, compassion produces the wrong incentives and therefore the wrong results. Franklin's God, who apparently gave lip service to compassion, actually had structured the world so as to punish the idle. In this view, biblical teachings about compassion must be discounted. The new original sin had become idleness, and the cure was to let the lazy suffer the harshest consequences appointed by the God of natural religion as portrayed by Franklin. This view anticipated the value system of nineteenth-century laissez-faire economic ethics.

Beginning to be visible in Franklin's thought was something new: *ethics must be congruent with the scientific nature of things*. Moral intentions devoid of scientific understanding are mere sentimentality and probably will harm things. This made scientific theory very important for morals: was nature generous or stingy—could humans afford to share, or did they always need to view their fellows as competitors for scarce resources? Here, too, Franklin gave an answer that anticipated the future of economic doctrine. His essay "Observations Concerning the Increase of Mankind," dated 1751, anticipated much in the scarcity-dominated thought of Thomas Robert Malthus. Perhaps Franklin's American environment saved him from drawing Malthus's gloomiest conclusions (367–74).

In sum, many of Franklin's ideas anticipated the classical political economists who restated similar ideas as economic law. The lesson of political economy in the nineteenth century would be that individuals should submit to those laws and that any effort to blunt the harsh consequences of economic law on the weak was mere sentimentality. Superimposed on this view of reality was a moral psychology that attributed human behavior to self-interest, guided by material incentives. Given wrong incentives, other humans were always potential parasites.

Benjamin Franklin, however, never succumbed to the full logic of all this. He never quite lost the transcendent reference point, never quite conceded that all could be reduced to economic law. In *Father Abraham's Speech* (1758), an exhortation on self-improvement that consisted of a string of maxims from Poor Richard, Franklin suddenly interjected a bolt from the blue. Wrote Franklin: in the end one's efforts "may all be blasted without the Blessing of Heaven," so "ask that Blessing humbly, and be not uncharitable" (1302). Perhaps Franklin foresaw where his ideas were pointing and recoiled from it. Perhaps he perceived that something transcending the harshness of nature commanded a charitable inclination and a true concern for the public good. As is well known, Franklin devoted his later life to the service of his new country. It would have been difficult to have predicted his later deeds from the values promoted in his earlier teachings.

Patriotic Clerics of the Revolutionary Era

As tensions with the British government increased, American pulpits expounded distrust of the British government, and government in general. Earlier Puritan thought had held that all those who governed were sinful mortals, who might govern unjustly; it also held, in that earlier period, that governing was a divine calling meant to serve the social good. This second point, which produced a balance, was lost in revolutionary-era sermons.

In 1774, the clergyman Samuel Sherwood upheld civil disobedience on the grounds of the fallibility of kings: "the will of none is infallibly right in all things and cannot therefore be complied with in all instances." Sherwood added the secular theory of John Locke that the origin of society is "in voluntary compact" among free individuals (Sherwood, in Sandoz 1991, 382–83).

And, as Locke had argued in promoting the idea, contracts are entered into voluntarily because they advance group members' interests. In a passage that foretold later attitudes toward government, Sherwood claimed that citizens may be oppressed in proportion to the strength of a government (385). While earlier Puritans were certain that governments could oppress, their operating principle was to judge governments by the merits of their actual behavior. Sherwood, by contrast, expressed a much more generalized suspicion of government, ignoring the possible goodness of particular governments. This prejudice against government continued even after independence. In 1785, Samuel Wales declared that those with the most power "are in the greatest danger of abusing it" (Wales, in Sandoz 1991, 852).

Already in 1747, Charles Chauncy was advocating a notion of government's role in economics that almost could have served as a model for laissez-faire. A "just" government had several functions, which may be clustered into two groups. The first group included aids to commerce by ensuring honest weights and measures, providing a sound currency, preventing injury to creditors, freeing trade from all "unnecessary burdens," and forwarding "those manufacturers which may be of public benefit." Except for the last item in this list, all the items are what laissez-faire would come to accept as the only legitimate economic functions of government. Chauncy added a second list of economic virtues that government should enforce on the population: discouraging "idleness, prodigality, prophaneness [sic], uncleanness, drunkenness and the like" and encouraging "industry, frugality, temperance, chastity, and the like moral virtues" (Chauncy, in Sandoz 1991, 163). This list certainly contained the economic virtues that laissez-faire would come to endorse. To be sure, laissez-faire would have ruled out governmental imposition of these virtues on autonomous individuals; however, in this respect Chauncy continued to exhibit one of the older Puritan tendencies—willingness to enforce virtuous behavior. In a final departure from his ability to foresee emerging laissez-faire ideas, Chauncy called on government to educate children. With this exception, his vision of the proper role of government was largely economic and largely minimalist.

WILLIAM PALEY: THEOLOGICAL UTILITARIANISM

By the late eighteenth century, Americans had moved a long way from the early Puritan and Quaker moralities, with their suspicion of self-interest. This is evidenced by the wide acceptance in American colleges of William Paley's *Principles of Moral and Political Philosophy* (1785, first edition). This book was to become a mainstay of American moral philosophy courses until an evangelical revolt against it in the 1830s led to the adoption of Francis Wayland's texts.

Paley was an arch-deacon of the Church of England, whose moral philosophy wedded utilitarian pleasures and pains to belief in an afterlife, a mixture sometimes called theological utilitarianism. That is, like the utilitarian philosopher Jeremy Bentham, Paley defined the good as that which provided pleasure and the bad as that which provided pain. Bentham, an atheist, had given a materialistic, this-world interpretation to pleasures and pains. Paley, however, sanctified Bentham's worldly utilitarianism by holding that the pleasures and pains would be meted out in an afterlife. This prospect, he taught, would motivate people to do the good (to gain pleasure) and avoid evil (to avoid pain). In this scheme, goodness was the result of a selfish calculation—namely, that the reward to oneself justified being good. Gone was any unselfish rationale, such as a duty to glorify God or to serve others in one's actions, or even pure love of the good. Paley presented essentially secular Enlightenment utilitarianism in a form palatable to the pious, provided they did not look too closely. As summed up by Jacob Viner, "except for its addition of pleasures and pains in the future life to the pleasure-pain calculus, it was a close counterpart of Bentham's completely irreligious hedonic utilitarianism" (Viner 1972, 74). Because Bentham was frankly materialistic and atheistic, America's Protestant colleges rejected his teachings. Yet, they accepted Paley's tepidly religious version of the same thing, which indicates that the old Puritan suspicion of selfish motives had been lost. Bentham and Paley both promoted a morality of selfish pleasures and pains, with the minor difference as to *when* rewards or punishments would happen.

Wilson Smith summarized three features of Paley's morality: a very liberal Christianity, utilitarianism, and natural rights similar to those of John Locke. According to Smith's reading, Paley reconciled these three by postulating a utilitarian God who required "only what will promote general happiness," understood as "the greatest amount of ultimately spiritual pleasure." In short, "future rewards (pleasures) or punishments (pain) became the sole motive for virtuous living" in Paley's teachings (Smith 1954, 407). This morality rested on a self-centeredness that earlier Puritans understood to be sin itself. That the timing of the hoped-for rewards was postponed beyond one's mortal life made the exercise no less selfish. In contrast, the earlier Puritans affirmed duty to the divine will *apart from personal consequences*. When actually living up to their doctrine, these Calvinists acted for the glory of God, not for benefit of self.

Americans in the era of Paley's morality also moved beyond the earlier Puritanism in their view of God, for Paley taught that that "what promotes the general happiness is required by the will of God" (Paley 1790, 55). In other words, God had become a social utilitarian, seeking society's happiness, rather than righteousness or holiness. The Puritan reliance on scripture was gone as well. Paley made no effort to support this theology with scripture—a sign of his Enlightenment bias. However, if scriptural support was lacking, Paley assured his readers that nature and reason pointed to the utilitarian conclusion.

In Paley's moral philosophy, happiness held a twofold meaning. As the previous passage makes clear, *general happiness* defined goodness; thus, Paley's utilitarianism was a social utilitarianism as far as defining the good. Yet, what would motivate essentially selfish individuals to do what was the good for society? Paley's answer was that *personal happiness* guaranteed in the afterlife would provide the motive force. Paley melded social utilitarianism, providing a moral goal, with egoistic utilitarianism, providing individual motive force.

Paley often repeated the maxim that "whatever is expedient is right." But Paley would immediately, and at length, point out that he meant not what was expedient in the particular case at hand, but what was expedient in general: "'Whatever is expedient is right.' But then it must be expedient upon the whole, at the long run, in all its effects collateral and remote" (78). Paley invariably found that when all an action's effects, "collateral and remote," were properly factored in, the calculation supported the status quo of morality and law. Paley conjured up the example of the assassination of a villain, the results of which all seemed good. Nevertheless, he concluded that such actions, if generalized, would harm the general happiness (73–74). His point was that existing rules generally produce social happiness. Paley thus supported conventional rules of behavior, which powerfully defended the social and economic status quo.

Paley's invocation of divine rewards and punishments, apportioned to individuals for their behavior, provided the motive for otherwise selfish people to act on behalf of the public good. Paley asked, "Why am I obliged to keep my word"? His answer was, "because I am [motivated by] the expectation of being after this life rewarded, if I do, or punished for it, if I do not" (59–60). He reiterated that personal happiness was the human motive, to be obtained by obeying divinely appointed rules. Paley thus managed to mesh the Enlightenment's emphasis on self-centered motivation with a pre-Enlightenment emphasis on authority (the will of God).

Even if Paley retained the "will of God," the clash of such a morality with the earlier colonial Calvinist morality was enormous. It would have been no surprise to the colonial Puritans that sinful humans were self-centered, just as Paley posited. However, to harness selfishness to motivate people would have confounded them, for selfishness was itself a form of sin. A sinful motive linked to a righteous end would be an unholy match, especially since God judged intent, not merely outcome. Immersed in scripture, the Puritans would have found little to support the notion that God supremely willed the happiness of society. For them, God willed a righteous society, as described in scripture.

Worse from the Calvinist view, perhaps, was that Paley's moral system had humans *earning* heavenly reward. This was heresy to the Calvinists, who held that salvation was by divine grace and could not possibly be earned. One's deeds and character would reflect the duty to glorify God, not a worldly-minded effort to influence God. Orthodox Calvinists placed little emphasis on an afterlife as a form of ethical motivation. Paley's ethic, to the degree educated Americans in the post-Puritan era accepted it, represented an abandonment of Calvinist theology and the adaptation of religion to the Enlightenment. Paley's theological utilitarianism would prove to be too unorthodox for the evangelical movement that emerged from post-Puritan, evangelical Protestantism in the early nineteenth century (see chapter 4 on Francis Wayland).

It may be as relevant to judge Paley against the secular trends of the Enlightenment as against the Puritan heritage of America. Viner (1972, 74) pointed out that in an environment hostile to religion Paley tried to uphold religion's social value, stressing the "importance of religious sanctions for civic morality." Enlightenment rationalism made incentives the reasonable motives for behavior. But it was obvious that rewards and punishments for behavior were not certain in this life. Thus, an afterlife was needed to guarantee rewards and punishments; Paley supplied this by invoking a certain aspect of revealed religion. This provided a very pragmatic counter to the Enlightenment tendency to reject revealed religion as superstition. The Enlightenment's self-interested individualists needed rewards and punishments to behave civilly. But where were rewards and punishments in this world? Finally, by assuring adherents of a "final accounting in a future life," the doctrine disarmed discontent with the injustices of the status quo. Thus, Paley's ethic was distinctly socially conservative. Viner (75) concluded that "This was a good deal for one body of doctrine to achieve."

CONCLUSIONS

The willingness of American colleges to adopt Paley's textbook toward the end of the eighteenth century reveals how far a significant component of American thought had moved away from its Calvinist beginnings. Even at the start of the century, the tentative beginnings of such a movement were visible in the writings of Cotton Mather. In between, secular writers such as Benjamin Franklin further anticipated the outlines of the economic morality that was to reach maturity in nineteenth-century laissez-faire.

The reasons for this shift have not been our main concern, but several possibilities suggest themselves. Average Americans no doubt adopted highly utilitarian, pragmatic ethics in their dealings with hardship and opportunity in a new land. In addition, wealthier and educated Americans were not sealed off from Enlightenment ideas. Further, Puritanism itself may have contained a logical dynamic that led in this direction. American Puritans had always argued with their Calvinist roots, trying to soften the absolute sovereignty of their Calvinist God and to reconcile his authority to human reason (Miller 1956, 74). Perhaps this logical dynamic eventually would have led to something approximating liberal religion, a larger role for self-interest, and utilitarian ethics. Finally, the American Revolution, as we have seen, caused even the orthodox to exaggerate the individualistic tendencies of Puritanism against government.

The early Puritan ethic had done much to establish American economic morality: it was individualistic, required that economic activity be undertaken as a primary duty, and legitimated fundamental economic institutions such as private property. Yet, Puritans distinguished between individualism and self-centeredness, and found the model for the good society in God's revealed will, which, as they read it, stated a relational ethic. The eighteenth century marked the transition from this Puritan relational morality toward laissez-faire and autonomy morality. Self-interest not only lost the taint of sin that it bore in Puritanism, but it was pressed into duty as the foundation of William Paley's ethic. Once self-interest was in place, the structure of morality took on a utilitarian cast: what was good was what produced outcomes desired by the individual. Even the social good had to be guaranteed by promising private rewards to motivate the necessary actions of individuals. Finally, the American Revolution produced distrust of both the British king and government in general. In place of the relatively balanced Puritan view of government, the revolutionary-era preachers produced an emphasis on distrust of government.

The eighteenth century produced hints of two ideas that would reach maturity in nineteenth-century laissez-faire. First, there emerged the view that a major role of morality and social policy was to provide harsh incentives to deter idleness, to which people were apparently naturally attracted. Second, because individuals were understood to be free enough to choose among incentives, they earned moral praise or blame for their own economic condition, which resulted from their choices. The next chapter considers full-blown laissez-faire—a potent blend of moral values and economic theory.

FOUR

Laissez-Faire for Americans

DURING THE EIGHTEENTH CENTURY, many American moralists progressively abandoned the earlier colonial ethics for the morality of the Enlightenment (chapter 3). This trend reached fullest form as nineteenth-century laissez-faire, which viewed self-interest as the engine of the economy and source of economic good for society. Notably lacking was the older Puritan wariness toward self-interest. The new political economy, to the contrary, claimed that the public good was *automatically* served by competitive behavior intended only to serve private interests; it supported this proposition with a set of economic laws. If the resultant economy seemed to contain ills, such as extensive poverty, that outcome was nevertheless believed to be the best that could be produced within the constraints of natural and economic law. This perspective minimized any moral obligation for individuals or society to alleviate economic ills. For if the status quo was the best that was possible, what could be done to make things better?

This chapter begins with a description of British laissez-faire. While it did not emerge fully elaborated from Adam Smith's writings, Smith's thought nevertheless set the direction of subsequent thought. A textbook by the Englishwoman Jane Marcet beautifully summarized the full laissez-faire theory. Her text, widely used in America, made explicit the morality promoted by the inevitable economic laws of laissez-faire. By the 1830s, a great American revival of evangelical Protestantism, the heir of Puritanism, confronted laissez-faire face-to-face in the denominational colleges. Could this revived evangelical outlook accept economic doctrine that viewed self-interest optimistically as the engine of human good?[1] Could a revived Protestant conscience, sensing its obligation to the will of God and equating self-love with sin, abide Enlightenment morality that revolved around self-interest in economic life? Could the American sense of progress and of open possibilities be reconciled with the static laws of scarcity in European economics? The unlikely answer to these questions turned out to be "yes." Francis Wayland, the Baptist president of Brown University, stripped laissez-faire of certain European elements, while taming evangelical ethics, so that the two could live at peace. Wayland helped evangelicals believe they could accept a thoroughly secular economic morality.

EUROPEAN BACKGROUND: ADAM SMITH

In his lesser-known, first book, *Theory of Moral Sentiments* (1759), Adam Smith portrayed morality as the result of the natural sympathy of humans for one another (an essentially relational perspective). However, Smith's outlook seemed radically different by 1776. In *Wealth of Nations* (1776), Smith envisioned economic actors who were motivated solely by self-interest. This startling contrast has often been noticed, but should not be exaggerated. The Smith of the *Theory of Moral Sentiments* believed that natural sympathy between humans weakened as social distance increased—in other words, one bonded most strongly to kin and neighbors, with lesser bonding at greater social distances. As social distance increased, self-interest was needed to replace the weakened bonds of human sympathy. In *Wealth of Nations* Smith argued that the division of labor, which placed people in specialized occupations, invariably increased the social distance between people. People would adopt the narrow outlook of those in their trade, while losing sympathy for those in different trades. Economic relationships between persons who were not socially close necessarily would be reduced to self-interest. Economic progress depended on the division of labor, which, in turn, weakened other social connections, leaving self-interest alone as the basis of relationships.

The *Wealth of Nations* opened with a primary truth: the division of labor is the basis of increased productivity, a benefit that is not to be taken lightly in any relatively poor society. Immediately following this, Smith's famous statement about self-love appeared: "It is not from the benevolence of the butcher, the brewer, or the baker, that we expect our dinner, but from their regard to their own interest" (Smith 1776, 14). In short, dinner can more surely be had by a paid transaction with the butcher, brewer, and baker than appeals to their love of humanity. As division of labor increased, desired output would increase; but social distance would widen, and so human interactions would have to occur on the basis of self-interest, not sympathy. Actually, as early as his *Theory of Moral Sentiments*, Smith had argued that self-interest was a sufficient basis for a society itself: "Society may subsist among different men ... from a sense of its utility, without any mutual love or affection" (Smith 1759, 86). That is, a durable society was one that served the self-interest of many people.

If self-interest were to be the foundation of the economy, then it needed to be given full play, and not be interfered with in the name of some higher good. Smith, in fact, had caustic words for people "of the greatest public spirit" who were "not very sensible to the feelings of humanity" (Smith 1759, 185). Casting public-spiritedness in a bad light, Smith set the tone for laissez-faire, which saw little good in government involvement in the economy. Self-interest might motivate greater production (clearly one social good); however, Smith's negativity toward the public-spirited exhibited unwillingness to see additional dimensions of a good economy.

Smith argued that self-interested competition was not only the engine of greater production, but that it imposed a *moral* discipline, for a workman found it in his interest to keep his customers happy: "It is the fear of losing [the customers'] employment [to competitors] which restrains his frauds and corrects his negligence" (Smith 1776, 129). Thus, competition would be a benign and active moral agent, policing against commercial vices. Almost every example Smith gave of self-interest gone bad required a noncompetitive environment. Competition was a moral force, reducing the need for explicit ethical rules (as least in dealing with customers).

If self-interest were given full play in a market economy, general output would increase, but there were bound to be winners and losers. Smith expressed little concern about economic inequality: the rich "are led by an invisible hand to make nearly the same distribution of the necessaries of life, which would have been made had the earth been divided into equal portions" (Smith 1759, 184–85). His meaning was clear: inequality of wealth hardly makes a difference in anyone's access to a basic standard of living. Thus Smith dismissed inequality as a relevant issue for moral discourse.

Adam Smith's understanding of human motivation raised a fundamental paradox for social morality. If everyone cared only about private interest, how would the common good (other than greater output) emerge? In the clash of self-interests, might not social disharmony emerge? But Smith denied that this problem existed. To the contrary, he asserted, self-interest in competitive markets would advance society's interest: the self-interested person's "study of his own advantage naturally, or rather necessarily leads him to prefer that employment which is most advantageous to the society" (Smith, 1776, 421). In short, self-seeking *unintentionally* produces social good. Though one's motive may be completely selfish, one is "led by an invisible hand" to promote society's greater interest. Added Smith, the self-interested person "frequently promotes [the interest] of society more effectually than when he really intends to promote it" (Smith 1776, 423). Smith's famous invisible hand, besides eliminating the problem of wealth inequality (see above), now disposed of problem of conflicting self-interests. Further, Smith again disparaged public-spirited motives, asserting them to be less effectual in achieving the public good, their stated purpose, than self-interested motives.

If the interest of society were simply to increase production, Smith's position was defensible, but, as a general moral truth, it presented problems. With the invisible hand, Smith severed the ethical connection between *the intention and the outcome* of an action—for the common good was supposed to result from intentions not aimed at the common good. This disconnection between intent and outcome surely required qualification: counterexamples easily can be found of self-interested motives leading down nonproductive paths (to mention only economic counterexamples). The minimizing of moral intent also countered centuries of traditional biblical morality, which had repeatedly stated that "God searches the heart." Even if viewed purely as great literature, the Bible embodied centuries of human experience and wisdom regarding the moral significance of intent. More than severing the intention-outcome link, Smith suggested that intentions were inversely related to outcomes. He stated that the selfish motive "more effectually" contributed to the public good than the well-intentioned motive did.[2] Twentieth-century British economist Joan Robinson questioned this, suggesting that Smith's invisible hand had "abolished the moral problem" (Robinson 1962, 54).

The disconnect between intent and outcome raises significant ethical questions that often go unasked. What is good about a version of public good if it is not worth intending to achieve it? Are intentions and outcomes truly irrelevant to each other? Might questionable intentions eventually subvert the outcomes? If the public good can always be produced by economic self-interest, is not such a public good too narrowly defined—too one-dimensional?

Despite his strong statements, Smith apparently did not believe that the invisible hand was all-powerful to produce good every time. Some self-interested actions went beyond what even Smith could accept, so he suggested moral boundaries to self-interest: "Every man, *as long as he does not violate the laws of justice*, is left perfectly free to pursue his own interest" (Smith 1776, 651—emphasis added). Apparently recognizing that self-interest was incapable of restraining itself, Smith spoke of external "laws of justice" to provide the missing restraint. Apparently, some self-interested actions *did* hurt the public good. Smith went so far as to affirm government's "duty of protecting, as far as possible, every member of the society from the injustice or oppression" of others (Smith 1776, 651). This statement recognized that self-interest may not always serve the greater good.

Smith, therefore, hesitated to move down the road of making self-interest the centerpiece of an ethic and letting it alone define the good. Clearly, if "laws of justice" were needed to restrain self-interested actions, Smith could not have believed that self-interest was an adequate foundation of an ethic. Indeed, when the "laws of justice" appear suddenly, late in the *Wealth of Nations*, they seem to come from out of the blue, perhaps as an afterthought. Smith, like Benjamin Franklin, seemed ultimately to question the adequacy of a pure self-interest ethic.

Later writers, however, did not draw back; they used Smith's writings, without his late qualification, as a map of the contours of emerging laissez-faire. For economic purposes, the actions of the self-interested would produce the public benefit of greater national output. This would make public-spirited motives irrelevant, and possibly even convert them into an economic hindrance if government got involved. The emerging laissez-faire could be blind to what public-spirited persons might think were additional dimensions of the public good.

JANE MARCET'S TEXTBOOK

By the 1820s, classical economics, crystallized as laissez-faire, appeared in popular form. Jane Marcet's *Conversations on Political Economy* first appeared as a text in England in 1816 (1823 edition cited here); it was used heavily both there and in the best colleges of the United States (Dorfman 1946, V.2: 515). The text explained the inevitability and harmony of economic laws. The volume takes the form of a conversation between a naïve girl, Caroline, and her tutor, Mrs. B, who convinces Caroline that a free-market economy is really the best for all involved—including those who come out on the short end. At the end of 400–plus pages, Caroline exclaimed, "All that you have said reconciles me, in a great measure, to the inequality of the distribution of wealth" (Marcet 1827, 473). Caroline was driven to acquiesce to the status quo.

In Marcet's book, the principles of political economy are viewed through the lens of their implication for poverty. The poverty of industrial workers is explained as the inevitable result of population pressure as expounded by Malthus. The tutor states that "as soon as the labouring classes find their condition improved . . . population once again outstrips the means of subsistence; so that the condition of the poor, after a temporary improvement is again reduced to its former wretchedness" (153). Population growth thus grinds away any temporary improvement. There is a moral subtext: if there is no moral obligation to change what cannot be changed, and if poverty is inevitable, there can be no ethical obligation to deal with poverty. If there is any responsibility at all, Mrs. B strongly suggests that it falls on the poor themselves. If the employers paid higher wages, or provided relief, it would merely cause more population growth.

Mrs. B also taught the wages-fund doctrine, which held that wages were paid, not from the product of labor, but from a fixed fund set aside by employers before they employed workers. Employers sought to spend the entire fund each year to hire the most possible labor and so to produce the most possible goods. At the end of the year, the goods would be sold, a profit realized, and the fund replenished. The wages fund, together with the size of the worker population, determined the actual wage rate. If the available workers were few, the bidding among capitalists for workers would drive up the wage rate; the wages fund would be exhausted paying a high wage to a relatively few workers, and vice versa.

The moral implication of this doctrine was one-sided. First, workers wholly relied on the *prior* action of employers to establish the fund. In effect, workers were dependent on the thrift of employers to create the fund. Further, in this theory the workers' claim to pay was a claim only against the preexisting fund; they had no claim at all on what their labor helped produce. Finally, since the wages fund was entirely spent each year, whether workers were numerous or few, workers only had their own large numbers to blame if wages were low.

The wages fund did not admit of government intervention. Being a fixed amount at any given time, the fund would support fewer workers if higher wages were legislated or if taxes depleted the fund. Worse, with fewer workers for the same expenditure of funds, the return on capital would be less and the fund in subsequent times would be less. Thus, the victim of meddling by government would be the worker—a common theme in laissez-faire. The same reasoning also undermined charitable motives, for funds diverted for charity diminished the wages fund.

According to Mrs. B, wealth was the result of individual effort and poverty the just reward for idleness: "By continued exertion . . . [the skillful and industrious person] becomes rich; whilst the less industrious . . . remains poor" (89). This served as a moral justification of inequality, for the industrious wealthy deserved what they have earned, while the "less industrious" got what they deserved. Paradoxically, even while teaching Malthus's law of population, which made poverty inevitable and so not a choice, Marcet charged poverty to workers' lack of industry, which her readers would have interpreted to be the workers' free choice.

One might suppose that wealth would impose an obligation to add to the wages fund, since a larger fund would be the one way to permit more productive employment. But no such admonition was coming, for Mrs. B remained reluctant to put obligations on the employer class (see Marcet 1827, 463–64). The wealthy had great discretion in the disposition of wealth, for property rights were absolute and trumped either productive investment or social reform.

Mrs. B is faithful to the writings of Adam Smith and portrays self-interest in economics as a positive force. She points out that owners of capital can discover the best use for their capital, to which Caroline, the student, replies, "Of their own advantage they are no doubt the best judges" (460). This was a classic debate-stopper of laissez-faire proponents whenever governmental intervention in the allocation of resources was suggested. Yet, that debate-stopper begged the question whether other ends besides those encompassed by personal advantage needed to be considered. Mrs. B simply rejected the possibility that self-interest might not produce the common good. In her view, "It is the active zeal of each individual exerted in his own cause, which, in the aggregate, gives an impulse to the progressive improvement of the world at large" (464).

Marcet, through the questions and answers of her characters, also stated that the economic status quo represented the best of possible outcomes. Did land rents and food prices rise dramatically during a famine, which fell heavily on the poor? Mrs. B turned that into good news: the high prices would draw more resources into agriculture and eventually end the famine. As Caroline learned, "if the poor are obligated to pay a high price for the necessaries of life, it is for their own benefit" (233). Something could be found to justify everything bad that happened. Falling wages should guarantee more employment for the working class, for the wages fund would stretch further. Caroline sums up: "The more I hear on this subject, and the better I understand it, the greater is my admiration of that wise and beneficent arrangement which has so closely woven the interests of all classes of men" (458). This "beneficent arrangement" hints at a providential design, which thereby bestows a divine endorsement on the status quo.[3]

MARCET'S DEBT TO MALTHUS

Mrs. B owed much to Thomas Robert Malthus, whose *Essay on the Principle of Population* (1798) held that population increases exponentially until it overtakes the ability of the earth to provide subsistence. Once this limit is met, poverty is imposed inevitably on at least some part of the population. After stating that the "power of population" outruns the ability of the planet "to produce subsistence," Malthus drew a conclusion with heavy moral import: "This difficulty must fall somewhere and *must necessarily* be severely felt by a large portion of mankind" (Malthus 1798, 71—emphasis added). Malthus's laws were entirely deterministic: "we know from experience that these operations of what we call nature have been conducted almost invariably according to fixed law" (114). These natural laws were "absolutely independent of all human regulations" (138). Thus, relief to some poor merely diverts the blow to others: "though [the English poor laws] may have alleviated a little the intensity of individual misfortune, *they have spread the general evil over a much larger surface*" (94—emphasis added). Malthus's laws, because they were immune to human control, destroyed all humane values, for humane values proposed doing the impossible. Who is morally obliged to change what cannot be changed?

Viewing the great inequality of wealth of his era, Malthus expressed a personal judgment that inequality was bad. However, he was unwilling to advocate policies to promote equality: "whether a government could with advantage to society actively interfere to repress inequality of fortunes may be a matter of doubt" (177). In this way, morality was reduced to mere personal preference, a sentiment; but if change is scientifically impossible, such a personal preference imposes no obligation to act—it may be classified as wishful thinking. Ethics were clearly subordinated to what were perceived to be economic laws.

The only optimistic aspect of the ideas of Malthus was that free markets make the best of a bad situation. Scarcity is inherent in nature, but the incentives given by unfettered markets to self-interested actors provide the most that can be hoped for. If inequality and poverty are the result, any alternative would be just as bad, if not worse. In effect, the economic world operates by its own laws, which render social reform, morality, and compassion irrelevant.

FRANCIS WAYLAND: LAISSEZ-FAIRE FOR THE EVANGELICAL MIND

It is hard to believe that Malthus's dismal vision of Old World scarcity would ever have had much appeal in America, whose opportunities drew people from that Old World. But even more than American abundance, American religion stood as an intellectual and moral obstacle to laissez-faire. The early decades of the 1800s saw a revival of evangelical religion, which had significant differences with laissez-faire (Frey 2002, 217–20). First, evangelical Protestantism was heir to the Puritans' Calvinism, which viewed the self as a potential idol that threatened to displace the love of God and neighbor from one's heart (see chapter 2). Conversely, laissez-faire held a benign, even enthusiastic, view of (economic) self-interest. Second, the post-Puritan evangelical acted under a sense of obligation to God's revealed will in scripture, for that divine will defined the good; for the Enlightenment utilitarian, rewarding outcomes defined the good. Third, as noted, the evangelical looked to divinely inspired scripture for authority, whereas the Enlightenment celebrated autonomous human reason. In political economy, reason was narrowly understood as rationality focused on attaining self-interested goals. More generally, the Enlightenment thinkers had little use for revealed religion. Fourth, the evangelical inherited the Puritan's civic activism, which had attempted to transform society into a righteous or holy commonwealth. As noted earlier, laissez-faire argued that the economic status quo was largely inevitable, the working out of natural laws that could not be changed. Fifth, evangelicals, along with other Americans, shared economic optimism that clashed with Malthusian pessimism.

The reawakened evangelical spirit, therefore, logically should have rejected laissez-faire or its manifestation in everyday capitalism. Mark A. Noll (2002, 272–74) argues that, in a variety of ways, American Protestants prior to the Civil War participated fully in the emerging American economy, yet without capitulating to its mentality, taking a stance much like the Puritans. Yet, it is difficult to partake of an activity while rejecting the values most closely associated with it; indeed, success in a laissez-faire economy might well elude an evangelical Protestant who did not rationalize behavior ultimately acceptable only to the ethics of laissez-faire. Evangelicals apparently made their peace with the laissez-faire values that accompanied economic activity in the new American Republic. One possible reason for this accommodation is that alternatives to laissez-faire were associated in Protestant minds with atheism and other kinds of radicalism (May 1967, 7–15). An alternative is that a respected, evangelical moralist rationalized away the differences between laissez-faire and Protestantism.

A Baptist minister probably did more than anyone else to harmonize evangelical Protestantism and laissez-faire. Francis Wayland (1796–1865) became the president of Brown University in 1827 and remained there twenty-eight years. Wayland had experienced a deeply-felt conversion and, after giving up his medical apprenticeship, had studied at theologically conservative Andover seminary in New England. As president of Brown, he was to produce two texts, *The Elements of Moral Science*, which first appeared in 1835 (though the 1837 edition become standard) and *The Elements of Political Economy* in 1837. In the first text, he challenged the utilitarian outlook of Paley's text on moral and political philosophy (chapter 3). Wayland repudiated Paley's theological utilitarianism and affirmed the earlier morality based on obligation to divine will. On the other hand, Wayland exploited the fact that Protestant morality had never condemned self, as such, but only exclusive selfishness. Wayland, thus, defined an ethical realm of "innocent" self-interest in which he let laissez-faire principles have full play.[4]

Against Paley, Wayland's *Moral Science* appealed to evangelicals by stoutly rejecting the utilitarian notion that something was good because its consequence was what the individual desired: "it is not proved that an action is right because it is productive of the greatest amount of personal happiness." Rather, he wrote, the "*will of our God alone* is sufficient to create obligation" (Wayland 1837a, 36). This was a classic Puritan outlook: righteousness was more important than happiness, and God defined the obligation. Contrary to Smith, Wayland reaffirmed the importance of a good, even holy, motive. He said that character "consists in yielding up the consideration of our own happiness as a controlling motive, and subjecting it without reserve to the higher motive, the simple will of God" (98).

Instead of living by the "simple will of God," one might follow self-love, which could be sinful. This was as much as the most orthodox Puritan had claimed. But, according to Frey (2002, 222–24), Wayland also made an argument that was to minimize the moral threat of self-love. Wayland argued that many choices are "equally innocent." And, in deciding between equally innocent alternatives, the decision could turn on self-interest (1837a, 99). If the realm of "equally innocent" choices were to be large, self-interest would have a large, morally legitimate playing field in everyday economic life. In this neutral realm, evangelical ethics and Enlightenment economics would converge. Yet, showing a key tendency of autonomy morality, Wayland tended to characterize "innocent" activity only as not actively infringing upon someone else's rights. He seemed unconcerned with actions that required more than refraining from harming someone.

In the neutral, or innocent, realm there was room for economic activity. After clearing the ethical path, Wayland then produced *The Elements of Political Economy* (1837b) only two years after his moral science text. In the economics text, he taught conventional laissez-faire economics. The denominational college faculties apparently were readily persuaded by Wayland, for both his texts were perennial best sellers (on the political economy text see Frey 2002, 215, n.1). Wayland's economics text, "the epitome of prewar clerical laissez-faire," continued his influence into the final quarter of the nineteenth century (May 1967, 136).

When Wayland wrote of economic wrong or evil, he generally understood wrong or evil as particular acts of individuals, which harmed others. He did not—with the exception of certain religious duties—consider it wrong to fail to take affirmative actions for the benefit of others or of a larger good. His evangelical outlook is evident in the fact that Wayland took particular care to discuss bad motives in commerce (see Frey 2002, 224). With his focus firmly on the individual, Wayland never questioned a commercial *context* that might constantly tempt the motives of individuals. For Wayland, the economy apparently never embodied systemic ills; all sin could be understood under the rubric of bad personal motives. Wayland labeled as "oppression" legislation that might deal with systematic economic faults. To the victims of unregulated capital markets, Wayland's measured judgment was only that investors "be somewhat careful how they speculate in stocks" (1837b, 379). He typically admitted in his economics text that unethical, or sinful, economic activity was a reality, but never suggested that individual wrongdoers faced temptations created by the nature of the economy in which they moved.

Wayland's laissez-faire economics fit with his heightened views on individual rights, which acted to shield the autonomy of the individual. His *Moral Science* stated that God endowed each individual with the same fundamental rights (Wayland 1837a, 174). This imposed a *duty of reciprocity*, namely, that each person should respect in neighbors the same rights he claimed for himself. Government would exist merely to enforce this essentially moral reciprocity. Individuals who respect the duty of reciprocity, Wayland wrote, should need to "*surrender nothing whatever* in order to form a civil society" (1837a, 316; see also 180). The mutuality of relational language was clearly missing. Civil society, then, would consist of a group of otherwise autonomous people who protected themselves collectively from other autonomous people who might infringe their rights. This was a classic statement of the role of government in autonomy morality, and it took more from John Locke than from the Bible. Wayland's "duty of reciprocity" as the justification for government did not affirm human relationship or commonality; clearly, any Puritan notion of *commonwealth* was absent. Wayland's government had no higher role than seeing that one did not infringe another's rights to act in free autonomy. This evangelical's understanding of government was purely secular and drew little on the Bible.

Even Wayland's minimal government was problematic, for governments, once instituted, would hold the power to oppress the individual. Wayland warned against democracy's "unprincipled majority" and stated that even elected government may use its power for the citizen's "injury and oppression" (1837a, 320), which included taxes (236). According to Wayland, government was to do only things listed in the constitution and to "leave everything else undone" (330). Obviously, this meant laissez-faire in the economic sphere.

The major human right for Wayland was the right of property, and the duty of reciprocity required the protection of property rights by government. Only if humans could lock up the fruits of their labor in property would they be industrious, argued Wayland. To the degree that property is respected, "civilization advances" (Wayland 1837a, 212). Wayland abandoned fully the Puritan sense that property rights were contingent on their service to God and the common good. Instead he made them absolute. His *Moral Science* stated that "the value of property depends upon the *unrestrained use* which I am allowed to make of it" and denied society the right to abridge those rights (1837a, 236—emphasis added). Here Wayland showed none of the Puritan fear of the sinful potential of the unrestrained human will or of the Puritan sense that ownership was stewardship.

Wayland suggested some religious obligation to extend charity to the more worthy poor. Yet, his political economy text argued that private relief was never to be superseded by government programs, which "are in principle destructive to the right of property, because they must proceed upon the concession, that the rich are under the obligation to support the poor" (Wayland 1837b, 126). Further, if the poor came to consider governmental aid as an entitlement or right, they might no longer feel the gratitude that dependent persons ought to feel (Wayland 1837a, 348). Wayland portrayed the poor as a threat to property rights, for systematic relief would require taxation of property. For Wayland the religious obligation to charity was kept limited and segregated from civic morality. A relational morality would not have made such a dichotomy, for fellow humans in need possess a claim whether one acts in a religious or civic capacity.

In contrast to Malthusian pessimism, Wayland's economic outlook was colored by American optimism. The one original contribution Wayland made to economics was his emphasis on technological progress—something missing from the classical economists. Wayland, who had studied medicine before his conversion, like the Puritans, greatly appreciated practical benefits of empirical science (Frey 2002, 231). Relational moralists, such as William Penn, also viewed the potential of nature optimistically, and they used this as a reason to support a fuller definition of the public good. Wayland, however, reached a different conclusion. Wayland's belief in abundance led him to the judgment that any American who was not an idler could support a family, for in America "distressing poverty, or poverty which shortens life, except it arise from intemperance, or from some form of vice or indolence, is very rare" (1837b, 340). Wayland's sense of progress led to the conclusion that *poverty was a choice* and therefore not of concern to others. Morality thus dictated doing nothing to reinforce such behavior, certainly not rendering aid.

Apparently to the satisfaction of his readers, Francis Wayland's reasoning bridged the gap between evangelical and laissez-faire morals. It is likely that Wayland articulated what many of his prospering Protestant peers thought, for his works retained great popularity in the denominational colleges to which they sent their children. To be sure, American Protestantism was not monolithic, but Wayland's autonomy morality—superficially harmonized with parts of the thought of the earlier Puritans—had a significant impact.

CONCLUSION

By the early nineteenth century, laissez-faire theory and values had gained an influential following in America. Yet there were reasons this might not have happened. The economic conditions in America did not approximate those of Europe, where Malthusian scarcity was plausible. As for moral thought, America in the early nineteenth century experienced the revival of evangelical Protestantism, whose doctrines clashed at many points with laissez-faire.

Laissez-faire—as a morality leaving maximum freedom to, and imposing the fewest obligations on, economic actors—was bound to find some follow-ing in America. But in order for laissez-faire to stake out a secure position, its dissonance with evangelical Protestantism had to be resolved. This task was achieved by Francis Wayland, who repeated the forms of Protestant orthodoxy while neglecting much of its substance; specifically, he shifted the boundary line between sinful self-interest and "innocent" self-interest far enough to cre-ate significant tolerance of most economic activity. In reality, Wayland went far beyond tolerating most economic activity; he advocated absolute property rights and rejected most socially imposed obligations on economic actors. In doing this, Wayland restated certain relational Puritan doctrines in ways, and with emphases, that converted them into supports for autonomy morality. Many of Wayland's Protestant peers obviously accepted his arguments.

The difference between autonomy morality and relational morality shows clearly in Wayland's "duty of reciprocity," which was a centerpiece of his ethic. The duty of reciprocity imposed few positive obligations toward others. Instead, it simply stated that the autonomy one wished for oneself should be respected in others. The basis of this duty was purely logical: if such a rule were not followed, then anyone's autonomy could be threatened by others. This was a purely negative obligation that implicitly denied relational ethics: leave others alone in the interest of being left alone. (This is not to ignore the importance of the reciprocity principle: Wayland used it to reach strong anti-slavery conclusions.) However, any notion that one had positive obligations toward others, or to contribute to a common good shared with fellow, related moral beings, was not an integral part of this ethic. Although the clergyman Wayland did allow for some religious obligation to others, these resembled irrelevant interruptions in the general flow of his autonomy logic. For Wayland, the moral significance of poverty was that alleviating it might impose property taxes—not that revealed religion taught love of neighbor. Lest government became the instrument to advance a greater vision of the common good, and in so doing infringe individual autonomy, Wayland stood solidly against anything but a minimal government.

APPENDIX: A FULLER SKETCH OF LAISSEZ-FAIRE

Few laissez-faire moralists gave a comprehensive mapping of all its doctrines, so a brief overview is justified. The major doctrines of classical economics were among the economic doctrines of laissez-faire. These economic laws included the idea of gains from the division of labor, the benefits of trade, a labor theory of value, and the quantity theory of money (i.e., that prices in the long run changed in proportion to changes in money).

For morality, the most relevant characteristic of laissez-faire was the view of human nature as self-interested. Self-interest was a good characteristic because—as Adam Smith had asserted—unintended public good emerged from self-interested behavior. Self-interest was understood in rational, calculating terms; material incentives were the weights that the calculator put onto the scales. Self-interest, of course, was whatever the autonomous individual defined it to be. A corollary was the need for liberty to follow where the incentives might lead. Laissez-faire also affirmed competition, which emerged naturally as calculated, self-interested behavior in the context of scarcity. A very high status for competition was justified in varying ways, for it was what regulated Adam Smith's system of "natural liberty."

These core beliefs were fortified with subsidiary legal doctrines. Private property was necessary if autonomous economic man was to pursue self-interest. John Locke had argued that property existed *prior* to the establishment of governments and so could not legitimately be touched by government regulation; that is, property rights were absolute rights. Application of this doctrine allowed even taxes to be viewed as theft. A similar right to contract became so embedded in American law that by the late nineteenth century courts regularly used freedom-of-contract doctrine to invalidate labor-reform legislation.

In addition to the economic doctrines listed earlier, other doctrines of classical economics were even more closely identified with laissez-faire. Among these laws were: Malthus's population theory, Ricardo's rent theory and law of diminishing returns, and the wages-fund theory. These four essentially portrayed economics as the study of scarcity in various ways. A law less focused on scarcity was Say's law, which stated that production generates an equivalent amount of demand in a system with flexible prices. While not focused on scarcity, Say's law effectively ruled out any need for government involvement in the economy for it essentially ruled out involuntary unemployment.

Because European laissez-faire viewed nature as harsh, moralities promoting values other than individual survival could be dismissed as sentimental or unrealistic. European laissez-faire's view of reality thus protected individual autonomy: no one could be charged with an obligation to handicap oneself in order to remedy ills of others that were inevitable anyway. However, as noted previously, laissez-faire also claimed the existence of enough moral choice that economic success was due to virtue, while poverty was due to vice. The difficulty in pairing inevitability and moral choice went unrecognized in most laissez-faire writings.[5]

The abundance of America represented a clear challenge to the scarcity doctrine while making it more plausible that economic failure was due to personal moral failure. Francis Wayland's sense of America's abundance made it more logically compelling that economic failure was due to individual moral vices. When criticism of laissez-faire finally emerged (chapters 9, 10), the critics blamed an unjust economy, not scarcity or vice, for poverty.

FIVE

Ethics Better than
the Morals of Hermits

THE ASSERTION THAT the public good could emerge unassisted from competitive, self-interested behavior was never without critics. Alexander Hamilton favored the federal constitution precisely because, in his view, it could *thwart* particular interests that would stymie the common good. Daniel Raymond, a lawyer-turned-economist with a Puritan heritage, rejected the Enlightenment's complacent view of self-interest, and also affirmed government responsibility for overall economic health. Horace Mann, pioneer of public education, scorned moral "hermits" who resisted even education taxes. His "hermits" were so psychologically disconnected from the rest of mankind that they denied all obligations to others. Mann articulated a moral commonwealth of intergenerational rights and responsibilities. At approximately the same time, as documented by Alexis de Tocqueville, average citizens were forging a commonwealth through voluntary societies for social reform.

ALEXANDER HAMILTON

Alexander Hamilton's ideas and policies reflected conservative instincts. His support of the federal constitution was motivated in part by distrust of popular democracy; his financial policies, whatever else their justification, were designed to keep the confidence of the "moneyed class" in the federal government (Dorfman 1946, V.1: 412). Yet, he articulated a positive role for government in economics because he believed that the public good would never emerge automatically from the interplay of purely private interests.

Hamilton addressed four great issues facing the young American republic: adoption of a constitution, financing the national debt, stimulation of domestic manufactures, and creation of a national bank. In each case, he argued that the common good could not be attained by relying on an invisi-ble hand. At a deeper level, Hamilton's federalist principles were consistent with his dim view of human nature. Citing examples from classical literature, he concluded in *Federalist Paper No. 6* that "men are ambitious, vindictive, and rapacious" (Hamilton, Madison, Jay 1787–88, 54). Self-interest inevitably meant shortsightedness, he said, stating that "momentary passions, and imme-diate interests" always dominate more long-term interests. In *Federalist No. 15* he noted that a carefully designed government was needed because "the pas-sions of men will not conform to the dictates of reason and justice without constraint" (110). A well-designed federal government would check those tendencies, he thought, allow virtuous leaders to rise, and so bring about the public good. A rightly structured government, which checked one set of pri-vate interests against another, might well produce great gain for the good of all. He collaborated with Madison who "designed the elaborate constitutional mechanism to filter and refine popular passions in hopes that in the main it would be men of vision and virtue who would reach office at the national level" (Bellah et al. 1985, 255).

Hamilton's thought went beyond the role of government in merely checking conflicting interests. Contradicting laissez-faire, Hamilton claimed that humans were *ineffective* in acting upon their true interests. Hamilton wrote in 1791 that in the economic sphere "the simplest and most obvious improvements, in the [most] ordinary occupations, are adopted with hesita-tion, reluctance and by slow adaptations" (Hamilton 1966, 266). Because self-interest was sluggish, progress may "require the incitement and patronage of government" (267).

Contrary to laissez-faire doctrines, Hamilton doubted that an ungoverned commerce would tend to the best possible outcome. In a newspa-per piece in 1782, he dismissed laissez-faire doctrine as a "cant phrase." He called the creed of self-regulation of trade, "one of those wild speculative para-doxes." It had hardened into an antigovernment doctrine "as little reconcilable with experience or common sense as the [mercantilist] practice it was first framed to discredit" (Hamilton 1956, 275). Hamilton possessed a wide range of experience, from which he apparently inferred that larger purposes do *not* emerge from competing private interests.

Despite opposition to laissez-faire, Hamilton was no opponent of private enterprise. His opposition to laissez-faire was to its dogmatic rejection of gov-ernment activity: "practical politicians know that it [the economy] may be beneficially stimulated by prudent aids and encouragements on the part of government" (Hamilton 1956, 262). Notably, his opposition to laissez-faire was based on practical experience.

Because the ineffectiveness of self-interest left vast room for improve-ment, Hamilton saw great potential for government projects to improve things. When Hamilton proposed federal projects, he argued that everyone would share the benefits. Noting that some believed that agriculture and commerce had antagonistic interests, Hamilton added that both would benefit from the constitution. In fact, he said in *Federalist Paper No. 12*, experience shows that "their interests are intimately blended and interwoven" (Hamilton, Madison, Jay 1787–88, 92–93). Later, Hamilton took a similar line in his *Report on Manufactures* (1791) insisting that both North and South could gain from increased domestic manufacturing (Hamilton 1956, 282–83). He even claimed that agriculture would gain (282). Government support for infant industries would eventually benefit all as competition slowly replaced any monopolies initially granted to new industries (282). Contrary to laissez-faire, government policies could create gains for all.

Hamilton invoked a variety of reasons for his plan to repay the public debt, which was left from the Revolutionary War. He argued in 1791 that the government was morally bound to repay, that "the established rules of morality and justice" apply to nations, and "that governments are bound to keep their promises" (Hamilton 1956, 248). As with his other projects, Hamilton also found benefits for everyone in his plan—although the most direct beneficiaries would be those holding highly depreciated government bonds (including speculators). In 1801, he claimed public benefits from debt repayment to be an "extension of commerce . . . and manufactures, the rapid growth of our cities and towns, the consequent prosperity of agriculture, and the advancement of the farming interest" (252). Finally, his national bank project also promised generalized benefits (270.) In short, government could benefit the economy because relying on individual action had not worked effectively.

Hamilton's dim view of self-interest, presumably honed by observation of finances during his government service, challenged the political economists of his era, whose well-reasoned antimercantilist views had evolved into a more general antigovernment doctrine. Yet, from his pessimism came grounds for optimism: the very failures of human nature presented the opportunity for gains, which could typically be broadly distributed. Hamilton's claims were not based on abstract considerations; in fact, he was constantly providing practical plans to better the economy. Ironically, the treasury secretary and practical financier had a much more sober view of self-interest and of the workings of markets than Adam Smith, the theorist.

This being said, Hamilton was an economic conservative. His focus was on government's role in advancing production and improving markets, including financial markets, but not primarily in promoting economic equality or supporting the economically weak. His programs had in common with the policies of laissez-faire that the primary impact would support the existing economic order. Nevertheless, Hamilton generally argued that the more distant effects of his proposals would benefit even the yeoman farmer or fisherman. These claims were not unchallenged; the Jeffersonian opposition to Hamilton disputed the outcomes Hamilton claimed. Yet, leaving aside specific proposals,

Hamilton's more general position was that governmental activism in the service of a common good was necessary. In his experience, the common good transcended the mere sum of individual interests and did not result from merely selfish actions. Hamilton did not articulate a full relational morality. However, autonomy morality drew plausibility from a theory of self-interest operating within unrestrained markets; Hamilton challenged that idea vigorously with the authority of experience. Thus, he made relational morality, as expressed more fully by others, that much more credible.

DANIEL RAYMOND: POST-PURITAN
AND RELATIONAL MORALIST

Daniel Raymond's major work, *The Elements of Political Economy*, appeared in 1819 with a revision in 1823. Raymond was a lawyer with New England roots, who turned to economic theory. Many of Raymond's ideas may be understood from the perspective of his late Puritan, New England background (Frey 2000, 607–28). Raymond possessed an almost foreboding sense of human sin; because of it, he had a deep mistrust of self-interest as the motive force of economics. More important than this similarity to Puritanism were the many characteristics of relational morality that appeared in his thought. In fact, Raymond echoed some of the themes of the colonial Quakers.

Raymond held that "man by nature possesses a disposition to violence and plunder" (Raymond 1823, V.1: 17). Successful plunderers live at the expense of others; the ultimate example of this, according to Raymond, was slave-owning. Self-interest of this sort was certainly not the moral basis for an economy or even a sound practical basis either. In the aggregate, a society could only prosper from the labor of citizens; effort spent enriching self at the expense of others produced nothing. Directly challenging the invisible-hand doctrine, Raymond held that individual interest and public interest "are often directly opposed" (V.1: 35). Like Hamilton, he argued that the self-interest of individuals is often shortsighted.

Raymond, like Hamilton, believed that government was obliged to take a relatively active economic role, contrary to laissez-faire: "the absurdity of this doctrine of not legislating at all, and permitting every man to pursue his own interest in his own way, is manifest, from its utter impracticability" (V.1: 163). The question was not whether there would be laws, but their wisdom, he wrote. And laws might indeed lack wisdom due to the pervasiveness of sin, thought Raymond. Although Raymond, like the Puritans, had no naïve faith in government, he sometimes sounded much like William Penn, likening government to "a good shepherd, who supports and nourishes the weak and feeble ones in his flock" (V. 2: 13). The almost biblical metaphor of a shepherd-government went on to suggest that government assist the weak to "take their chance with the strong." Raymond delineated an ideal role for government, far greater than its minimal role in laissez-faire, always knowing that government could fall far short.

Raymond rejected absolute property rights that exempted owners from social responsibility. Instead, he argued, property existed only by the action of society. Because property is created by society, private rights are always subordinate to the public good. Here, by a different logic from the Puritans' biblical ideas of stewardship, Raymond came to the same position on property. He wrote that "the public grants no title to property in derogation of the public weal" (V.2: 205). This contradicted the very heart of autonomy morality (see Francis Wayland's view of property, chapter 4).

Like the Puritans, Raymond was uncomfortable with exaggerated differences in incomes and wealth, and he doubted that observed economic inequality was the result only of natural differences. On the contrary, Raymond wrote, "the powerful ones in society . . . are not usually those who are so by nature" (V.2: 12, 13). Much existing economic power is based more on artificial advantage, often created by laws, than on natural differences, he held.

In addition to his theory of artificial advantages, Raymond attacked the theory of poverty promulgated by laissez-faire as he understood it. In that theory, any healthy and strong person in poverty could fend for himself and therefore deserved no aid. Raymond, on the contrary, claimed that "the pauperism of those who have health and strength to work is often involuntary" (V. 2: 33). The idea of *involuntary* poverty denied the rationale that vice caused poverty.

To the prescription that the poor needed to reform, Raymond retorted bitterly that if this prescription succeeded, the only result would be to "substitute virtuous and industriously disposed paupers for vicious and lazy paupers" (V.2: 65). Thus he rejected emphatically the vice-poverty link, which he saw as a convenient rationalization to ignore the plight of the weak. In fact, he stated that relief should not be conditioned on inability to work. In company with other relational moralists, Raymond rejected the idea that the weak were shameless parasites—certainly no more than some who were well-off. He denied "that the poor will voluntarily place their dependence for support upon public charity; the great mass of mankind have an innate feeling of independence and pride, which scorns to receive charity" (V. 2: 80). In effect, people possess an innate human dignity—a proposition similar to the view of early Quaker thinkers (chapter 2) and similar to that found in much relational morality. The poor have a claim on society, for God provided the earth in common to all. The law should enforce this claim because "private charity is not adequate." Charity was inadequate not merely in the sense of too few dollars, but also the moral sense that charity is an act of mercy to someone *who has no claim to aid.* Raymond believed, to the contrary, that the poor were *entitled to aid as a human right.*

At a time when laissez-faire argued that economies left alone perform as well as natural laws allow, Raymond argued that economies were subject to systemic ills. In malfunctioning systems, certain self-interested actions would make things worse. Inadequate demand would feed on itself, for owners of an unsold surplus of goods "may throw it into the consumption of some following years, but . . . by so doing they would interfere with the future production to an equal extent" (V.1: 124). The postponed sale of surplus goods might serve the owner's interest, but harm the public good by extending economic depression.

Having suggested that a sick economy is not self-curing, Raymond proposed a role for government: in case of surplus production "it is as much the *duty* of a legislator to make provision, if possible, for its immediate consumption, as it would be to adopt measures for the supplying the nation with food" (V.1: 123). He suggested that the nation could become ill and in that condition required governmental medicine. This recommendation came close to twentieth-century macroeconomics (see chapter 11). But, as important, Raymond framed it as a moral duty of government. Keeping hands off, while the economy continued sick, was not a moral course.

Raymond reversed the attitudes of autonomy ethics: he taught obligation to a common good and suspicion of self-interest. In addition, he emphasized innate human dignity: the poor had pride and would not demean themselves with voluntary dependency. He denied the popular view that the poor were more likely to try to live at others' expense than some of the rich. If the social body did host parasites, Raymond held that they were members of all social classes.

Raymond's work demonstrates that economic morality does not stand alone; it is congruent with society's understanding of how an economy works. If the accepted economic view is that exclusively self-interested actions, taken without regard to the public good, nevertheless produce the common good, then selfishness is well on its way be being accepted as a virtue. Raymond was very adept at giving examples in which the good of an individual was counter to the good of the larger economy; the public good, he argued, was not simply the sum of private goods. The conflict of public and private good occurs especially when the economy is a system that operates by laws unique to a system.

Again, Raymond showed how accepted theory interacts with morality. If the accepted perspective is that poverty is due to inherently lazy people, then there is little ethical duty to act on their behalf. Indeed, aid may provide an incentive for sloth. Raymond proposed the alternative perspective, that able-bodied people were without work, not by choice, but because the economy left them that way. Linking this economic statement to an ethical proposition, he suggested that an innate human dignity made the poor willing workers. This position greatly diminished the great role assigned to material incentives in fostering work by Enlightenment thinkers such as Franklin (chapter 3). Raymond in effect argued that society had moral obligations to address social ills, and that governmental action created the public good.

HORACE MANN: PUBLIC EDUCATION
AND PUBLIC MORALITY

Horace Mann (1796–1859) was a Massachusetts state senator who became secretary of the state board of education in 1837. In his position with the board, he authored twelve annual reports that expounded the philosophy and morality of free public education in a republic. In one report, he contrasted the republic with the "doctrine of No-government" and dismissed that doctrine on the grounds that it would "forfeit all the power that originates in concert and union" (Mann 1957, 57). In his writings on education, he outlined a clash between no-government individualism and republican mutual obligation.

Mann held that the common heritage of humanity belonged to children by right, and that the citizens of a nation were obligated to transmit that heritage—that is, he taught obligations that self-interest individualism denied. Mann's tenth annual report, for the year 1846, concluded with three ethical propositions: "The successive generations of men, taken collectively, constitute one great Commonwealth. The property of this Commonwealth is pledged for the education of all its youth," he said. And added that "the successive holders of this property are trustees" (77–78). Children possessed a natural right, he said, to intellectual nourishment as well as physical nourishment, with the obligation to fulfill this right falling to the preceding generation. His great commonwealth extending through generations expressed human relatedness through time. The commonwealth metaphor, in his mind, implied that education had a lien on property because the function of property was ultimately social.

Mann, nevertheless, encountered resistance to education taxes on the grounds the taxes infringed property rights. Most of the tenth annual report was devoted to refuting this proposition, making the case against the "arrogant doctrine of absolute ownership." How, Mann asked, can anyone imagine that property exists apart from society and human history? "We have seen how insignificant a portion of any man's possessions he can claim, in any proper and just sense, to have earned." All wealth derives from the efforts of multitudes working over ages of time, argued Mann: "Resources developed, property acquired, after all these ages of preparation, after all these facilities and securities, accrue not to the benefit of the possessor only, but to that of the next and all succeeding generations" (70). An owner of property is merely a beneficiary of those who went before, he argued, and in turn must be benefactor of those to come. Mann's ethic of relationship implied duty: humans are bonded to one another by history and experience, so have obligations to one another; failure to fulfill these is a breach of trust. Mann likened the morality of self-interest to "the philosophy or the morals of hermits" (71). That is, the morals of those sensing

themselves isolated from, or alien to, other humans, and so without obligation to others.

Mann also rooted his advocacy in an analysis of contemporary trends.
Noting that Massachusetts was one of the most industrialized states of his era,
Mann concluded that it was unthinkable that Americans should tolerate
"those hideous evils which are always engendered between Capital and Labor,
when all capital is in the hands of one class and all the labor is thrown upon
another" (86). Universal education, he thought, could guarantee that such a
division between classes would never occur, for universal education would dif-
fuse property ownership. Mann held that economic outcomes were not
inevitable; rather, the good of society depended on the acceptance of collective responsibility for education. Greater equality could be had, and class strife
avoided, if humans collectively fulfilled their duty to educate their children.

In propounding a relational morality, Mann did not forget that relationships
were among individuals, and that obligations existed for the *good of individuals*.
In fact, he emphasized a kind of education that took heed of the individual differences of children. One commentator notes that Mann wrestled with the problem of how "the values of individuality" can be "reconciled with the necessity of
teaching children in groups" and advised that teaching methods be adjusted to
children's individual differences (Cremin in Mann 1957, 17). A major purpose of
education, according to Mann's brief, was to educate citizens capable of self-government in a republic. In spelling this out, Mann showed the utmost respect for
the child as a reasoning, moral being: "as soon as his capacity will permit," he said,
"the reasons on which [the law of the republic] is founded, should be made as
intelligible as the law itself" (Mann 1957, 59). Acceptance of the law was based
not on obedience to authority, but through moral comprehension. Mann's relational morality naturally expressed a sense of humans being moral beings and so
deserving treatment that respected the dignity of that status.

Writing in the 1840s, just before Marxism broke on the world scene,
Mann highlighted class divisions as a potential threat to the republic. Instead,
Mann held that education would eliminate stark class divisions, into which
individuals were submerged. This helps to underline that Mann's relational
morality was an individualistic morality. Indeed, education explicitly develops
the full powers of individuals. The opposition of relational moralists to autonomy morality never pushed them into the socialist camp—they were individualistic from the first. Mann's message was that humans have an obligation to
act collectively because the interdependence of individuals requires older people help youth develop fully as individuals.

VOLUNTEERISM AND REFORM

Alexis de Tocqueville observed in the 1830s that "no vice of the human heart
is so acceptable to it as selfishness" (Tocqueville 1835, V.2: 109). But Toc-

queville marveled that American democracy resisted the tendency to let self-interest dominate society. First, the American democracy threw persons together to work out the details of the common good, thus thwarting the temptation to look only inwardly. But, more important, because no individual alone could have a significant impact on the community, Americans banded together in a vast array of voluntary societies to advance every possible public purpose. Tocqueville wrote of his admiration of how Americans "succeed in proposing a common object for the exertions of a great many men and in inducing them voluntarily to pursue it" (V.2: 115). He added that Americans with a social vision instinctively "look out for mutual assistance; and as soon as they have found one another out, they combine" (V.2: 117). Voluntary associations existed for every possible purpose: temperance, evangelizing the frontiers, prison reform, poor relief, Sunday schools, antislavery, women's rights and education, the founding of hospitals and colleges, world peace, and more. At the extremes were religious and secular socialist communes.

Unlike hierarchical cultures, in which aristocrats could do great things, said Tocqueville, in America only the cooperation of many would accomplish great things. He noted Americans' willingness to give up *narrow* self-interest and to work for "self interest rightly understood," which involved the common good: "an enlightened regard for themselves constantly prompts [Americans] to assist one another and inclines them willingly to sacrifice a portion of their time and property to the welfare of the state" (V.2: 130). Tocqueville attributed all this to democracy, but he might have looked for additional influences.

America of the early nineteenth century was still deeply influenced by the Puritan heritage of reform. The movement had been a reform movement in old England, and the migration of the Puritans to America had been to establish a holy commonwealth—with scripture as a guidebook. The history of New England was a long story of successive migrations from an old order to found a better order (e.g., the founding of the Connecticut colony from the Massachusetts Bay colony). As noted (chapter 3), Puritan clergy had been forceful in supporting the American Revolution. The inspiration of American voluntary efforts might have included far more of a tincture of Puritanism than the French visitor recognized.

When Puritan Cotton Mather (chapter 3) proposed voluntary societies, the proposal emerged from less than a general vision of the common good. Mather's original proposal envisioned the proposed groups being supports for pious living among the members (as they were among German Pietists); their activities would essentially be Christian evangelism. Even in their nineteenth-century form, voluntary reform groups did not pose a direct challenge to the market economy or to the broader society. As private groups, they were an alternative to more general governmental action. Although some voluntary associations (such as the abolition cause) ultimately precipitated government involvement, voluntary efforts could also become a reason to postpone more comprehensive solutions to problems. Although the reform movements allowed anyone to go beyond narrow self-interest, each was so tightly focused on one problem that no one cause could embody a comprehensive vision of the common good. Being voluntary in nature, these reform groups depended on those with a social conscience and rarely posed a challenge to those who felt no responsibility (Ralph Waldo Emerson was famous in this respect). A culture that relied almost exclusively on voluntary groups to deal with its problems was a culture denying that the common good was compelling enough to require that all contribute.

In another sense, however, volunteerism implied a criticism of laissez-faire and the status quo. The large number of causes suggested that a competitive economy had either created flaws in society, or at least had failed to address them. Further, the proliferation of voluntary and charitable causes showed that many people did not believe that social ills were inevitable. The existence of reform societies raised questions whose answers challenged autonomy ethics.

CONCLUSION

Laissez-faire was never unchallenged. Some moralists clearly saw the dominance of self-interest to be an obstacle to the creation of a responsible society. Both Hamilton and Raymond portrayed self-interest as shortsighted. The common good, they suggested, is achieved when self-interest is checked. Hamilton favored governments designed so that interest groups would check each other—with the common good finally emerging. Raymond suggested that property rights should be limited for the sake of the common good. He also proposed that when the economic system falls ill, self-interested responses might actually worsen the systemic sickness. To describe the economy as a system implied a moral proposition: all passengers on a single economic ship shared a common fate and self-interested behavior might harm the ship.

The moralists of civic responsibility expressed themes of relational ethics, understanding human existence to be fundamentally social. Mann observed that no individual exists outside a great human commonwealth. Both Mann and Raymond held that private property—that central institution of individualism—is the creation of society and subject to social rules. Even self-reliance, a cardinal virtue of individualism, is only possible within a social framework, they thought. Mann and Raymond were not socialists; but, for them, the individual—as a fact of existence and of ethics—must be oriented, not inward toward the self, but outward toward the commonwealth.

Even at the time Raymond and Mann were writing, laissez-faire was hardening its doctrines into a scientific defense of the economic status quo (chapter 4). Among other things, this meant preserving, and morally justifying, large economic disparities. With the possible exception of Hamilton, whose proposals were accused—at least in terms of their first-order effects—of increasing disparities of wealth, the other moralists of this chapter argued that economic disparities were neither inevitable, nor morally acceptable. The changes advocated by these writers ranged from fiscal policies to end recessions, to direct support of the poor, to universal and free public education. Hamilton, Raymond, and Mann understood the economy to be the product of intentional human actions and institutions—not untouchable economic laws. If outcomes were intolerable, then change was both possible and required. Hamilton proposed a trial-and-error process for government policy—thereby implying that economic reality was more open-ended, less constrained by economic law, than laissez-faire decreed.

Although Hamilton held a less egalitarian vision of society than Raymond and Mann, he shared their belief that unregulated markets were not the way to achieve the good for society. Hamilton shared with the others an understanding of the role of government as an agent of the good economy. Ultimately, all had a vision of the social good that required intentional actions by many acting in concert and that placed obligation on all members of the society. This, they saw as better than the morality of hermits, who cared nothing about those to whom they never even acknowledged a connection.

The ideas of these relational moralists were not without flaw. Mann certainly promised too many potential benefits to education. Raymond's general wariness of self-interest seemed to be held in abeyance when he discussed the motives of the poor. And Hamilton made only an indirect contribution to relational morality; his skepticism of laissez-faire lent credibility to more cooperative theories of economic life. Tocqueville properly noticed the uniquely American institution of voluntarism. But he failed to note its negative side: the implication that the service to the common good was merely a voluntary concern that was binding on no one. Yet, each articulated at least portions of a relational morality that interpreted individualism within a framework of human relationships. Mann, in particular, explicitly added the historical dimension to relational ethics: people, he affirmed, were beneficiaries of those who had preceded them, and were trustees for those who came after them. Human relationships extended through time as well as place.

SIX

Religious Socialism

The Communal Moravians

═══════════════════════

AS MORALISTS OF the two forms of individualist morality debated their differences, other people were practicing socialist economics and morality. By the later colonial period, and throughout the nineteenth century, intentional socialist groups continually sprouted in America. Almost all eventually abandoned their communitarian ways, or disbanded entirely—some rather quickly. One of the shortest-lived socialist communities, New Harmony (1826–1827), was secular in outlook. The more enduring socialist groups were motivated by a variety of religious beliefs, including perfectionist and millennial beliefs (e.g., Oneida or the Shaker communities). Others sought to live closer to New Testament norms (e.g., Harmony, Amana, Ephrata, and the Hutterites—who continue to the present). The group on which this chapter will focus began at a far earlier date than most and persisted for decades. The colonial-era and federal-era Moravians revealed key elements of religious socialism.

The Moravians provided a moral critique of individualism that other socialists would have shared. The Moravians, as did other socialist communities, also provided a natural experiment, which tested key assertions about human nature made by autonomy morality. Autonomy morality and classical economic theory supported each other by asserting *material incentives* to be the driving force in economic behavior of self-interested people. The socialist experiments provided some evidence as to whether material incentives are really so important in economics, for socialist groups typically severed any tight link between one's income and one's contribution to productive effort. The standard political economy predicted that high moral ideals could not substitute for linking material incentives to work effort. The Moravian experience finds material incentives to be less clearly linked to economic success than the secular economists declared with such certainty.

The Moravian communities began much earlier in American history than most socialist groups and endured longer than most. Lessons from their experience might also be more easily generalized because they did not base their practices on relatively extreme beliefs, such as millennialism. The closed Moravian communities functioned under both purely communal and semi-socialist arrangements over an extended period that began about 1740 and ran until the middle of the nineteenth century—though existing in form only after about 1830. Over the several generations that the Moravian communities operated under varying degrees of church control, they interacted (sometimes unwillingly) with the intruding American culture. This interaction forced them to produce a moral critique of that culture. In large measure, Moravian ethical views must be inferred from their daily practices and from documents intended mainly for other purposes.

MORAVIAN BACKGROUND IN BRIEF

German-speaking Moravians settled in Pennsylvania and North Carolina during the middle third of the eighteenth century. These Moravians claimed religious descent from Czech Protestant reformer John Hus, who preceded Martin Luther by a century. In the decades following Hus's death, a group of his followers in Bohemia and Moravia organized a church, the *Unitas Fratrum*. However it was decimated and scattered during the Thirty Years' War (1618–1648). In the 1720s, some refugees who recalled this fading tradition, along with non-Moravian religious refugees, found asylum on the German estate of Count Nicolas Von Zinzendorf, a Lutheran nobleman. Zinzendorf found his meaning in Pietism, rather than in his duties as a nobleman, and soon became spiritual leader of this group. The religious brotherhood that coalesced around Zinzendorf combined the Lutheran Pietism of the eighteenth century with influences of the older *Unitas Fratrum*. Eventually, this group came to consider itself the renewal of the *Unitas Fratrum*.

A mark of Pietism was its emphasis on small groups for spiritual growth. At Zinzendorf's estate, these groups evolved into choirs, which were not singing groups, but groups for spiritual development stratified by age, sex, and marital status. This grouping allowed persons of like status in life to encourage each other in faith and allowed choir leaders to exercise a close spiritual discipline. This close supervision eventually extended to overseeing the choir members' participation in economic life. Separate communal housekeeping arrangements by choirs began in the late 1720s in Herrnhut, the town built by the refugees on the Zinzendorf estate in Saxony. Eventually, this town and others became Moravian "congregation towns." The communalism of these Moravian towns has been characterized by one historian as "social communalism" (Atwood 2004, 118). However, according to this historian, when the Moravians founded Bethlehem, Pennsylvania, in the early 1740s, the "full sharing of a communal economy" would emerge (118; see also 175).

THE GENERAL ECONOMY OF
BETHLEHEM, PENNSYLVANIA: 1742–1766

Starting in 1742, Moravian settlement of Bethlehem and Nazareth, Pennsylvania, was accomplished by European settlers, many of whom were fully organized aboard ship as highly disciplined "sea congregations," complete with choirs. The towns were to be guided by rules known as the General Economy (Sessler 1933, 80–92). Under the General Economy, adults worked without compensation in the trades or agriculture, or as missionaries. Ownership of land was held by representatives of the church. A simplified explanation of the system is that members donated their labor "in exchange for no other compensation than food, clothing, and shelter for themselves and their children" and for "the joy of seeing the gospel preached" (Sessler 1933, 85). Others, however, argue that the interconnections between Moravian devotion, theology, and everyday life were more complex than that, as living became an act of liturgy (Atwood 2004, 176–77).

During the years of the General Economy, Bethlehem proper was a community of "trade and manufacturing," surrounded by farming communities (Atwood 2004, 119). Under the leadership of August Gottlieb Spangenberg, who arrived in 1744, the commune prospered, but when he was recalled to Germany in 1748, his successors in a few years turned prosperity to economic failure. When Spangenberg returned in 1751, the older patterns were reinstated with success. Significantly, when Spangenberg proposed to convert the nearby Moravian community of Nazareth into a less rigidly regulated town (as an alternative for those who did not care so much for the General Economy), lack of enthusiasm for the plan among Bethlehem's residents caused it to be abandoned (Atwood 2004, 131). A Brotherly Agreement—a document common to all Moravian congregation towns—was drafted and signed in 1754.

The Brotherly Agreement of 1754 articulated communal values in eight articles (Sessler 1933, 229–32). The first article made clear that the Lord's will guided both the internal functions and the mission functions of the community. The article also committed the signers to being "helpful when and where the Savior may need us." The "when and where" would be determined by the church. Much of the first article spelled out the support the members of the community would provide for those serving as missionaries; specifically, missionaries' children would be raised by the communal institutions that raised and educated all the Moravian children.

The second article affirmed that the signers belonged to the Savior and the corollary that "what we have, that all belongs to Him." Pious Christians anywhere might have accepted the sentiment expressed by Article Two—that all belongs to God in an ultimate sense. However, the Bethlehem Moravians meant that the Lord, *acting through church leaders*, could literally control one's efforts and resources in the here and now—a clear distinction between a socialist system and either of the rival individualistic value systems that held sway elsewhere.

The third article explicitly rejected the employment relationships of the outside world, which reduced people to "men-servants or maid-servants, who serve some man for the sake of wage." Instead of work being motivated by money, in Bethlehem it ideally was an expression of one's relationship with the savior. The third article continued that "we are here as brethren and sisters, who owe themselves to the Saviour, and for whom it is, indeed, a token of grace that they may do all for His sake." Those who owed all to Christ could not "pretend to any wage or have any reason to pretend to any."

To be "brethren and sisters," as the Brotherly Agreement stated it, was to relate as kin rather than on the basis of material considerations or for the self's advantage. This relationship of the Moravians to each other was based on the relationship of each to their savior. The willing renunciation of a mercenary relationship to the community was a natural corollary to the believer's affirmation of a relationship to the suffering Christ.

The Brotherly Agreement continued in the fourth article to criticize the outside world's misguided notion of freedom, as the philosophy of living "according to our own notions." The outside world, it suggested, equated freedom with self-will or autonomy, whereas those led by the savior freely turned from self-will and chose the ordered life of the Lord's community. The fifth and six articles proclaimed the signers to be "satisfied" and "content" with what the Lord had provided. Discontent with one's material status showed worldliness in one's outlook. Instead, one's focus on Christ's suffering should replace the goad of selfish material incentives. Two final articles adopted a less theological perspective and seem aimed at preventing the outside world from gaining legal leverage over the Moravian community.

Under the Brotherly Agreement, Bethlehem continued relatively successfully in its communal ways until 1761 when the General Economy was disbanded under orders from Europe shortly after Zinzendorf's death. Population and economic statistics can be read to suggest that the move away from communalism (and simultaneously from Zinzendorf's theology) reversed growth and led to decades of decline (Atwood 2004, 224–25). This suggests that, at least in the 1760s, economic failure or major dissatisfaction was *not* the cause of the abandonment of communalism. The centrifugal forces of individual autonomy apparently had not overcome the unity of spirit engendered by the vivid theology of the suffering savior who sanctified all of life.

A MIXED ECONOMY AND
SALEM'S BROTHERLY AGREEMENT

Although it was ended in Bethlehem in 1761, the General Economy continued for several more years in the North Carolina frontier settlement at
Bethabara, which was founded in 1753. The economic arrangements at
Bethabara were similar to those of Bethlehem (and many of its residents had
moved from Bethlehem). They are described succinctly: "In the common
housekeeping, individuals could retain their own personal property, but
income from farm and industry went to the congregation, and food, clothing,
and housing were supplied as needed to each member" (Crews and Starbuck
2002, 48). The church owned all productive inputs "except labor, which individual brothers and sisters provided in return for food, housing, clothing,
medical care, and education" (Thorp 1989, 41). Thorp (69) characterized the
General Economy as providing "security from cradle to grave" especially for
families. The General Economy traded with surrounding settlers, and it was
expected to remit any profits to the church in Europe (a prospect that largely
failed to materialize).

Was the communalism of the General Economy accepted enthusiastically
by all? The founding of the nearby town of Bethania, which provided consid-
erably more individual freedom than in Bethabara, might have provided an
outlet for individualists. However, Thorp provides an alternative explanation
for its founding.[1] And Crews and Starbuck (2002, 32) state that "the records
simply do not bear out" the hypothesis that Bethania was founded due to dissention with the General Economy. Nevertheless, uncooperative individualists
did indeed exist and were invited to leave entirely (Thorp 1989, 101–104).
However one couple moved back to the General Economy from the less regulated town of Bethania. Internal dissention with communalism does not
seem to have been a major reason for the end of the General Economy in
Bethabara. Rather, Bethabara had been destined to be a temporary settlement,
diminishing when the congregation town of Salem was established; ending
the General Economy at that point was logical.

By 1772, when many of the Bethabara residents moved to the newly
constructed Salem, the General Economy was left behind. A recent history
notes that "communal economy was not a tenet of Moravian religion,"
although it was an expression of unity (Crews and Starbuck 2002, 47). It
may have emerged from a combination of pragmatism in adapting to frontier life, an extrapolation of trends in European Moravian towns, Spangenberg's leadership, and perhaps from the interplay with Zinzendorf's theology. While abandonment of the General Economy had been imposed on
Bethlehem from church leaders in Europe, in North Carolina the change
seemed more acceptable to the local members. At Salem, in place of the
communal economy, a mixed system, which might be called socialist, was

put in place. It would prove to be a transition phase on the way to a more worldly and individualistic economics.

The Brotherly Agreement of 1773 for Salem, North Carolina, which amounted to the constitution of the community, revealed a transitional Salem economy, which nevertheless was far more regulated than economies in most American towns of the era (Brotherly Agreement, 1773).[2] The tension between the General Economy and the newer, only partially socialized economics is obvious in the document. The Salem Agreement did not disparage wages as the Bethlehem Agreement had. Indeed its fifth article (section 11) admonished each member to earn a living. This included paid employment as well as running one's own shop or trade. Salem governing boards had some say about the nature of employment contracts.

The 1773 Brotherly Agreement envisioned the future to lie in the direction of individual enterprise. The fifth article (sec. 14) encouraged all with the skills to operate businesses. Yet, this was not unregulated enterprise, for church boards would control entry into, and oversee conduct of, business. The Brotherly Agreement formally expressed disapproval of monopoly. However, it is evident that that when additional competition providing a particular good or service was deemed harmful to the community, boards were slow to approve more entrants into that trade (see Crews and Starbuck 2002, 82). A board (*Aufseher Collegium*) was to oversee prices in the town. Explicitly ruled out by the seventh article (sec. 3) was pricing by haggling—perhaps because haggling tempted some to misrepresent goods or hide true intentions.

The seventh article (sec. 1) also stated that the goal in a trade should never be gaining wealth, but instead rendering service to one's fellow men. The potential for economic inequality developing under the Salem Agreement surely was perceived as a threat to the fundamental spiritual equality based on God's love bestowed on every person without distinction. While not ruling out economic inequality, which was an inevitable result of allowing private enterprise, the Brotherly Agreement of Salem made some effort to reaffirm the ideals of equality: the fifth article (sec. 3) affirmed that residence in town would not be granted on the basis of wealth, and (sec. 5) that in the Moravian schools children would be treated without regard to economic standing of parents.

In the Brotherly Agreement of Salem, self-interest had bounds set around it: all were urged to look to the general good, not merely personal good. The general good under the Salem agreement was not left to individual conscience. The congregation town provided a wide array of services, including schools, night watchmen, and a public piped-water supply. The Brotherly Agreement's fifth article (sec. 17) obligated all citizens to contribute to the expense of these services. In addition, the shared cultural life of Salem—while not explicitly spelled out—far exceeded that of frontier towns. A high standard in the arts (especially music) was almost guaranteed in Salem, given the skills of occupants of the various church offices also confirmed by the agreement. This was a philosophy of shared support of public facilities, services, culture, and church that was largely at odds with views prevailing on the American frontier.

Ultimate control over businesses and citizens was made possible by the church's ownership of all land in the built-up town (Crews and Starbuck 2002, 82). Residence in Salem was strictly controlled; only members of the church of good character were permitted to reside there. Nevertheless, the fifth article (sec. 8) recognized private ownership of property.

The Brotherly Agreement was ambivalent toward private economics. The brethren recognized that private economics is motivated by self-interest, which could become the wedge that would split apart communal institutions. The community seemed to perceive that private economic activity, which it was endorsing, tended to reduce human interactions to the level of economic transactions. To begin relating in terms of transactions was at odds with the religious ideal of the Moravians—that love of their common savior related all as brothers and sisters. Significant regulations were imposed on private economics, possibly in an effort to thwart this tendency and other self-centered tendencies inherent in private economics. The preamble to the Brotherly Agreement significantly notes that the regulations about to be constituted by the document are needed because of "human frailty."

Problems for Communal Values in Salem

The General Economy had persisted as a viable system for about twenty years each in Bethlehem and Bethabara. The Brotherly Agreement for Salem intentionally moved away from that model, recognizing individuals as economic actors, while retaining substantial community control; that model contained internal tensions. In addition, Salem would face external challenge: the American Revolution and the encroachment of slavery.

The American Revolution posed problems for socialist institutions and values among the Moravians at the same time as it provided the occasion to reaffirm the communal ideal. The Moravian economies could not be insulated from the effects of war—particularly instability in the value of the currency. In Salem, official price oversight was eroded as businesses found it impossible to charge the amounts the board would approve and still cover rapidly inflating costs. Rather than force local businesses to fail, price oversight was eased. Finally, as the situation became critical, businesses in the interest of survival were permitted to price items as best they could. For a time, the *Aufseher Collegium* also attempted to control currency exchange rates in the face of disparate inflation rates among the various colonial currencies in use (Frey 1988). Official control of prices and currency exchanges symbolized that the general good came before private interest. Thus the wartime inflation, which undermined community control of currency values and prices, also undermined the communal ideal.

Rapid inflation produced outbursts of self-interested behavior on the part of single brothers, who found the regulated wages of their choir to be increased too little and too late. In 1777, the Salem single brethren went on strike, thus breaking community solidarity with a demonstration of organized self-interest (see Crews and Starbuck 2002, 108–109). When the Revolutionary War finally ended, Moravian records note that young people were leaving to practice their trades more profitably elsewhere. Clearly, a mixed system that required persons to care for their own livelihood, combined with wartime circumstances that made life difficult, increased self-interested behavior.

Slavery also challenged the moral basis of the communal way. When the Moravians first settled in colonial North Carolina, the slave-owning culture they found was foreign to them. In addition, their craft-oriented activity did not use large teams of enslaved workers as was the case on plantations in other locations. Even so, with the passage of time, shortages of particular skills, or extraordinary efforts, as when the community was constructing large projects, argued for augmenting their own labor. At first, specific needs were met either by hiring free day laborers or hiring slaves from outsiders. They "accepted the limited use of slave labor if it supplemented, but did not replace, the toil of white Moravian hands" (Sensbach 1998, 64–65).

In the late 1760s, the inevitable question of purchasing a slave arose because a hired slave expressed his desire to convert to Christianity, according to Sensbach (64–65). Perhaps it is an indication of the nature of the question to the Moravians that the deliberation occurred in the Elders' Conference, which was charged with spiritual, not temporal issues. The question was finally put to God by the lot (a Moravian practice at the time). When the lot favored purchase, the issue was settled for both that case and future cases.

The decision to purchase slaves, despite initial reluctance and uncertainty, in the long run evolved into patterns of slaveholding that were largely indistinguishable from those of the southern culture in which Salem was located. At first, however, there were differences as the slaves "had just as much freedom as legally free white Moravians—freedom in Christ, the only kind of freedom that really mattered" (Sensbach 1998, 81).[3] This spiritual freedom could extend as far as the right to be heard by church courts in the case of disputes with white members, membership in appropriate choirs, and some schooling. In the early years, at least, the African brothers and sisters participated in religious life on an equal basis, states Sensbach (104). However, religious equality applied only to converted slaves, only a portion of all the slaves. With time, the southern fear that the slaves' presence was a threat spread into the Moravian town and segregation occurred—mandated by state laws.

Slavery undermined the communal ethic in a variety of ways. Compulsion, in its very nature, denied the foundational concept that a member's work was a voluntary offering to the Savior. In the case of non-Christian slaves, it created a resident class that was not composed of brothers and sisters. It also undermined communalism's rejection of self-interested motives. The unconverted slave did not share the community's ideals, and presumably was motivated in other ways; material incentives were one obvious way to try to motivate. Thus, to motivate slaves, even if only some, the managers or co-workers surely resorted to material punishments or rewards. Thus, motivating slaves amounted to practice in worldly thinking.

THE END OF THE COMMUNAL IDEAL

Although Salem's communal structure formally dissolved in 1856, the dissolution of the ideal began far earlier. As one commentator noted, the mixed economy expected the impossible in that "the church wanted its members to make money in the marketplace but not to act or think like the other traders there" (Thorp 1989, 203). In business, who else would watch out for one's interest if not oneself? The very act of trading resulted in some Moravians becoming "more and more 'this-worldly'" (Sessler 1933, 200–201). The mixed economy produced mixed values.

Despite accumulating problems, the system continued until well into the nineteenth century. The decisive decade may have been the 1830s, when church-board regulation of businesses was challenged by numerous citizens of the town who began engaging in economic activity without permission (Crews and Starbuck 2002, 256–57; also 300 n.). Discipline theoretically continued to be enforced by the church's ownership of the land of the town, which residents only leased. Yet, ongoing disputes with residents led to a church board deciding in 1836 that the lease system could not continue as the means to enforce regulations, according to Crews and Starbuck (257–58).

In the 1830s, the Industrial Revolution also arrived: both cotton and wool mills were established at the edge of the town, and church officials seemed to have been eager to obtain these firms. Surely, the inability of the hand-trades of Salem to compete with manufactured goods helped create this desire. These mills employed a relatively large workforce of non-Moravians, whose various requests and disputes brought the church boards a host of new issues to decide. This was a highly visible measure of non-Moravian values entering the local society. The Industrial Revolution forced the community to face the values and issues of an emergent capitalist economy. Church regulation of trades ended in the 1840s.

In 1856, the church relinquished its last economic leverage by selling Salem land to its occupants. It had become more and more reluctant to enforce its own regulations. Finally, the inability of potential investors in the community to buy land was considered a deterrent to desired investment (Crews and Starbuck 2002, 323–24). Obviously, if the authorities were themselves motivated by a desire to attract privately owned industry, the communal ideal was gone. The communal economy in both Bethabara and Salem had lasted a little more than a century, but in form only during the last few decades.

THE ESSENTIALS OF THE
MORAVIAN ECONOMIC ETHIC

In the General Economy, and to a lesser degree in the mixed economy of Salem, responsibility for economic decisions resided with church authorities rather than individuals, a major difference from the individualistic outside culture. In this communal context, the major virtue for the individual was a cooperative attitude. Cooperation was overlaid with religious meaning, for one's love of God was naturally expressed in a brotherly spirit.

Although cooperation with congregational authorities made the system work, at least one decision had to be made individually. A member, or potential member, had to decide on affiliation, or continued affiliation, with the church. Individual choice in the matter of affiliation could not be avoided. At a practical level, nothing could stop someone from simply leaving the tiny Moravian communities. But something more fundamental was at work, for a heartfelt *personal* response to the savior's love was a central precept of Moravian Pietism.

The Moravians distinguished this free, personal response to Christ from worldly, economic notions of freedom. Christ, who emptied himself for others, upon whom the communal liturgies focused, was a model of the opposite of self-interest. As noted, Bethlehem's Brotherly Agreement suggested that the freedom held by outsiders amounted to selfish disorder; the Moravian notion of religious freedom was the ability to set the self's worldly desires aside to serve each other (as portrayed by the apostle Paul in Galatians 5:13). At a functional level, this meant subordination of the self's desires to church boards. An index of the increase of worldly values in Salem in the later years was the increase of individuals' disputes with, or disobedience to, church boards.

Under the General Economy, when needs were met by the community, freedom took on other meanings as well. Freed from material insecurity and the threat of want, the Moravians believed they could order their lives to answer a higher calling. In contrast to individualists who were absorbed in providing for self, members saw the General Economy as freeing them to engage in the Lord's work that otherwise might have left their family obligations unmet. Even in the mixed economy of Salem, one's personal economic success did not affect one's access to a high level of public services and integration into church, choir, and community activities.

In contrast to the outside society, the Moravian community acknowledged that it had material obligations to its members—for each person had an infinite worth to the Savior. Even during the transition to market economics, the fifth article of Salem's Brotherly Agreement (sec. 10) stated that the congregation recognized an obligation to provide "for the basic needs of any of its members" who could not support themselves. The obligation was only to those who could not support themselves. However, in that era the outside society did not formally accept even that obligation in many places in America. The 1773 document singled out orphans—in an age when there were many orphans. This stated commitment by the community to the weakest and most vulnerable members was a natural expression of the belief that all had an infinite worth to Christ, who had sanctified their lives by his life as a human.

The Moravian community held a view of human psychology that complemented this ethic. Their economy was built on the proposition that intrinsic motivation was sufficiently strong to substitute for material motivations: specifically, one worked for the Lord and—by extension—for one's brothers and sisters. Bethlehem's Brotherly Agreement of 1754 explicitly stated this proposition.

CONCLUSION: RELIGIOUS SOCIALISM AND INDIVIDUALISM

Socialist communities represented a critique of Americans' conventional economic values. When these socialist experiments dissolved, laissez-faire thinkers felt confirmed in their belief that self-interested values were more in tune with human nature. By the logic of early political economy, the lack of material incentives to motivate essentially self-interested people would doom socialist communities. Ironically, the Moravians essentially agreed that self-interest was an important ingredient in human nature—but of human nature without the light of the savior. Self-interested ways were the ways of fallen humanity, so Moravians never discounted self-interest. But, for them, self-interest played the *opposite* role morally as it played for the laissez-faire moralists. The various Brotherly Agreements spelled out the norms of character and behavior precisely because of the tendency to lapse into self-interest if love of the savior cooled.

If laissez-faire were correct, the failure of the Moravians to rely heavily on self-interested motives in their communities could by itself account for the demise of their socialist arrangements. Yet the long life of the Moravian communities makes that explanation seem too simple. Moravian communalism succumbed only after several decades—even if one dates the end to the 1830s. Bethlehem's General Economy apparently was healthy at the time it was ordered disbanded. As noted, the end of church control in Salem may have been due to a mismatch between the technology of the Industrial Revolution and the small, hand-trade economy of the community. This would rule out lack of material incentives as the dominating cause for the demise of Moravian socialism.

Moravian socialism encompassed the economics and values of a community that believed itself to be redeemed. To carry on their Lord's work, the active agents were church officials and boards—although these always relied on the willing obedience of members. When love of their savior motivated people, the importance of material incentives diminished in proportion. Freedom was defined by the apostle Paul's notion of freedom as freedom *from a worldly self.* Self was an obstacle to obeying the Lord and serving others.

While individual autonomy was diminished, the relational aspects of human life were magnified by the Moravian notion of brotherhood and sisterhood. This spiritual family existed, it believed, because God's love gave worth, or dignity, to all. But, in addition to this spiritual dimension, brotherhood also had a very concrete dimension. Members lived day-to-day with each other in a small community and related to each other in a multitude of everyday dimensions. The common good was almost literally the well-being of what amounted to an extended family. Even the controlling church boards were members of that family.

Although the Moravians were wary of the values of outsiders, they believed that Christ had lived and suffered for them, too. Thus, even the "stranger" was endued with worth far beyond his or her economic value as a customer or supplier. For example, during times of turmoil on the frontier, Bethabara provided safety and sustenance for refugees; Moravian physicians and clergy served nonmembers as well. In all this, the Moravians affirmed the value of all persons to God.

While a secular socialism might subordinate the individual to a collective good, the Moravian Christian faith provided the ultimate protection against such a tendency: for their savior loved each individual even during the period that their economy was socialist. Moravian relational morality, while it protected the individual, was not relational individualism in the early years, for major economic decisions in the religious community were not assigned to the individual. Yet, by the time the mixed economy of Salem adopted its Brotherly Agreement in 1773, the Moravians were moving closer to the norms of relational individualism, which allowed for market activity but placed more or less stringent restrictions on it. In the case of Salem, the community's restrictions were very stringent; the expectation was that individual Moravians would maintain a personal outlook that would continue to reflect a sense of human kinship.

APPENDIX: A CONTRAST OF RELIGIOUS AND SECULAR SOCIALISM

Moravian (and other religious) socialists were *practicing socialists*, whereas the secular socialists of the late nineteenth and early twentieth centuries were advocates of a socialist ideal set in the future. The religious socialists' experi-

ences, therefore, revealed much more about the morality of a working socialism (on a small scale) than did the writings of the secular socialists. The latter socialists were primarily critics of capitalism and theorists of the path to
socialism. Aside from very general principles, these socialists said little about
socialism when implemented. Even Edward Bellamy's utopian-socialist novel
Looking Backward (1889), which was intended as a map of socialist society, left
many blank spots.

Perhaps the most significant American socialist was Eugene Debs
(1855–1926), who eventually ran for U.S. president five times—receiving six
percent of the vote in 1912 (see Constantine 1991). Debs's ideas reflected a
humanistic spirit, which apparently showed in his personality. Although his
ideas contained elements of Marxism, they were heavily modified by American influences such as democratic ideals.

As noted, except for Bellamy, the secular socialists were vague about the
details of a socialist society. Debs in an undated essay ("Socialism") defined
socialism as a political movement that "aims at the overthrow of the prevailing capitalist system by securing control of the national government" (Debs
1908, 142). Significantly, this definition focused on the *process of getting to
socialism*, not what socialism would be like—other than being noncapitalist.
At a very high level of generality he added that under socialism "the collective
people will own and operate the sources and means of wealth production" and
"all will have equal right to work" (Debs 1908, 142–43).

Debs noted that the highest values promoted by autonomy individualism
were mocked by the industrial system that had actually emerged in the United
States. He asked, "Is [the worker] in any sense . . . a free man" (Debs 1908,
149)? Mocking the role of incentives in individualistic thought, Debs said it
was inconceivable that "a slave who is robbed of all he produces . . . has great
incentive to work and is highly individualized" (151). But the ultimate point
for Debs was ethical—that industrial capitalism dehumanized the worker. In
the language of factory managers, a worker becomes a factory hand, "no head,
no heart, no soul" (154). Debs saw the results of the Industrial Revolution and
condemned them.

This would be ended only by the victory of the working class and state
ownership of the means of production. Debs accepted that class consciousness
and class struggle would be required for this to happen (445). In this we see
the rejection of individualism—at least until class-conflict ceased. The
emphasis on class consciousness raised its own questions about reducing
humans to a single dimension.

After the victory of socialism, classes would disappear. What would be
the status of the individual in the socialist society? Given his understanding
of the effects of capitalism, Debs thought that the status of the individual
surely would be improved under socialism, but details were few. In attempting to answer, Debs resorted in a 1908 speech to visionary statements. After

the revolution, workers *automatically* would rise to a full humanity: "give [the worker] a chance and he rises as if by magic to the plane of a man. Man has the divine attributes" (489). Debs's hyperbole showed his great faith in human nature. Yet, such assertions are the socialist equivalent of Adam Smith's assurances that an invisible hand would automatically resolve problems of achieving the public good. In contrast to Debs, the Moravians, practicing socialism, had found that the communal way of life required a special calling, which apparently not even all Moravians possessed. The Moravians outlined the moral and legal code needed to fend off the old human ways from reasserting themselves.

The Moravians and the secular socialists shared at least one major perception: that when the insecurity, uncertainties, and false values promoted by market economies were eliminated, humans would be free to serve higher ends. Debs spoke of the freeing of people, but was not clear about the ends to be served; perhaps he thought that human nature had within itself certain implicit ends. For the Moravians, freedom meant freedom to serve their savior and in that service to relate to each other. However, service to the savior was defined by church leadership; this distinguished the communal Moravians from individualists. Debs did not address such differences between ends set by individuals and by leaders.

The Moravian communities in later years struggled with the reality of members who lapsed from that higher freedom and seemed to accept freedom as defined by markets. Given the Moravian experience, Debs's hope that the end of capitalism would, by itself, free the human spirit to serve higher ends seems too optimistic. Perhaps self-interest would reassert itself in ways conforming to the rules established by state-ownership of wealth—as happened in the late Soviet empire. Debs seems not to have foreseen this question, much less to have offered an answer. The Moravian communities provided a fuller expression of socialist morality than Debs, and most secular socialists, found possible to give.

SEVEN

Abolition

Human Dignity as a Boundary to Markets

SLAVERY WAS RECOGNIZED as an evil in colonial times by Quaker John Woolman (see chapter 2), who affirmed the human kinship of free and enslaved Americans. Later, Daniel Raymond (chapter 5) saw slavery as the prime example of self-benefiting exploitation. The intrusion of slavery into the community of Salem (chapter 6) contradicted the community's religious-socialist ideals. Slavery forced society to consider moral boundaries: where to divide the economic from the noneconomic spheres. What should never be considered property and so never subject to buying and selling? How absolute are property rights? When must economic motives and relationships give way to other kinds of relationships?[1] What standards should be used to judge what is, and is not, legitimately within the sphere of the market?

The literature of the antislavery movement answered these questions by emphasizing slavery's denial of human dignity, a dignity shared by all people. In so doing, abolitionists appealed to broad biblical principles (e.g., that all humans are "of one blood"—Acts 17:26); this use of scripture differed greatly from the Bible-citing proponents of slavery (Noll 2006, 20). Abolitionists also confronted other widely accepted principles, such as absolute property rights, which had come to be accepted by conservative Protestants (Stackhouse 1987, 38). Abolition, thus, became a watershed in such areas as biblical interpretation and economic morality. The outcome of the Civil War meant society's official acceptance of the abolitionist principle: that all persons possessed essential human rights that forbade them being treated as marketable commodities. But the implicit moral logic led to broader conclusions: an economy could also be judged by how well its practices and institutions affirmed full human dignity.

The abolitionist case had two important features. First, human dignity and human kinship, or relatedness, were intertwined concepts. It is readily apparent that anyone who held two biblical principles—that humans are created in God's image and are also "of one blood"—was simultaneously upholding dignity and relatedness. Part of the moral genius of Harriet Beecher Stowe's abolitionist novel (see below) was in showing that the two moral principles are twins. Second, the abolitionist case was built on a robust *moral psychology*, which was visible as early as in the thought of John Woolman (chapter 2), but reached full flower among the evangelical abolitionists. These projected an American Protestant understanding of slavery based on the concept of how wounded the human psyche was by sin.

In the following sections, we review writers of the period before the Civil War who emphasized the rights implicit in a common human dignity. For contrast, an appendix explains the utilitarian logic of economists as they reason about slavery.

FRANCIS WAYLAND REVISITED

Although Francis Wayland supported maximum economic freedom (chapter 4), he ultimately defined limits to self-interested action. Wayland's *principle of reciprocity* required that any moral being recognize in others the same rights he would demand for himself. Wayland argued this as a matter of pure logic. Accepting the principle that Mr. A may infringe Mr. B's rights would abolish the very idea of rights—for if everyone had an equal liberty to violate others' rights, then rights would effectively protect nothing and so be meaningless (Wayland 1837a, 177). Participants in a system of self-interest must restrain themselves from infringing others' interests or the system collapses. If all are free to infringe on all, then the conditions needed to pursue one's own interests do not exist—a logical contradiction. Thus, Wayland based reciprocity on logic rather than on its being integral to kinship. Nevertheless, in reciprocity he found reason to oppose slavery.

Wayland must have known that many slave owners would object that the principle of reciprocity did not apply to slavery by denying that slaves possessed full human status. Instead of contradicting this premise head-on, Wayland argued that *any moral being* was due rights: "suppose the inferior class of beings were not *truly men*; if they were intelligent moral agents I suppose that we should be under the same obligation . . . under the principle of reciprocity" (177). Even an angel, he said, had no right to infringe upon a lesser moral being. How much less right did the slave owner? He concluded "slavery thus violates the personal liberty of man as a *physical, intellectual and moral being*" (188). In sum, although Wayland's approach brilliantly circumvented the slave owners' argument, it did so by tacitly accepting their premise: Wayland chose to argue in terms of abstract "moral beings" instead of fellow humans. Other abolitionists (see below) chose the opposite approach: to argue for the human kinship of all.

Having thus determined slavery to be intrinsically wrong, Wayland also analyzed its negative effects. First, it destroyed the morals of both master and servant by "presenting objects on whom passion may be satiated without resistance" (189). Here Wayland for once reflected a deeply Protestant sensibility to the sinful potential of the unbounded human ego (compare with Wayland's treatment of sin in chapter 4). Second, Wayland made an argument that slavery was harmful to national wealth in that it rendered labor "disgraceful" by portraying labor suitable only for slaves; he also observed that capital accumulation in the slave states was slower than in free states. However, he never made economics the fundamental moral objection to slavery.

Wayland also sought to rebut the scriptural arguments of slave owners, who said that the Bible condoned slavery because it did not explicitly forbid it, and that its instructions concerning the treatment of slaves in ancient Israel were tacit approval of slavery. Quoting the commandment to "love thy neighbor," Wayland argued that slavery denied neighborliness to the slave. (The language of neighborliness is that of relational morality. However, Wayland seemed to limit "neighborliness" to refraining from harming the neighbor, while ignoring more affirmative actions usually associated with neighborliness.) Wayland found no condoning of slavery in biblical verses that told first-century Christian slaves to show obedience and goodwill toward their masters.[2] Nothing in the master–slave relationship commanded obedience and respect in its own right (Wayland 1837a, 192–96).[3]

Wayland then asked what must be done with the system of slavery and answered his own question: the system "must be abandoned," and "immediately" (196). He remained highly individualistic in outlook and addressed the individual consciences of slaveholders to provide the remedy. Having a clearcut answer to the wrongness of slavery, Wayland failed to say anything about societal actions to correct the wrong. Wayland demonstrated that both autonomy and relational morality could find reasons to oppose slavery; but, when compared to other abolitionist moralists, he also demonstrated the differences between relational and autonomy morality.

WILLIAM LLOYD GARRISON

Unlike Wayland, the academic moralist, William Lloyd Garrison was an activist, the abolitionist publisher of the *Liberator*, which for more than thirty years promoted emancipation. During the thirty years leading to the Civil War, a variety of other issues became tangled with the main issue of antislavery. However, the abolitionist's moral perspective remained constant through all this.

Committed to pacifism as well as abolition, Garrison would not justify violence against slaveholders. He addressed the 1858 New England antislavery convention at a time when warlike sentiments were rising. Even in words directed to the issue of slaveholders, his basic moral principles were clear: even the detested slaveholder "is a man, sacred before me." Given that fact, "all I have to do with him is to rebuke his sin." Garrison had "no other weapon to wield against him but the simple truth of God, which is the great instrument for the overthrow of all iniquity" (Garrison 1966, 251). Garrison's theology recognized an obligation to speak against evil, but no obligation to guarantee an outcome, which is to try to do God's job.

The most important claim of Garrison's statement was that the slaveholder remained a moral being, who may be called to repentance. If even the greatest sinner, the slaveholder, retained moral status, then how much more did the same apply to his victim? In short, slavery wrongly denied slaves their full dignity as moral beings.

The basis of Garrison's belief in human dignity was revealed in 1836 in his attack on the famous preacher Lyman Beecher, who had published a lecture on contemporary social evils, but had omitted slavery. In a long essay that covered almost every American evil that Beecher had neglected, Garrison finally arrived at labor relations: "Man is not regarded as man—his inherent and perfect equality is not understood—his princely and indestructible dignity is not recognized—even though the heavens and the earth were created for him . . . and though he is created in the image of God and though Jesus . . . died that he might live" (106). Addressed to nineteenth-century Protestant evangelicals, this was the most emphatic basis for human dignity that could be found.

As editor of the *Liberator*, Garrison in 1837 published the remarks of the freedman Theodore Wright, a preacher, who even more precisely defined human dignity. The remarks were made at a time when the abolitionist cause was gaining popularity, and Wright feared that the newcomers did not fully understand the underlying moral principles. He insisted they understand that the human family was one and all people kin: "to call the dark man a brother . . . that is the test" (Wright in Garrison 1966, 126). He continued a little further on: "Every man who comes into this society ought to be catechized. It should be ascertained whether he look upon man as man, all of one blood and one family" (in Garrison 1966, 126). If humans are "of one blood," then any dignity that anyone would claim for one's self logically must apply to one's kin. Wright emphasized moral kinship as the key element: the white man acknowledging his relationship with the dark brother and therefore that if either is a moral being, then both are moral beings.

Garrison, like other abolitionists, had a long list enumerating the defacements of human dignity by slavery: "stealing the liberties" of millions of God's creatures, "invading the holiest relations of life," and of "tearing the husband from his wife, and the mother from her babe" (74). Underlying this indictment is the reason these actions are crimes: they violate the inherent rights held by humans given by creation. This dignity is inseparable from its expression in human relationships—between husband and wife, and parent with child.

Although Garrison's pacifism restricted him to appeals to people's consciences, that did not mean he believed that this would bring the end of slavery. Garrison did not feel himself morally free to seek war, but a just God might achieve the end of evil through war. Thus, Garrison's mixture of pacifism and abolitionism produced some mixed messages. When John Brown's raid brought nearer the likelihood of war, Garrison said that despite being a "peace man . . . I am prepared to say, 'Success to every slave insurrection'" (266).

Abolitionist Garrison did not explicitly address economics. However, the case he made had profound implications for economic life: human dignity was a fundamental moral precept that required that boundaries to economic activity be set. And this dignity was intrinsically bound up with the relatedness of humans as children of God.

THEODORE DWIGHT WELD

In 1839, Theodore Weld published *American Slavery as It Is: The Testimony of a Thousand Witnesses*, which reported a massive number of eyewitness accounts to discredit the rationalizations used by the apologists of slavery. Weld's commentary on these accounts singled out the warping effect of slavery on the psyches of slaveholders. Responding to objections that the reported cruelty toward slaves was not credible, Weld proposed a psychology of the slave master: "he who holds human beings as his *bona fide* property, *regards* them as property, and not as *persons*; this is his permanent state of mind toward them. He does not contemplate slaves as human beings, consequently does not *treat* them as such" (Weld 1839, 110). Denying fundamental humanity, or human dignity, makes the slaveholder capable of virtually any crime against the slave. Weld analyzed the slaveholders' use of language to dehumanize their victims, noting that identical terms were used for slaves as for animal stock. Again, Weld dissected human psychology, noting that "the greatest provocation to human nature is *opposition to its will*." He followed this shortly: "The idea of property having a will, and that too in opposition to the will of its *owner*, and counteracting it, is a stimulant of terrible power to the relentless human passions" (111). The very resistance of the slave was testimony to the eternal human will. The "unceasing opposition" to the owner by the slave turns the owner, as measured by his behavior, into an irrational brute (111). Weld here used the very treatment of slaves as an unintentional affirmation of their humanity by their owners: only the opposition of human will to human will can evoke the cruelty observed under slavery. Weld kept a lens on the slaveholder, exposing a psychology of slaveholding that made cruelty inevitable.

Weld addressed the objection of southern apologists for slavery that "it is for the interest of the masters to treat their slaves well" (132). This was essentially an economic argument; even modern economists would argue that the amount of cruelty used by slave masters should have been very measured, rationally calculated by a cost-benefit analysis (see, e.g., Fogel and Engerman, 1974). The slavery apologists argued that slaves are to their owner an investment from which a return must be earned; poor treatment would reduce the return. Weld responded with Hamiltonian skepticism: "Even if it were for the interest of masters to treat their slaves well, he must be a novice who thinks *that* a proof that the slaves are well treated" (132). Then he added, "The whole history of man is a record of real interests sacrificed to present gratification." Weld argued that even when indulging their lusts and appetites harmed the slave owners' monetary interests, such indulgence occurred (132).

Finally, Weld pointed out that there were times when cruelty actually was *in the interest of the slaveholder*. The owner had financial motive to neglect the old and "worn out" slave, the diseased and maimed, the physically and mentally disabled and sickly infants. In addition, it was in the interest of slaveholders to badly treat runaways and slaves who otherwise resisted the system. After pages of documentary evidence, Weld concluded that "we have thus shown that it would be 'for the interest' of masters and overseers to treat with *habitual* cruelty *more than one million* of the slaves in the United States" (138).

Weld's treatment of self-interest reflected the Protestant tendency to link self-interest and sin. The abolitionists such as Weld showed that self-interest did not always have the benign results portrayed by laissez-faire. Weld attacked faith in the moral contribution of self-interest in two ways. First, he argued, like Alexander Hamilton, that prudent, and legitimate, versions of self-interest were often forsaken to gratify immediate passions. In short, there were different kinds of self-interests: which one will dominate? Second, and more damning, Weld argued that under slavery cruelty might align perfectly with the self-interests of the slaveholders. Slavery was wrong because it presented the opportunity for self-interest to transgress the moral limits defined by respect for human dignity.

HARRIET BEECHER STOWE

Abraham Lincoln is said to have attributed the Civil War to Harriet Beecher Stowe's *Uncle Tom's Cabin* (1852). There are several major, ethical themes to the book. First, Stowe argued that *evil may be systemic*, and that good individuals must fail within such a system. Second, she argued for the significance of community and human relationships in creating a moral order; an evil of the slave system was to shatter human connections (most obviously, family connections) among the slaves that are essential to moral growth. Third, echoing themes of Woolman, Weld, and more generally of the Protestant sense of sin,

Stowe held that to give a master absolute power over a slave invariably produced depravity. With Weld, she emphasized that the worst abuse would arise when slave's will opposed master's will. Fourth, Stowe made clear that morality and self-interest are often on opposite sides—especially under the perverse conditions imposed by the plantation system.

Finally, in common with almost all the abolitionists we have considered, she made the case in a variety of ways for the inherent human dignity of the enslaved persons—showing them to be moral agents—constantly facing choices between good and evil. Her book's central theme was the love between enslaved parents and their children, a bond universal to humanity. This manifest love of parent and child was meant to show to her readers that the slaves were full members of universal humanity. Indeed, the major cruelty of the slavery system, constantly emphasized in the book, was the arbitrary destruction of this bond between parent and child at a master's whim. And in this destruction of human relationships, the source of morality is destroyed as well. Addressing her evangelical Protestant readers, Stowe continually affirmed that Christ had come to redeem all, including the Africans. Indeed, Uncle Tom, of the book's title, proves to be a martyr of the faith. Finally, to any who would deny the human dignity of the Africans, Stowe emphasized that any negative behaviors were the expected human response to the depraved conditions in which the slaves were forced to live. Before developing these points, a short synopsis of the book is in order.

The opening scenes occur on the plantation of the otherwise kind Shelby family, who own the slaves Tom and Eliza, among others. However, when he falls into debt a kind disposition does not prevent Master Shelby from selling Eliza's son, Harry, and Uncle Tom to a slave trader. This tears Tom from his wife and children, besides threatening to tear Eliza from her very young son. Tom decides to go without protest, as his sacrifice for his community, when it is put to him that the alternative is the selling off of the entire slave population, sundering many family bonds. Eliza, unable to bear the loss of her son, flees with him. Miraculously, Eliza is reunited in flight with her husband, thus reestablishing relationships.

Tom, meanwhile, is transported down-river, but is purchased before reaching New Orleans by a kind new master, Augustine St. Clare, who is also a detached (and cynical) observer of the contemporary scene. Through St. Clare's observations, Stowe develops the idea that the "system is educating [the slaves] in barbarism and brutality" and "breaking all humanizing ties" (Stowe 1852, 291). St. Clare indulges his slaves as his way of acknowledging that they are innocent victims of a system from which he has benefited. Although Tom is promised his freedom, St. Clare dies suddenly—leaving Tom to be sold by St. Clare's unsympathetic wife.

Tom passes into the hands of Simon Legree, who relies on cruelty and fear to control his slaves, and who works them to death because he considers that cheaper than treating them as humans. Legree quickly perceives Tom's piety and challenges himself with driving Tom to despair and to abandon his faith. Tom does not resist the harsh treatment and labors on faithfully, while simultaneously bringing compassion to the brutalized slave population. When Legree finally orders Tom to inflict punishment on another slave, Tom for the first time disobeys. Legree perceives that this refusal is prompted by Christian faith, which infuriates him all the more—ultimately leading to Tom's martyrdom. Stowe portrays Tom as victorious in his death, which not only is given spiritual meaning but also wakens the humanity in his fellow slaves.

Stowe's first morally significant claim was that evil may be systematized. Speaking directly to her reader in an epilogue, she stated that slavery was a "system which confounds and confuses every principle of Christianity and morality" (481). Further, efforts of good individuals to work with the system, to compromise, forever proved futile. The book is populated by well-intentioned masters whose personal good intentions are negated with slaves being sold and human relationships cruelly severed. So long as a system that permits cruelty exists, cruelty will occur—despite individual efforts to resist. An equally bad impact of systemic evil is that persons are hardened to it a degree at a time, "the owner growing more and more cruel, as the servant more and more callous," according to St. Clare (269). St. Clare adds that he would not start down this path in order "to protect my own moral nature." Reflecting this same reasoning, Tom refuses to make the first compromise with evil (by acting as Legree's agent in beating another slave). Tom recognizes that the very act would begin to corrupt his character (390–91). Tom's need to resist amounted to the claim that the system will overwhelm the individual. Tom's only recourse as a moral individual, within an evil system, was to accept inevitable death.

Second, Stowe presented the case that humans become moral beings only by human relationships. This point is made with the slave-girl Topsy, whose thoroughly amoral behavior is attributed to her having been stripped of normal human relationships. St. Clare's spiritually precocious daughter, Evangeline, asks the other girl why she behaves badly—suggesting that good behavior comes from love. Topsy answers that all she loves is candy. The daughter perseveres, stating that surely Topsy loved her parents. Topsy answers, "Never had none, ye know" (306). With these chilling words the poor girl makes the author's point that human morality grows from the human relationships that slavery destroys. The scene ends as Evangeline, whose very name meant one who proclaims the gospel, gives Topsy good news, "Oh, Topsy, poor child, *I love you!*"

Third, Stowe illustrated, through the character Legree, the demonic possibilities of the human will, of one ego possessing absolute power over other human beings. When Tom informs Legree that he cannot obey an order to do wrong, Legree responds in a fury: "What have any of you cussed cattle to do with thinking what's right? I'll put a stop to it" (386–87). Here Legree would deny another's moral character. Because the slave system, as portrayed by Stowe, placed no limits on Legree's ego, he claimed a right he could not possess: to dictate another's moral and spiritual nature. Ultimately, Legree did his worst with Tom because he found an opposed will.

Fourth, Stowe argued that not all motivation is self-interested, especially if self-interest is understood in materialistic terms. Indeed, the last fifth of the book is taken up with Tom's titanic clash of wills with Legree, a clash in which Tom's self-interest—as understood by political economists—would lie in submitting to Legree. Tom resisted the demand to commit an evil *simply because it was evil*—that is, because of moral necessity, even at the cost of his life.

Finally, the center-point of Stowe's morality was universal human dignity. Because all share this dignity, a slave system that demeans such dignity could not be right. Simple membership in humanity confers equality, according to Stowe. Throughout the book, she argued that the slaves share the same bonds of love between parent and child as other humans. These relationships are the sign of humanity and such human love confers dignity. Stowe closes the work by telling how the dying Tom is received by his redeemer, leaving her evangelical readers with the assurance that the Lord himself has affirmed the full manhood of Tom and his enslaved brothers and sisters.

Stowe, with the other abolitionists, added a dimension to economic morality: moral boundaries to the market marked out by the imperative to protect universal human dignity. Slavery would fall outside the bounds of what markets were allowed to handle. Stowe's novel also challenged sharply the adequacy of materialistic versions of self-interest as explanations of human motivation. Instead, she suggested that humans were motivated, constrained, and shaped as moral beings by relationships within families and communities. She reaffirmed the fundamental evangelical Protestant suspicion that the human will, freed from restraints—as was the case for slave owners—was capable of unlimited, systematized evil. She also showed, in Tom, the potential of the free human will to suffer for the right instead of following self-interest.

CONCLUSION: WHAT THE ABOLITIONISTS ADDED

The existence of slavery exposed fissures in pre-Civil War American moral thought. Slavery implied that *no one had fundamental rights*, because if slaves—for whom the case was made by abolitionists that they were human kin—could be denied rights, then anyone could be denied rights. Given the abolitionists' point, that slaves shared in common human dignity, control over the slaves was only an accident of history.

Abolitionists also cast doubt on the political economists' view of human nature: given absolute control over another human, would the slaveholder really respond only by rational, self-interested calculations of profit and loss?

Or would absolute power unleash uncontrolled impulses? Was economically rational behavior, itself, always benign? Abolitionism thus made an indirect critique of the logic of political economy: self-interest and markets, which had expanded into buying and selling humans, have no self-limiting mechanism. Abolitionists argued that society had to draw boundaries around markets—for they would not limit themselves.

Stowe made the significant case that human dignity and human kinship (or relationship) were not two distinct pillars of morality but were intertwined, twin supports. Her premise was that the common humanity of her readers would allow them to recognize the human dignity of the slaves; they would recognize in them people like themselves. With her character Topsy, Stowe also made the case that humans grow as moral persons only through those very human relationships that had been denied the child by slavery. The abolitionists were part of, and shaped, American relational morality in their affirmation that shared humanity has meant equality of rights and a doctrine of human dignity.[4]

Abolitionism advanced a relational morality, and so was in many ways antithetical to the autonomy morality associated with laissez-faire. Yet, that fact does not mean that laissez-faire thinkers necessarily *favored* slavery. Even Francis Wayland, the great evangelical compromiser with laissez-faire, stated on purely logical grounds that the rights anyone would claim for self must be granted to all moral beings. However, Wayland's "reciprocity" was simply a logical protection of the negative right not to be exploited. As an autonomy moralist, Wayland fell back on pure logic that lacked the richer understanding of human interactions and motives shown in other abolitionist writings. Indeed, other abolitionists made the point that logic was too weak to deter other human motives.

As a clergyman, Wayland also countered pro-slavery, scriptural arguments. When Wayland sought to counter the biblical arguments of pro-slavery thinkers, he very instinctively slipped into the language of relational morality. He denied that slavery was consistent with "love of neighbor," thus bestowing a normative status on a form of human relationship. Wayland's notion of neighborliness, however, seems to have been very limited. Nevertheless, his appeal to a relational concept reveals the power of relational language in dealing with slavery.

The principle of human dignity, as enunciated by the abolitionists, possessed the potential for far more expansive applications. If humans possessed a fundamental dignity, then it could be argued that society should order all economic relations to respect that dignity.

APPENDIX: UTILITARIAN WELFARE AND SLAVERY

Two modern economic historians have presented evidence suggesting that slavery was profitable enough for slaves to share in the benefits. Specifically, they claim that the "average pecuniary income" of a "prime field hand" was about fifteen percent that above what he could have earned as a free agricultural laborer (Fogel and Engerman 1974, 239). These two economists never proclaimed slavery to be morally acceptable on the basis that the victims' incomes were increased. But, of significance for moral reasoning, was the way they inferred the wrongness of slavery. In keeping with the utilitarian tradition in economics, they expanded the notion of the slaves' welfare (or utility) to include not only pecuniary income but "non-pecuniary income" (i.e., non-material, psychological factors). Then they argued that nonpecuniary losses to slaves in gang labor far exceeded their pecuniary gains. In short, they asked if the extra income was enough to compensate for the psychological pain of such a condition. Fogel and Engerman finally presented calculations to show that if the slaves had been given the choice, they would have decided that their overall welfare was worsened due to slavery (244–45). Measured by the proper definition of welfare, the consequences were negative for slavery's victims.

Fogel and Engerman's argument against slavery (based on slaves' subjective balancing of pecuniary and nonpecuniary aspects of slavery) contrasts sharply with the abolitionists; abolitionists did not view cost-benefit calculations of slavery to be the decisive issue. They reasoned in terms of human dignity, human kinship, and rights. Suppose—contrary to what they actually argued—that Fogel and Engerman's calculations had led to the conclusion that the slaves' subjective welfare was somehow raised by slavery. Such evidence would have undercut any utilitarian arguments for considering slavery wrong. Yet, such a finding would not have led the abolitionists to waive their moral objection to slavery. While the utility consequences of slavery are not irrelevant, they did not ultimately determine for abolitionists whether slavery was intrinsically evil. The case of slavery illustrates the narrow frame of reference that self-interest thinking imposes (self-interest is typically defined in terms of such cost-benefit calculations). When Fogel and Engerman did raise the question of the separation of families, they commented only on how it raised the subjective, nonpecuniary costs of those threatened.

In conclusion, it is worth noting that despite his general support of the political economy of his day, Francis Wayland did not resort to utilitarian arguments to make his antislavery case. He believed that evangelical orthodoxy required rejecting that utilitarian reasoning was morally normative (chapter 4). To the degree, therefore, that he accepted evangelical premises, he had to forsake much that created the logical and moral coherence of political economy.

EIGHT

Social Darwinists of Different Species

EVOLUTIONARY IDEAS BEGAN to emerge in social thought in the middle of the nineteenth century; Herbert Spencer wrote even before the publication of Darwin's *Origin of Species*. Spencer in England was followed after some years by William Graham Sumner in America. Neither owed much to Darwin's actual work, but both restated existing economic morality in terms of a struggle for survival. Social Darwinism reaffirmed laissez-faire doctrines using evolutionary terminology. A well-known follower of Social Darwinism was the steel magnate Andrew Carnegie, who strangely blended the evolutionary philosophy with admonitions to his fellow rich men to engage in philanthropy of a paternalistic sort.

By the end of the century, however, the evolutionary approach was being used to reach different conclusions. Thorstein Veblen, a radical sociologist, wrote his best-selling *Theory of the Leisure Class* (1899), in which he mixed evolutionary anthropology with caustic wit to ridicule the class-structure of nineteenth-century capitalism. He portrayed the business class as a parasite class, reflecting ancient predatory habits, and the American economy as anything but the highest achievement of evolution. The economy, he claimed, was in the thrall of primitive cultural values. Veblen's evolutionary methodology envisioned change, but contained no premise that change would be progressive.

THE BRITISH SOURCE: HERBERT SPENCER

Although the doctrines of Social Darwinism bear the name of Charles Darwin, they owe their existence primarily to Herbert Spencer, a British sociologist who advocated a type of evolutionary theory prior to Darwin's major works. Though pre-Darwin, Spencer's ideas shared with Darwin the inspiration of Thomas Robert Malthus (Hofstadter 1955, 39).

Herbert Spencer had linked evolutionary ideas to society as early as 1851, eight years before Darwin's *Origin of Species*. In 1884, he approvingly quoted his 1851 *Social Statics*, in which he had argued that the natural hardships faced by animals ensured the improvement of their species. The 1851 piece continued that humanity might attain its "ultimate perfection" through the working of the same "severe discipline" (survival of the fittest). This discipline "never swerves for the avoidance of partial and temporary suffering" (Spencer 1884, 107). He claimed that the poverty of "the incapable" was decreed by evolution. By 1884, he disclaimed the teleological tone of his earlier statement, but otherwise concluded that time had given him no reason to change his mind. Indeed, the "beneficial results of the survival of the fittest prove to be immeasurably greater than those above indicated" (108). The everyday working of social evolution relied on nothing more than old standards of laissez-faire: that one's earnings should be determined by markets so that those who offered something of value would thrive and produce similar offspring (106). The proper working of evolution also required property rights, the sanctity of contracts, and freedom of market activity. Asked Spencer (104), who would "contend that no mischief will result if the lowly endowed are enabled to thrive and multiply as much as, or more than, the highly endowed"? Malthus had found the suffering of poverty to be inevitable, now Spencer declared it to be *desirable*.

The modern state, to Spencer, represented the greatest potential threat to evolutionary progress if it burdened the successful members of society with obligations toward their fellow citizens. The state might become the instrument for the softhearted to tax all in order to support evolutionary misfits. Worse, the state would accomplish this unworthy end at the expense of the economically fit and so burden them in the evolutionary struggle (113). The main functions of the state should be limited, he said, to protection of the economic freedoms of the individual, enforcement of property rights, and of contracts.

Spencer aimed to defend individual rights against state authority, for, in a regime of individual liberty, evolution would work best. In particular, Spencer devoted much attention to refuting Jeremy Bentham, whose utilitarianism contained the seeds of government activism (despite the alliance of the Utilitarian philosophers with laissez-faire economists on the issue of free trade). Bentham had favored democracy because he believed it was most compatible with his principle of the greatest happiness for the greatest number. He had rejected natural-law doctrines because historically they had been used to thwart the will of the people. Spencer supported natural rights as a way to stymie state activism and concluded that "Bentham's proposition leaves us in a plexus of absurdities" (141).

Having demolished—to his own satisfaction—Bentham's opposition to natural rights, Spencer then made a case for them on the grounds that the value of life itself must be granted and so "there must be a justification for the performance of acts essential to its preservation." In turn, this justified "those liberties and claims which make such acts possible" (150). It would be difficult to put rights on a more fundamental basis than those things that make life itself possible. Thus, because government did not create life itself, it could not legitimately abrogate those rights needed for living. Natural rights in Spencer's thought protected individual economic liberty from governmental infringements. In principle, these rights protected all, although they were of most value to those with the most to protect. Natural rights of this sort had a strong tendency to protect the economic status quo. In short, as envisioned by Spencer, they worked exactly as Jeremy Bentham had feared they would work.

When the exercise of the natural liberties of one person in proximity to another infringes those of the other, mutual restraint is necessary. This was the notion of ethics advanced by Spencer: ethics adjudicates competing claims when liberties conflict, and government's role is limited to protecting those individual rights established in ethics. This, of course, was very similar to Francis Wayland's principle of "reciprocity" (see chapter 7); the reciprocity principle, or something like it, keeps appearing in the history of autonomy morality.

A variety of technical criticisms (based on biology he could not have known) may be laid at Spencer's door, perhaps the largest being that his notion of economic "fitness" required learned, not heritable skills.[1] Still, Spencer managed to restate for another generation the old doctrines of laissez-faire morality in a fresh scientific idiom. With Spencer, absolute versions of property rights, freedom of contract, hostility to poor laws, tolerance of inequality, and so on, were validated by the grand process of evolution. Spencer made laissez-faire congruent with the dynamic world of evolution and replaced eternal scarcity with evolutionary progress. As a rhetorical feat, Social Darwinism was a strong reaffirmation of old values. As a logical feat, it was something less: how could it be that human values should never evolve alongside evolving humanity?

WILLIAM GRAHAM SUMNER

William Graham Sumner (1840–1910), after a short period in the Episcopal ministry, became a professor of political economy and sociology at Yale in the early 1870s. Over approximately the next decade he engaged in heavy polemics supporting laissez-faire and refuting economic-reform proposals on evolutionary grounds. In his later career, his agenda turned less polemical, although he did not retract his earlier work. Ironically, one of his students at Yale was the future radical Thorstein Veblen. Sumner was decidedly gloomier than Spencer.

Sumner held that nature rewarded the industrious and thrifty while grinding down the slothful and improvident. Only thrift and industry could accumulate the capital that made possible any improvement of the human condition. Conversely, the human race might at any time succumb to decadent habits and squander the capital that was its only leverage against nature. In 1883, he argued that the human strategy must be capital accumulation: mankind "can bring the productive forces of Nature into service. . . . How has the change been brought about? The answer is, By capital" (Sumner 1920, 59–60). Sumner attacked economic reforms favoring the poor because he said they would dissipate capital. In one essay ("Socialism"), he argued that the stinginess of nature made "our fellow-men" into "our competitors for the meager supply" (Sumner 1963, 76). This may be the most succinct and explicit statement of the ethical theme of laissez-faire: that competitive self-interest is justified by natural scarcity. Competition increased in proportion to the Malthusian pressure of population (Sumner 1963, 74).

Although Sumner recast the defense of competitive economics in the evolutionary terminology of his times, little was new. More than Spencer, his vision of the world remained the static world of Malthus. Therefore it is no surprise that Sumner endorsed the traditional individualist values of "liberty, equality before the law, responsibility, individualism, monogamy, and private property" (1963, 92). When he looked at human motivations, he saw self-interest at work, not moral forces (1963, 79).

That there would be economic cripples was inevitable, Sumner thought. But support for the weak would divert society's capital and thus threaten humanity's chance for success. Sumner sarcastically attacked reformers, "friends of humanity," whose sentimentality resulted in programs that produced "a transfer of capital from the better off to the worse off." Sumner resented capital being transferred "to a shiftless and inefficient member of society" (1920, 124–25). The wages-fund doctrine served its purpose again, Sumner arguing that charity diverts capital from wages of those willing to work. Sumner assessed aid for the weak by the metric of capital: because aid to the weak decreased capital (as embodied in the wages fund), such aid was wrong.

Departing from Spencer's positive view of natural rights, Sumner denied them lest a version of natural rights arise that guaranteed everyone a claim to basic support by society. In his world, no one had natural-law claims to subsistence, for this would amount to claims on others to provide the subsistence. In an essay ("Forgotten Man") Sumner argued that any person's claim on "the social product is measured by the energy and wisdom which he has contributed to the social effort" (1963, 117). In short, for fear of a highly unlikely occurrence—that natural-rights ideas would produce social entitlements for the poor in nineteenth-century America—Sumner rejected natural rights. Ironically, Bentham had opposed natural rights for exactly the opposite reason—that they only protected the privileged.

Sumner dismissed the idea that anyone held claims against anyone else. Except when the obligation has been voluntarily adopted (as with marriage), he held that no one should be morally or legally obliged to support another. Indeed, liberty, understood as the freedom *from* obligation and the freedom to act exclusively for self, was one of Sumner's fundamental values. The protection of personal autonomy was, for Sumner, the only legitimate function of the state: "*each man is guaranteed the use of all his own powers exclusively for his own welfare*" (1920, 34—emphasis in original). By disclaiming affirmative natural rights, Sumner created a vacuum that he named individual "liberty" and which he invoked like a negative natural right to limit government.

As did laissez-faire thinkers, Sumner wanted the smallest possible state. The assault on nature was best directed by self-interest, whereas the state mostly misdirected economic effort. Sentimental reformers would capture an activist state and use it to promote their unproductive schemes, while special interests would rush to create privileges for themselves.

If the state was to be negligible, what was to be the organizing structure of society? Sumner envisioned an aggregation of autonomous individuals who organized themselves by means of voluntary contracts: "the social structure is based on contract. . . . Contract, however, is rational—even rationalistic. It is also realistic, cold, and matter-of-fact" (1920, 24–25). The virtue of the indifferent contract was that it is the way "free and independent men" relate. Here, in sharp contrast, was a fundamental difference between autonomy morality and relational morality: Sumner's ethic saw goodness in keeping others at a distance; the relational morality treated others as close kin. Sumner's contractual individualism meant that one need not care about the person with whom one contracted business; persons related only in one dimension—that of necessary business transactions. Sumner seemed to revel in the idea that economic relations that were "cold, and matter-of-fact," for this protected the autonomy of the individual.

Sumner justified large concentrations of capital, inequalities of wealth, because of the leverage they provided against nature. He claimed concentration of resources was a "necessary condition" for social progress and continued: "If we should set a limit to the accumulation of wealth, we should say to our most valuable producers, 'We do not want you. . . .' It would be like killing off our generals in war" (1920, 54). Great inequality, therefore, was justified on a pragmatic level—what it could accomplish. Also, Sumner argued that the prospect of great wealth is an incentive for people to save: "Capital is only formed by self-denial, and if the possession of it did not secure advantages and superiorities of a high order, men would never submit to what is necessary to get it" (1920, 77). By calling saving "self-denial," Sumner attributed moral virtue to accumulation. Sumner did not ask whether the greatest accumulations of his day indeed represented the fruits of self-denial.

In his essay "The Forgotten Man" Sumner portrayed as a victim of meddlesome reformers the hardworking, middling person who is required by law to contribute through taxes to the social welfare (1963, 111). That is, Sumner asserted that social legislation came at the expense of the productive and middle-class Mr. Forgotten Man. Sumner stated that Mr. Forgotten Man had a legitimate grievance for being asked to do his share as part of the larger society. In statements reminiscent of Adam Smith's much earlier, disparaging observations about persons of public-spirit, Sumner painted the reformer, who *did* have a sense of the common good, as the opposite of the ideal Forgotten Man.

Sumner's Social Darwinism had very little evolution in it. Once the unfit for capitalism had been purged—along with any values that handicapped economic individualism—the economy and society would presumably have achieved the best that could be achieved, and so cease to evolve. Sumner did not consider the possibility that evolution doesn't end, that it would turn a corner and enter an era in which cooperative virtues would best suit an evolved humanity. Sumner was in the end as inconsistent as Spencer: using an evolutionary metaphor, he promoted static values that in effect denied the evolution of humanity.

CARNEGIE: THE GOSPEL OF WEALTH

The steel magnate Andrew Carnegie was a personal friend of Herbert Spencer and apparently gained an almost religious comfort from Spencer's doctrines (Hofstadter 1955, 45). Improbably, Carnegie converted one loophole of Social Darwinism—the freedom to spend one's money as one liked—into the basis of large-scale philanthropy, which he believed would not violate the major principles of Darwinism. Carnegie expressed his ideas on philanthropy in 1889 in a pair of magazine articles jointly known as *The Gospel of Wealth*.

Carnegie tried hard to keep his philanthropic recommendations consistent with Social Darwinism. The great advances in civilization, according to Carnegie, had occurred because of individualism, private property, wealth, and competition. These four "laws" were the "best and most valuable of all that humanity has yet accomplished" (Carnegie 1889, 6). For the accumulation of wealth, the four laws of Social Darwinism were unsurpassed; however, once accumulated, wealth had to be distributed. Carnegie defined philanthropy carefully so that it applied to the distribution of wealth in a way that did not interfere with the operation of the laws that applied to production and accumulation.

Carnegie's version of philanthropy, he believed, was compatible with the laws of Darwinism. The wealthy man was to turn his superior skills—attested to by the fortune itself—to the problems of the community, because, he thought, the rich can solve community problems far better than the community itself can. Another principle was that any donation should always promote self-help. The public library or university met this standard admirably, for library users and students must also make a personal effort. Conversely, "it were better for mankind that the millions of the rich were thrown into the sea than so spent as to encourage the slothful, the drunken, the unworthy" (14).

Here, again, was the durable conviction that the weak were blameworthy and that assistance to them created perverse incentives.

It was a wonder that the philanthropic impulse grew at all in such soil. Therefore, it is all the more surprising that the amount of giving required by Carnegie was very great. The man of wealth was to live modestly, to provide only moderately for his dependents, and "after doing so, to consider *all* surplus revenues which come to him simply as trust funds" that were to be administered "for the community" (13). Carnegie considered it shameful if a rich person should die in possession of great wealth.

Despite his efforts to make philanthropy consistent with Social Darwinism, Carnegie had to reach outside Social Darwinism to find grounds for the philanthropic impulse. Social Darwinism and laissez-faire might grudgingly permit philanthropy as an exercise of individual freedom, but they provided no affirmative reason for philanthropy. Carnegie justified philanthropy in language that would have been foreign to Sumner: "Men who continue hoarding great sums all their lives, the proper use of which for public ends would work good to the community from which it chiefly came, should be made to feel that the community . . . cannot thus be deprived of its proper share" (10). To hold back was to *hoard*, in Carnegie's negative terminology. He also wrote of the proper use of wealth, again suggesting some moral frame of reference unknown to Social Darwinism. Although he seemed to favor the axioms of autonomy for producing wealth, he apparently thought such principles inadequate to define the good in dispersing one's wealth. Carnegie's ethic appears dualistic, and dualism is often problematic.

Although Carnegie may have been a free thinker in matters of religion, his essay appealed to the religious impulse of his readers. His philosophy was a *gospel* of wealth. In philanthropy lies hope for "the reconciliation of the rich and the poor—a reign of harmony" (1889, 11). This is a prophetic vision and invokes religious words such as reconciliation—which refers to the healing of relationships. He concluded with the statement "the gospel of wealth but echoes Christ's words." This might have been little but convenient rhetoric to Carnegie. However, it may have been more: Carnegie may have recognized that without the resort to Christian, relational norms, his Social Darwinism could provide no compelling basis for his philanthropy; in fact, Sumner had promoted a general presumption against philanthropy.

Carnegie needed to transcend Social Darwinism to find a motivating vision for his gospel of wealth. He believed that the wealthy had to recognize themselves as parts of a community; he went as far as Horace Mann (chapter 5) in recognizing the community as the source of wealth. He excoriated greed, a vice for which Social Darwinism had no critique. He quoted Jesus, whose words would have been discounted by most Social Darwinists. In short, Carnegie accepted relational moral principles to support the philanthropic use of wealth, which he would have rejected if he truly had applied the values of Social Darwinism.

Carnegie presented an understanding of the economic world (Social Darwinism) and a value system to support philanthropy (a sense of obligation to community) that essentially conflicted. In contrast, Sumner's work had no such tension because the nature of the economy as he saw it and his value system were completely congruent: the evolution that worked itself out in the economic world defined what was morally good. However, Carnegie's philanthropy had an independent foundation, possibly in Christian teaching, from his Social Darwinism. The result was an inconsistency between Carnegie's ethic of philanthropy and his avowed Social Darwinist ethic of production. Whether such a position is logically or psychologically possible is open to question. Jesus said that one cannot serve God and mammon; Carnegie seemed to try.

THORSTEIN VEBLEN

Thorstein Veblen (1857–1929) was a systematic thinker whose evolutionary ideas led to radical conclusions. His view of society was truly evolutionary in the sense that as society changed, values changed, too. Veblen eked out a small living from an academic career, held back, no doubt, because he never accepted the orthodoxies of his era. That he was tolerated at all (at a time before academic freedom was protected) attests his immense learning (see, e.g., Edgell 2001). His writing was learned, ironic, and dismissive of his era's capitalist culture.

Veblen's first book, *Theory of the Leisure Class* (1899), opened with a challenge to the orthodox theory of property. Ignoring John Locke's widely accepted view of property, Veblen stated that property originated in the plunder of war (Veblen 1899, 27). In his 1904 book *Theory of Business Enterprise*, Veblen again discredited Locke and natural rights explicitly. After noting Locke's theory of property, he added that "no doubt, such was not the pedigree of modern industry or modern ownership; but the serene, undoubting assumption of Locke and his generation only stands out the more strongly and unequivocally for this its discrepancy with fact" (Veblen 1904, 78–79). According to Veblen, this natural-rights doctrine of property served as the legal basis for the capitalism of his day (1904, 82). Ironically, he said, just as natural-rights ideas were being embedded in the American founding documents and laws, the industrial age dawned. And the realities of the Industrial Revolution were incongruent with natural-rights metaphysics:

> The discrepancy between law and fact . . . has had repeated illustration in the court decisions between bodies of workmen and their employers or owners. These decisions commonly fall out in favor of employers or owners; that is to say, they go to uphold property rights and the rights of free contract. (1904, 278)

Property rights and rights of free contract, which served to stymie legislative reforms in labor relations, were not adequate to address the realities of the new industrial age, Veblen held. In fact, in response to the realities of modern industrial life, the industrial (worker) classes no longer even thought in terms of property and ownership (1904, 327). Veblen was calling the natural-rights idea of property *a sociological invention*—appropriate for one time and place, but not for his own era. These ideas of property and contract belonged to a time of handcrafts.

The ancient roots of property lay in the ages when life was warlike and predatory, and property was synonymous with captive slaves, said Veblen. Soon, classes emerged: an enslaved class, which performed productive industry, and an owner class, which continued the warlike, exploitative tradition. This owner class then evolved into a leisure class, free from productive work, but devoted to periodic war, politics, priestly functions, and preparing for war. With the passing of the warlike phases of culture, accumulation of wealth, often by means not far removed from predation, came to be the main mark of this class. Given the *real* function of wealth (bestowal of status on the possessor), the desire for wealth could not be sated (Veblen 1899, 32). Thus, the accumulation motive is driven by an endless competition for status.

Those successful in the primitive stage of civilization could live at leisure because they lived off of plunder and the efforts of slaves. But with the evolution of culture, leisure itself became the mark of success (Veblen 1899, 38). Further, members of this leisure class were pressured to be profligate—in order to display their success. Veblen had turned laissez-faire on its head, for it claimed the rich got that way by diligent work and thrift.

Over the ages, the leisure class had ceased being engaged literally in warfare for a living and had adapted to the new industrial society. Although the richest of the rich might waste time conspicuously on extravagant hobbies, in travel, and so on, most of the males were employed. But they were *not employed productively* as laborers, tradesmen, supervisors, and engineers. Instead, the leisure class related to industry in a way analogous to their former existence as predators, argued Veblen, in "a pecuniary relation—a relation of acquisition, not of production; of exploitation, not of serviceability" (1899, 209). In other words, the former predators now engaged in financial predation at the expense of the productive class. The predatory class (transformed into businessmen) pursued mergers and acquisitions that created railroad trusts and inflated railroad stock. They did not actually construct or run a railroad—or any other business:

> they will aim to manage the affairs of the concern with a view to an advantageous purchase and sale of its capital rather than with a view of the future prosperity of the concern, to the continued advantageous sale of the output of goods or services produced by the industrial use of this capital. (Veblen 1904, 157)

Veblen juxtaposed this interest of businessmen—manipulating assets for a profit—with the "permanent interest of the corporation as a going concern" and with the "community at large," which demanded efficiency and good products (1904, 157–58). Veblen's key theme is easily stated: the business managers seek their success in financial manipulations, whereas the working class's interest and the general community's interests lie in the actual productive process.

How different were Veblen's views from those of Sumner, whose business "generals" were the source of all progress! Real progress, said Veblen, came from purely industrial advances and outran the ability of the leisure class to adapt because that class (unlike the workers) was under no necessity to adapt (Veblen 1899, 193). With adjustment slowed by the leisure class, economic progress probably will be "less than might be if the scheme were altered to suit the altered conditions" (1899, 194). Thus, Veblen converted the rich from an engine of growth to a retarding factor: that class "consistently acts to retard that adjustment to the environment which is called social advance or development" (1899, 206–207).

This assessment was opposite those of the conservative evolutionists. These latter had used "survival of the fittest" to promote belief in "the natural superiority of the dominant class and the inevitability of competitive capitalism" (Edgell 2001, 112). Veblen's understanding of evolution was that real change preceded institutional change; thus conventional values and institutions were better fitted to the past. Accordingly, "to the extent that circumstances change all the time . . . contemporary institutions are always out of step with them" (Edgell 2001, 113). The leisure class-business class, of course, was a creature of the past and a retarding factor. According to Edgell (113), if the conservative economic evolutionists basically claimed that "whatever is, is right," Veblen stated that "whatever is, is wrong." Veblen was reluctant to make explicit affirmative ethical assertions. Nevertheless, he played a negative role as moralist by scrutinizing laissez-faire's version of evolution and making the case that its values were inconsistent with actual economic conditions.

In all this, Veblen kept the pose of the scientist who was merely setting out the theory of the leisure class without making a moral judgment about it. Yet, it became progressively more difficult to maintain that pose as he discussed the values of the respective classes. The values of the leisure class, which was really a "barbarian culture," were: "ferocity, self-seeking, clannishness, and disingenuousness—a free resort to force and fraud" (Veblen 1899, 225). Of course, he said, modern economics would be better served by cooperative traits (1899, 227–28). The business-leisure class thought in conventional terms, in terms of doctrines embedded in the established legal system, which had served them so well. This mind-set, argued Veblen, meant that social changes were forced into the old intellectual framework instead of the old framework being changed in the light of social changes (1904, 319).

Veblen made explicit the obvious conclusion, that such a mind is profoundly conservative and is literally incapable of questioning the moral and economic framework that has served its interests well (1904, 320). In contrast to the business class, Veblen argued, the industrial class dealt with machines directly and every day. The machine was a material reality and its operations emphasized a cause-and-effect mentality. The machine created "workday ideals and skepticism of what is only conventionally valid" (Veblen 1904, 323). That is, the industrial class habitually adjusts to change and ignores outdated frames of reference. Thus, unlike the conservative Darwinists, Veblen did not see the business-leisure classes as agents of evolution, but as brakes on evolutionary change. Real change was produced by the industrial classes.

Nineteenth-century economic morality never stood apart from a scientific story of how things worked. The morality of original laissez-faire had its foundation in the science of scarcity and incentives. The conservative evolutionists viewed the world through the lens of "survival of the fittest" and, in so doing, they justified the values associated with the status quo. Veblen provided an alternative evolutionary interpretation. In his interpretation, scarcity was not the dominant reality; to the contrary, the industrial age allowed for conspicuous consumption and waste. More, Veblen taught that economic evolution was not driven by the dominant classes, who actually held things back. Instead, he spoke of the new values blossoming within the industrial classes, which faced the new industrial world.

A CRITICAL CONCLUSION

The ethic of Spencer and Sumner extolled competitive values in a world of scarcity. The term "competition" seemed sometimes to refer to competition of humans as a species with nature and at other times to competition of human with human. Nevertheless, person-with-person competition might not be the best strategy for the "struggle" of the species with nature. The Social Darwinists never demonstrated that cooperative values at the individual level would not produce better results for the human species in its struggle with nature. They seem to have taken it for granted that person-to-person competition automatically was the best strategy for the human species against nature.

Using a new, scientific metaphor to defend old values led to some ironies. One commentator notes that Sumner's virtues were simply the old Puritan virtues (Hofstadter 1955, 61). After the latest scientific idea of evolution had been adopted as the framework for economic ethics, what emerged were truncated religious values—old ones at that. As a further irony, the old religious ethic had been far more nuanced than Social Darwinism. The Puritans, for example, had recognized that even virtues could go wrong (e.g., thrift could become miserly). Sumner made no such distinctions: the good was measured very simply by the accumulation of capital.

The conservative evolutionists added two elements to the old laissez-faire. First was an important change in tone. Especially as told by Sumner, the struggle for survival sounded much like war. And, in war, victory often justifies any tactics. As a matter of *logic*, both laissez-faire and Social Darwinism required that no economic actor should infringe the rights of the others (one recalls Wayland's duty of reciprocity). That is, restraint, not war, is the right model for social behavior. But how persuasive is the mere logic of restraint in war? If economic life is a battle for survival itself, then victory becomes all-important. It seems likely that Sumner's bellicose tone and imagery could have had a larger impact on economic morality than his actual arguments. Victory in war—with or without fair play or respect for limits—may become an all-justifying end. Sumner's hyperbolic vision of life as a war for survival might have undermined not only "sentimental" ethics, but *any* ethical restraint at all.

The second potential amendment of Social Darwinism to laissez-faire was the language of change, dynamics, or evolution. The old laissez-faire posited scarcity in an unchanging world. Darwinism made progress a staple of nineteenth-century thought and Spencer incorporated some sense of economic progress in his writings. Strangely enough, the American, Sumner, failed to grasp the dynamic aspect of evolution. His version of natural selection never moved things beyond adaptation to Malthusian scarcity. It was never clear from his writings what changes would occur if the "fit" did survive and the "unfit" perished. We can infer that capital would accumulate faster. That was Sumner's favorite measure of progress. Sumner's essays convey the sense that any progress would be at best an asymptotic approach to some Malthusian limit. Eventually, an unchanging economy would be filled with as much capital as it was worth having—or perhaps even more than it was worth having (for Sumner specified no limit to accumulation). At some point, one might infer, all capital investment would go simply to replace the huge depreciation of a monstrously large capital stock. Sumner's end point seems dehumanized: a huge capital stock, the accumulation of which defines human virtues and purposes.

Sumner never conveyed the sense that he had an appreciation for the idea that species evolve when they adapt to *new* environments—whether created by natural disasters, or by changes of climate, or encountered during migrations, or even by capital accumulation itself. That is, significant evolution is driven by changes in environment. If values are simply what make for success in a *particular kind of environment*, then those values would need to change if environment changed. But this was the last thing Sumner wanted to argue.

Andrew Carnegie's mixed approach to economic morality might at first glance seem a form of desirable compromise between autonomy and relational morality. However, in order to work, Carnegie's approach required that economic life be divisible into self-contained units (earning vs. spending or production vs. distribution) to which completely different moralities would be applied. Carnegie claimed to apply autonomy morality (Social Darwinism) to earning or accumulating income and a truncated form of relational morality (philanthropy) to spending income. This is not really a combining of the two ethics but a segregating of them into two realms. However, such a segmentation of one's economic life into pieces is probably impossible. What psychologically well-integrated owner of a firm, who was engaged wholeheartedly in antagonistic labor relations, could *genuinely* seek the reconciliation of the classes as a philanthropist? Would not attitudes and principles employed in one sector have difficulty coexisting in the same psyche with the contradictory habits and principles employed in the other? In Carnegie's own life, the incompatibility of the two moralities became apparent in 1892 when he left town while a lieutenant waged a brutal battle against the Amalgamated Association of Iron and Steel Workers; incongruously, Carnegie claimed to support unions.

If the human personality cannot be segregated into self-contained compartments, neither can economic functions. And if earning and spending are intertwined, then the moral principles by which they operate cannot be segmented. This intertwining occurs at the simplest level: as William Graham Sumner would have been quick to note, income given in charity is income that cannot be reinvested in economic expansion. At the aggregate level, production and consumption are intertwined: strong consumer demand is a short-run cause of increased production and investment. The very act of deciding on the amounts of productive activity one will engage in relative to philanthropy forces one to decide which is more important. In turn, this forces a decision on which set of moral principles should dominate the other. Perhaps the tycoon-philanthropist in dividing time and resources simply satisfies some personal preferences. In that case, such preferences then become a *supermorality* that chooses the degree to which one engages in production or philanthropy. Such a supermorality would be another form of autonomy ethics (i.e., egoistic utilitarianism, maximizing the fulfillment of self-defined preferences). It seems difficult to have it both ways, as Carnegie tried to do.

In Veblen's work, evolution was truly dynamic: the realities of economics changed, and new adaptations constantly emerged. Yet, what happened earlier in history continued to matter, for patterns of behavior, once fitted to an early era, remained as holdovers that in a new era might function in parasitic ways. At the intellectual level, Veblen's work appeals as original and interesting, whereas Sumner's is repetitious and even boring. Veblen used evolutionary ideas to paint an opposite view of reality from that promoted by Sumner and Spencer. He made explicit that those who win in a capitalist society may win on the basis of old rules that do not favor economic progress in the present. The past remained in one form or another, shaping the present and future— and not always for the best. Thus, for Veblen, nineteenth-century capitalism was not the highest accomplishment of evolution.

. Veblen's mind ranged over long eras of human history. Veblen was well-versed in the anthropology of his time. Yet, a modern reader may find his portrayals to be more the imaginative creations of his fertile mind than anything that could be established by modern standards of evidence. In this failing Veblen was no different from the conservative Social Darwinists—but far more original.

Veblen was not a moralist in the sense that he gave explicit reasons for the values that he favored, although it was clear what economic values he did favor. Yet, he was a moralist in another sense: he attacked the value system of laissez-faire and conservative Social Darwinism by arguing that the economic world that fit those values simply did not exist. Veblen was also what might be called a meta-moralist, paying little attention to the values of a particular morality, but establishing a perspective on how all value systems evolve with changing circumstances. In that sense, his meta-morality implied moral relativism. Yet, it was not individualistic relativism (one defines one's own values), but a cultural relativism: values are more or less well suited for the economic culture of a given era.

NINE

New Influences in Economics

EVEN IN THE LATE nineteenth century, most of America's recognized economists continued to accept laissez-faire (Heilbroner 1972, 209–10). However, the disparity between laissez-faire—its theories and values—and the actual economy no longer avoided continuous intellectual challenge. Henry George was a journalist-turned-economic writer, who recognized that laissez-faire formed a self-reinforcing package of ideas that blinded adherents to the need for reforms. He attacked it in a best-selling book *Progress and Poverty* (1879). The book also launched a highly visible political and speaking career for George. Richard Ely was an academic economist, and one of a few Americans holding an earned doctorate at the time. As a religious liberal, he saw similarities between laissez-faire economics and the kind of religion he disliked—doctrines that seemed divorced from experience. He set out to make empirical observations and historical analysis, methods being used in liberal religious scholarship, a part of the methods of economics. Along the way, he anticipated the ethics of the Social Gospel movement (see chapter 10). His long-running economics textbook articulated the case for reform in economic theory and practice. John Bates Clark's early writings contained many of the emphases apparent in Ely's writings. In his later career, Clark overthrew a major pillar of laissez-faire, but then gave his theory a moral interpretation that was potentially as supportive of the economic status quo as laissez-faire had been. However, Clark seemed to harbor the suspicion that the status quo was intolerable, and sought hope in economic dynamics. Ultimately, Clark appeared to believe that an abstract ethical principle—even one he had contributed to formulating—could not be taken as the last word if it condoned intolerable lives for members of the economy.

HENRY GEORGE

Henry George (1839–1897) moved from the East Coast to California, where he became a journalist and educated himself in economics. His *Progress and*

Poverty (1879) was stimulated by his wonderment at high land values in post-Gold Rush California juxtaposed against poverty, and by his deep, but nonorthodox, religious liberalism (Sklansky 2002,128). The book was simultaneously an economic and moral treatise that targeted both static and evolutionary versions of laissez-faire. Worldwide, his followers promoted tax reform, based on the idea of a single tax on land replacing all other levies. Because George's theory focused on the unearned rents that accrued to the owners of scarce land, it is not surprising that it provoked some vehement objections from England's landed aristocracy (see Samuels, Johnson, and Johnson 2005).

According to George, classical political economy had a three-part foundation: the wages fund, Malthusian population theory, and David Ricardo's rent theory. Ricardo held that land rents were proportional to the fertility of soil relative to the least fertile land in production. As less fertile land came into production under the pressure of population, landlords would be enriched and workers impoverished (George 1879, 165–72). While rejecting the wages fund and Malthusian ideas, George drew heavily on, and expanded, Ricardo's rent theory.

Before presenting his own theory of poverty, George restated for his readers how the triumvirate of wages fund, Malthus's population theory, and Ricardo rent theory had been used to rationalize the inevitability of human poverty. Population pressure implied that wages fell as more workers divided the fixed wages fund among themselves (97). Meanwhile, the same population pressures also "forced cultivation to less and less productive lands . . . thus explaining the rise of rent." George (99) summarized the obvious conclusion of laissez-faire: "poverty, want, and starvation" are "the inevitable results of universal laws, with which . . . it were as hopeless to quarrel as with the law of gravitation."

To the wages fund, George retorted that wages were paid from labor's *current production* and not from a fixed pool of capital. The only limit to wages was labor's own productivity. A worker gathering eggs or berries is paid out of the gathered eggs or berries, and whalers are paid from the oil they themselves bring to port (George 1879, 50). Although modern income and product accounts have come to view wages as being paid from production, George was attacking the orthodoxy of the time. He was also undermining its implications, which put workers at a disadvantage. First, George undermined the notion that the worker should feel dependent on, and thankful to, employers, whose thrift and sacrifice created a wages fund. Second, at the moral level, George had recast wages as the workers' legitimate claim on production itself, rather than as a contracted claim on the preexisting wages fund—thus leaving employers as the rightful claimants of all current production.

George attacked Malthusianism for implying that "there could be no solution to the poverty question," and providing the "elite with a rationale for inaction" (McLaughlin-Jenkins 2005, 45). He gave examples of growing populations that enjoyed increasing—not decreasing—prosperity. And he argued that the poverty of India and Ireland was due to the rapacity of British colonial policy rather than Malthusian pressure. George held that "the injustice of society, not the niggardliness of nature, is the cause of the want and misery" (George 1879, 141). The reason population did *not* outrun sustenance, according to George, was that "the denser the population . . . the greater the economies of production and distribution" (150). Malthusian theory was "utterly inconsistent with all the facts" (150).

If a Malthusian explanation is ruled out, how would he explain poverty? The key, George thought, was Ricardo's theory of rent (219). It held that the least fertile land in production would earn no rent, for no farmers would bid to till such poor land. More fertile land would command rent, however, because farmers would bid competitively for the right to till more productive land; farmers would bid the most for the right to till the most productive land, and so on down the line. However, there would be no competition to win the right to work the *worst* land—which would earn no rent. Ultimately, landowners would collect as rent all the difference in production between the more fertile and the least fertile lands in use. While landowners reaped the benefits of their land's fertility, non-owner farmers labored for a wage equal to what could be produced by the least fertile land.

George amended Ricardo's rent theory by insisting that land would earn rents, not only because of superior fertility, but because of superior productivity in *any* use. After all, some manufacturing firms, or office buildings, may be more productive in certain locations than others. Because of increasing productivity over time, land rents would rise, especially where economic activity was the greatest, as in urban areas (235–43). Thus, the fruits of economic progress in general, the creativeness of an entire society, were being captured by rent.

Because human productivity was growing, poverty could be eliminated if productivity grew faster than the landlords' rent share increased. However, if the share of landowners increased faster than productivity, workers could still be impoverished despite rising productivity: "Private ownership of land is the nether millstone. Material progress is the upper millstone. Between them, with an increasing pressure, the working classes are being ground" (357). In the race between rising productivity and the increasing rent share, the landowners won (282). George seemed to view this more as a truth based on observation than something to be proved deductively.

If land rent was diverting the benefits of society's progress from the vast majority of people, this put private ownership at issue. George asked "what constitutes the rightful basis of property" (334)? His answer was that a human has a self-evident right to "everything produced" by his or her own labor. But human labor produced no land so "no one can be rightfully entitled to the ownership of which is not the produce of his labor" (336). Thus, private land ownership is wrong, and from this "we have traced the unjust distribution of wealth" (342).

How, then, did private ownership arise? To George, private ownership had been grasped by the powerful ones in society (George 1879, 342). In his emphasis on land acquisition by violence, George anticipated Veblen's later work (chapter 8). Given the morally questionable basis of land ownership, the terms of ownership could be changed by society. This left George free to propose a solution to poverty: specifically, to tax away virtually all the landlords' rent. George was convinced that the proceeds of this tax would be so great as to eliminate all other taxes—and so it came to be called the single tax. The proceeds of the single tax would be redistributed to the population in various ways, thus eliminating poverty.

George resorted to religious imagery to condemn poverty as "the open-mouthed, relentless hell which yawns beneath civilized society" (1879, 457). The constant threat and insecurity naturally evoked selfish human behavior as self-defense. George denied that selfishness was integral to human nature, arguing that it comes from the insecurity of want: "For poverty . . . means shame, degradation; the searing of the most sensitive parts of our moral and mental nature" (457; see also Sklansky 2002,128). He held it amazing that humans were not more selfish than they were (461). In a final attack on the old economics, George declared, "Shortsighted is the philosophy which counts on selfishness as the . . . motive of human action. " He soon added, "It is not selfishness that enriched the annals of every people with heroes and saints" (462). To George, higher motives were at the heart of the human psyche. George was very aware of the Darwinist recasting of laissez-faire and noted the parallelism of the two (George 1879, 479). He thought Spencer's evolutionary processes to be materialistic and so to exclude moral choice (George 1879, 478, 480). George also pointed out the essentially static view of society presented by the Social Darwinists and the dynamism of true evo-lutionary theory (McLaughlin-Jenkins 2005, 45). Attacking the very heart of conservative Social Darwinism, George scorned the notion that economic virtues or vices could be inherited: "A child no more inherits his father's knowledge than he inherits his father's glass eye" (504). Finally, George asserted that evolution did not guarantee progress, and that it could move into blind alleys: one such blind alley was the rise of rent to create mass poverty.

The passage of time has shown that George had some of the economics wrong: in the years since he wrote, rent payments to landlords have not swal-lowed up all increases in economic productivity. Instead, much technical change has economized on land, making it relatively less scarce. And if George was wrong on this issue, he would have been wrong about the ability of a single tax on land to fund all government. But on other large issues, he was correct. Malthusian scarcity has failed to describe developed nations for the last two centuries.[1] Indeed, increasing productivity, which George high-lighted, has been the basis of growing standards of living for two centuries. George also anticipated modern national income and product accounts; these modern accounts treat wages as paid from current production, not from a sta-tic and preexisting wages fund. Modern theory of urban economics takes as a given George's extension of Ricardo's theory of land rent. Finally, George was correct in singling out productivity growth as *the* overriding factor in eco-nomic change.

When George attempted to show that poverty was not inevitable, he was making a theoretical argument. However, his theory had a moral impact, of which he was fully aware: for if poverty is not inevitable, then an obligation to act on the problem can no longer be dismissed. As a theorist, his other point was that poverty is a human invention, a function of human institutions, which can be reformed. He also argued, as a moralist, that failing to end poverty is a crime against human dignity. Ending poverty would free a new side of humanity that was previously buried under layers of behaviors spurred by insecurity. Remove a system of insecurity and shame, and the goodness of human nature will emerge. In this approach, George hit many of the themes common to relational morality.

RICHARD T. ELY

Richard Ely (1854–1943) earned a doctorate in economics in Germany in the 1870s. German economics was oriented to documenting facts and studying the history of social ideas (such as property rights); Anglo-American eco-nomics, by comparison, was abstract and deductive. With this educational background, and a set of liberal religious beliefs, Ely began criticizing laissez-faire on his return to America in the 1880s (see Bateman and Kapstein 1999, 252). Anglo-American economics, as he saw it, consisted largely of deductions from axioms, which had seemed plausible to Enlightenment rationalists. Yet these deductions seemed at odds with more recent economic facts as Ely read them. Ely advocated that economics shift focus to the description of poverty and working conditions, and to the history of economic institutions and ideas. Ely (with mixed success) helped organize economic associations designed to foster this approach.

Ely's adherence, simultaneously, to such economics as well as to liberal religious beliefs might seem to be a coincidence—a chance joining of unrelated convictions. This would be an incorrect reading, for Protestantism had many links to empiricism in natural science (see Harrison 1998, 5–8). But even fur-ther, the type of empirical *social* science that Ely learned in Germany had been a direct outgrowth of liberal German Protestantism, whose founder, the the-ologian Friedrich Schleiermacher, "saw religious experience as the antidote to speculative philosophy and theology" (Herbst 1965, 78). Schleiermacher's influence turned religious scholarship toward historical studies of religious experience. The "higher criticism" of scripture complemented this as it posed questions such as, what was the enduring meaning of this or that biblical concept given its ancient context? Or, what was the purpose of those who introduced this concept in an ancient culture? This predilection of liberal Protestantism for empirical, historical, and critical research led to the economics Ely learned in Germany. German economists had "deliberately aligned themselves with the . . . higher critics in philology, theology, history and jurisprudence" (Herbst 1965, 131–32). The German economists, with whom Ely studied, opposed the speculative Anglo-American economics as part of their movement of historical, critical thought.

A relatively young Ely became "one of the best-known proponents of social Christianity in America" during the 1880s and 1890s (Bateman and Kapstein 1999, 250). He proclaimed in the 1880s the essence of what would become known as the Social Gospel: that true "Christianity is primarily concerned with *this* world, and it is the mission of Christianity to bring to pass *here* a kingdom of righteousness." He labeled as error the idea "that Christianity is concerned primarily with a future state of existence [for the individual]" (Ely 1889, 53—emphasis added). His father, a Connecticut Yankee, who was "a humanitarian and a believer in social progress," had turned the young Ely in this direction. According to Ely's autobiography, his father believed that "whatever may be our Fate in the Hereafter, it was our job to make the present world better" (Ely 1938, 23). His father's reforming brand of Calvinism, though conservative, had an affinity for the reforming impulse in the younger Ely's liberal religion.

In the 1880s, a decade of labor turmoil, Ely put his empirical research in the service of social reform. His first book, *The Labor Movement in America* (1886), consisted of a number of descriptive and historical case studies of various types of labor organizations, including communal groups such as the Shakers. His approach was not the abstract, deductive approach of which he accused orthodox economists. His case studies described labor and communal organizations in which the Christian ethic of brotherly love actually seemed to work. He also applied historical-critical methods, similar to those of biblical scholars, to dispute conservative opposition to industrial reform. Opponents of reform used arguments "drawn from Adam Smith and intended for entirely different circumstances" (Ely 1886, 317). Even the great Smith's ideas had to be understood in context. Though he did not challenge Smith head-on, he stated that Smith's ideas only had a contingent validity. Finally, Ely's direct observation of his own times contradicted the Malthusian axiom of scarcity: "sufficient goods to satisfy all rational wants of men can be produced" (Ely 1889, 94).

Ely critiqued the prevailing economics as a dogmatic "orthodoxy." He approvingly repeated a quote that "critical study of [economic] phenomena is as unpopular as free thinking in religion" (Ely 1938, 125). As a religious person himself, he was sensitive to the religious pretensions of orthodox economics: in classical economics, he said, competition had usurped the role of divine providence (Ely 1938, 125). Like a religion providing a worldly salvation, the natural laws announced by laissez-faire, if obeyed, allowed a society to reach "the highest state of economic felicity possible to mankind" (Ely 1938, 126). Continuing to portray laissez-faire as a type of secular religion, he argued that its proponents preferred people to be ignorant of economics than to have heretical views (Ely 1938, 127).

Ely's understanding of economic ethics was obviously shaped by his view of biblical ethics. Especially in the 1880s, Ely consistently cited Jesus's ethic of love of neighbor as the starting point for economic ethics—particularly in labor relations, which were in turmoil during that decade. Like the abolitionists before him, Ely thought that general Christian principles, such as brotherly love, had direct implications for society. He had no sense that this would be applying Christian principles where they were inappropriate. First, most of the employers, who practiced bad labor relations, were his fellow churchmen. They had no excuse to continue to ignore the ethics to which they at least nominally subscribed. Second, Ely believed that Jesus's words expressed a truth about human solidarity that was inherent in human nature, and so was true for everyone.

As an economist, Ely was deeply involved in forming the American Economic Association as an instrument for opposing laissez-faire. Ely's prospectus for the association had asserted that "the doctrine of laissez-faire is unsafe in politics and unsound in morals" (Ely 1938, 136). As secretary of the new association, Ely received notes from many who rejoiced in an alternative to the old orthodoxy, which they characterized as "opposed to the recognition of any ethical element in our economic life," and as deifying "a monstrosity known as the economic man" (Ely 1938, 144).

A LATER WORK OF ELY

The third edition of Ely's long-running introductory *Outlines of Economics* appeared in 1916, representing Ely's mature thought. To Ely (1916, 11), economics remained an "approximate and partially descriptive science" due to its subject, man. Economics' human subject is highly changeable through time, he claimed, which "invalidates theories, laws, general principles, institutions and enterprises" (6–7). Because humans interact with each other and the world in many ways it is "impossible to divorce economics completely from ethics and politics" (14). In short, he still was opposed to economics that was based on abstractions and generalizations, such as "economic man," rather than down-to-earth description.

Ely still attacked the remnants of laissez-faire. According to Ely, change had been particularly hard on the Malthusian subsistence theory of wages, which "does not square with the facts of today" (438). Ely was explicit about the ethical abuses of laissez-faire, which thrust the responsibility for poverty "upon the poor themselves; the rich were soothed with the assurance that they were not primarily responsible" (746).

He emphasized the evolution of economic institutions in contrast to the static view of classical economics. For example, private property is not based on an eternal natural law, but is an evolving "creation of man" that "did not always exist" (22). This human creation is subject to the state's "continually placing limitations and restrictions on the right" (23; also 696). He took a similar position with respect to the right of contract (25). Not only is a labor contract not absolute (which gave leverage to employers), but regulation of contracts actually is the historic norm.

Ely's textbook challenged the autonomy values of laissez-faire. Its negative freedom—the right to be left alone—may be relatively meaningless for most people most of the time (27). Conversely, true freedom would be increased by "laws which limit the power of the strong to oppress and which help to open the gates of opportunity" (27–28). Ely saw the dominance of autonomy individualism in America as an accident of history: "The triumph of individualism, as a philosophical system, came at the critical period when our State and federal constitutions were in the making, and it thus became intrenched [sic]" (96). American economic individualism thus was the result of an accident of timing. The general message was that there are no unchangeable economic laws and that the economy is a human invention and should be changed if the human good requires it.

The text covered many of the reforms that Ely favored at the time of its writing—ranging from public regulation of monopolies to minimum wages, and from social insurance to progressive taxes; he even hinted at the desirability of prohibition of alcohol. By 1916, Ely's text avoided formal ethical arguments for these reforms; he only suggested that people were competent democratically to discern needed reforms.

Ely's historical and empirical methods were closely connected to liberal Protestantism, which had first applied the historical-critical method in religion. At the same time, they were the methods that opposed what Ely saw as the methods of economic orthodoxy. Ely's work was based on the conviction that virtually all economic practices and institutions were the creations of time-bound and place-bound humans. Thus, he rejected making absolute any principle, whether of laissez-faire or Marxist origin. Such principles subordinated ethics to economic "laws" and, as a result, subordinated people to dehumanized abstract principles.

His concern for method was rooted in ethics, for he believed that laissez-faire economics served to rationalize the conditions that had led to the labor crisis of the 1880s and other shortcomings of the American economy. As he noted, laissez-faire allowed those who benefited from the economy to avoid responsibility for the weak in the economy. Especially in the decade of the 1880s, Ely explicitly promoted a liberal version of Christian ethics as the model for labor relations. His economic case studies attempted to show the feasibility of an ethic of human brotherhood.

JOHN BATES CLARK

John Bates Clark (1847–1938), when young, expressed ideas that reflected his German education. In this he was similar to Ely. But in his later career Clark focused much more on abstract theory, to which he contributed the marginal-product theory of labor. It advanced moral thought in that it replaced the wages fund, a key element of laissez-faire. However Clark was to find an ethical interpretation for the marginal-product theory that protected the status quo as much as laissez-faire had done. The Clark of this theory seemed to retreat toward impersonal ethical abstractions that corresponded to his theory. Yet, he seemed to sense that a definition of justice based on the marginal-product theory would prove inhumane and therefore untenable.

THE YOUNG CLARK

Like Richard Ely, after study in Germany, the young Clark opposed the American economic orthodoxy for explicitly moral reasons—though his morality was not as clearly religiously informed as was Ely's. Clark's *The Philosophy of Wealth* (1886) was based on articles published during the first ten years of his career. While *Philosophy of Wealth* was clearly ethical, and stated premises that sounded much like Ely's, Clark's ethic was not explicitly grounded in a Christian framework as was Ely's.

In his early book, Clark sharply critiqued the "economic man" of laissez-faire. He argued that the old economics was "erroneous" in the "motives attributed to men" (Clark 1886, 32). The caricature of a human in classical economics "is too mechanical and too selfish to correspond with the reality" and suffers from "an abnormal love of acquisition" (35). The young Clark also explicitly affirmed a relational basis for morality: "So close is the relation between [a man] and others of his race that his conduct is dictated and his nature transformed by it" (37).

Clark complemented this with a moral psychology. The drive to do what is right is assured by a hierarchy of wants, at the apex of which is "the love of right action, and the aspiration for worthy character" that "may subordinate every lower impulse" (44). The moral *content* of these highest wants is unselfishness, which finds no room in "economics based on selfishness" (45).

Early in his career, Clark wished to discover the principle by which national income was distributed between labor and capital. He sensed that the answer lay in understanding the workings of demand and supply under a "regime of competition in the true sense free" (Clark 1886, 110). At this stage, Clark did not yet know how supply and demand operated under competition to distribute income. The young Clark had already decided the wages-fund theory was deficient and stated the proposition (along with others such as Henry George) that wages "are the workman's share in the value created by the industry in which he participates" (130).

Clark, in showing some other characteristics of relational morality, also expressed the need for moral boundaries around competition: "Competition without moral restraints is a monster," he wrote (1886, 151). Restraints were most necessary to avoid predation: "freedom unqualified by law is not freedom, but license. The commercial code which authorizes a trader to depart from the standards furnished by the general market gives him, as it were, letters of marque, authorizing him to prey upon the weak at will" (166). Clark also observed that competition always threatened to become a race to the bottom (168). Said Clark, as well, "competition at best exists by sufferance, and the power that tolerates and controls it is moral" (204). Without moral limits, competition would provide "immoral books, poisonous beverages and adulterated articles of food" (205). By the end of this book, Clark held that unregulated competition could be "supremely immoral." But, showing a conservative side, he also held that competition may be tolerated in order to avoid even worse results (219). The meaning of this unclear statement he did not elaborate.

The early Clark accused laissez-faire of relying on assumption without checking the facts: "The assumptions of political economy need to be subjected to a comparison with facts. It is on the anthropological side that the traditional science is most defective" (Clark 1886, 35–36). What had seemed obviously true about human nature to the rationalists of the Enlightenment seemed a century later to be out of touch with reality.

THE OLDER CLARK

Clark's early book had claimed that "true" competition might produce a just distribution of national income, but lacked details. Clark's later work showed how competition could indeed divide the national income.

A later book of Clark's on the subject, *The Distribution of Wealth* (1899), was an explanation of the marginal-product theory of labor, capital, and land (the three "factors of production"). In it, he explained how competitive markets equate the payment to each factor to its *marginal product*. Marginal-product theory assumed that payments to the factors of production are made from what the factors have helped produce (not from a preexisting wages fund). And the payments for labor are equal to the contribution, or production, of the marginal worker, who thus becomes the representative worker for purposes of wage payments.[2]

Under competition, workers earned what the representative (marginal) worker produced, and Clark held that such wages were just.[3] The theory also implied that capital's share of the national output was just because it, too, earned its marginal product. In short, so long as markets were reasonably competitive, and so set payments equal to marginal products, a form of justice prevailed—namely, that factors earned what they produced as defined by marginal products. This potentially justified the economic status quo, although economists could debate just how competitive markets actually were.

Clark's theory has become standard in modern economics, but the theory is not our main interest. Rather, of interest for economic morality are his reasons for the claim that marginal-product wages amount to just wages. He stated that under competition:

> the amount they [workers] get, be it large or small, is what they produce. If they create a small amount of wealth and get the whole of it, they may not seek to revolutionize society; but if . . . they produce an ample amount and get only a part of it, many of them would become revolutionists, and *all would have the right to do so*. (Clark 1899, 4—emphasis added)

Taken literally, Clark said that workers, as a collective factor of production, have a right to what they produce (i.e., the marginal product). The fulfillment of that condition presumably defined justice. This definition of justice coincided with what marginal-product theory claims is the outcome of competitive processes.

Clark was not done with the question of justice, and later in the introduction returned to the question "whether a rule that gives to each man his product is, in the highest sense, just" (1899, 8). He noted that there are alternative notions of wage justice: for example, socialists have defined justice as "work according to ability and pay according to need." However, the socialist formula is faulty for it "would require the taking from some men a part of their product in order to bestow it on others. . . . It would violate what is *ordinarily regarded* as a property right" (8). Although Clark claimed that "pure ethics" are outside the economist's realm, he used an ethical argument, based on rights, to attack socialism. All that remained was for Clark to state the grounds for a right in what one has produced. He simply asserted that there exists "the claim of a producer to what he creates" (9). This must have seemed self-evident to Clark, or at least convincing enough simply to be asserted. Marginal product was Clark's measurement of what workers create (see, e.g., 1899, 168–72).

Some would argue that this is the sum of what Clark said about wage justice. But that is not quite true. In *The Distribution of Wealth*, Clark emphasized the differences between a static economy and a dynamic economy, which is constantly changing for various reasons (1899, 68–76). Given competition and static conditions, an economy would settle toward marginal-product wages. On the other hand, Clark said very clearly that the actual economy was

not static, but dynamic. Thus, shocks, such as new inventions, kept the economy from reaching the static state; presumably the marginal-product wage
might never actually occur in a dynamic situation.

The existence of dynamics makes Clark's view on wage justice more complex. Despite his talk of marginal-product wages in a static society, Clark
seemed to recognize that in a static society wages, even those to which workers strictly had a right, might not seem adequate. Dynamic change was the key
to a tolerable society: "the social structure grows and improves daily, and will
do so to the end of time; and it is this growth that makes the social condition
tolerable" (Clark 1899, 400). Clark's argument seemed to say that workers
would earn what they produced in a static economy. However, he also suggested that to reach a tolerable social situation, dynamics were more important. Many commentators have criticized Clark's suggestion that marginal-
product wages essentially defined just wages. What the critics fail to notice is
that Clark seemed unsure that such static wage justice was even an attainable
norm—and, if so, whether such a wage would be tolerable by some unstated,
higher social norm. He seemed to suggest that abstract notions of justice, such
as that defined by marginal product, were in some way incomplete.

ASSESSMENTS OF CLARK

Later commentators have not agreed with each other on the validity of Clark's
marginal-product ethic for wages. Both Richard Ely (this chapter) and Paul
Samuelson (chapter 11) sharply criticized the ethical content that Clark added
to marginal-product theory.[4] Samuelson (1947, 211) dismissed Clark for presenting marginal-product wages as "a 'natural law' which is 'morally justifiable.'" Contrary to Samuelson, another Nobel-winning economist, George
Stigler, saw in the marginal-product wage a productivity ethic that commanded "wide support" (Stigler 1982, 19). Stabile (2000, 585) cites another
interpreter who argued that the later Clark abandoned ethics altogether in
favor of "technical aspects of economics very narrowly constrained."

All this misses the fact that Clark presented the marginal-product idea in
conjunction with a static economy, while advocating the idea that modern
economies were actually dynamic. Dynamic change led to ever-changing
wages that rendered moot questions of marginal-product ethics. Clark may
have decided that abstract formulas of wage justice (such as marginal-product
wages) were secondary to economic changes that gave people grounds for
hope. This was what might be called Clark's paradox: a static economy was
necessary for marginal-product wages (which defined a sort of justice), yet, a
dynamic economy, which would disrupt marginal-product wages, was necessary to have a tolerable society. Although it may be impossible to tell exactly
what Clark meant, one interpretation of this paradox is that Clark recognized
the moral inadequacy of an abstract, marginal-product notion of wage justice.

SUMMARY AND CONCLUSION

These three economists attacked laissez-faire in a variety of ways. George challenged the premise of scarcity by emphasizing sources of productivity growth, thereby blaming poverty on the unjust division of the fruits of progress. He challenged the wages fund on grounds now accepted by national income accountants: workers are paid from what they produce. George also held that rent and land ownership depended on social custom, not on unchangeable natural laws. Social reform on a grand scale was not only possible, contrary to laissez-faire, but should be undertaken in order to transform humanity for the better. In George's statements, one finds echoes of relational moralist William Penn, who also held that nature was characterized by abundance, not scarcity, and that unjust human institutions were the cause of human ills.

Richard Ely perceived that laissez-faire was much like a highly doctrinal religion that ran counter his own liberal religion. Just as religion was a human expression of religious experiences, so economics was the product of humans; no a priori system of interlocking economic truths and values should impose itself on human society. So Ely sought to challenge laissez-faire with the study of history and empirical facts. Ely's religious stance and his science merged: if thought systems were expressions of human communities, they had to be held tentatively, always subject to possible refutation, for human understanding is never complete. Claims by Marxists, on one side, or by laissez-faire economists, on the other, mistakenly treated as absolutes those insights that were only conditional and relative. Ely's economic method reflected the religious proposition that nothing in economics (or any other human discipline, including religion) captured eternal and universal truth, for only God is absolute.

John Bates Clark seemed to be at least two different economists. The young Clark rejected the assumptions on which the "economic man" of laissez-faire was built. His early writings reflected a relational ethic (though often stated without the depth of feeling of other relational moralists). The older Clark of marginal-product fame seemed to have left these themes behind. Further, he proclaimed a certain moral status for competitively obtained marginal-product wages.

Critics have noted that the marginal-product theory did indeed have reactionary potential, since it justified the wages that static markets paid, and, if one believed that actual markets produced marginal-product outcomes, this lent itself to the defense of the status quo. Yet, a fair assessment of marginal-product theory in its context would note that it actually was fatal to laissez-faire; it replaced the wages fund, which had been so crucial to laissez-faire. As well, Clark's theory undercut the extreme individualism of laissez-faire, for *every* worker shared the wage of a marginal worker. Even at face value, marginal-product wages proclaimed that workers were related in a common outcome.

But, more to the point, Clark's position seems to have shifted by the end of his second major book. Clark entertained the idea that dynamic improvements in society were more important than whether a society achieved marginal-product wages. In fact, he argued that in a dynamic economy marginal-product wages would not occur.

Each of these economic thinkers found fault with the state of economic theory and economic institutions in his time. However, it would be a great mistake to conclude that the attack on laissez-faire amounted to an endorsement of socialism of some type. For example, Henry George, in blaming land rents for social ills, exempted capitalists from blame (in sharp contrast to the anticapitalist views of socialists). And his attacks on land ownership were never attacks on private property as such, on which he held a conservative opinion. Both Ely and George denied that human affairs are deterministic—a central premise of Marx as well as an implication of parts of laissez-faire. The morality of these economists thus was in the tradition of relational individualism, a middle position between extreme autonomy of the individual and the collectivist denial of individualism altogether.

TEN

The Social Gospel and Catholic Thought Around 1900

ALTHOUGH LAISSEZ-FAIRE was under challenge by economists in the last quarter of the nineteenth century, Francis Wayland's alloy of autonomy ethics and classical economics continued to be "the most popular college textbook" (Hofstadter 1955, 145). In many Protestant churches, the moral sentiments echoed those of Wayland. However, a liberal Social Gospel addressing economic morality was emerging to challenge the conservative Protestant strain of economic ethics. It was visible as early as 1871 in the novel *The Silent Partner*. Social Gospel ideas had appeared in the work of economist Richard Ely (chapter 9). The full set of ideas formally called the Social Gospel was best seen in the work of theologian Walter Rauschenbusch slightly after the turn of the century.

The growth of the non-Protestant population also promised challenges to the prevailing economic morality, although Catholic thought was slow to address the American economy. Pope Leo XIII's encyclical *Rerum Novarum* (1891) addressed the problems of industrialization, but seemed more directed to radicalism in Europe than the American situation. Only in the first third of the twentieth century did Monsignor John A. Ryan fully develop an American Catholic economic ethic.

THE SOCIAL GOSPEL

The failure of traditional Protestant thinkers to address industrialization, urbanization, and poverty was illustrated by Henry Ward Beecher in 1874, who viewed new realities through the old lens: "no man in this land suffers from poverty unless it be more than his fault—unless it be his *sin*" (quoted in May 1967, 69). He went on to blame poverty on individuals' lack of the minor

Puritan virtues such as frugality rather than recognizing a social ill; Beecher thought all that was needed to attain prosperity was liberty and more liberty. Many in his congregations must have found validation of their own economic success in Beecher's words. Yet analyses like Beecher's seemed increasingly irrelevant to the poverty, class divisions, child labor, labor strife, and huge business trusts that people observed every day.

LITERARY PRELUDE TO THE SOCIAL GOSPEL

The novel proved to be the "Social Gospel's most spectacular and eventually most successful secular medium" (May 1967, 207), and Elizabeth Stuart Phelps's *The Silent Partner* (1871) established this genre. The "silent partner" of the title was Perley Kelso, heiress to the major share of a nineteenth-century textile mill. The other partners made it clear that she, as a woman, would have no say in decisions—that is, be a silent partner. This treatment, combined with her chance meeting with a mill worker, transformed Kelso from a pampered rich girl, oblivious to her own employees' lives, into a social activist. In the process, Kelso liberated herself from class bias and the limitations placed on women.

Phelps described the hardship of the workers through relatively few characters. Sip Garth was a toughened mill-girl, who had survived most of her family and continued to care for a deaf-mute sister. Through Garth's experiences, Phelps told of the hardship of mill life, and the dignity of mill workers. Phelps personalized the evil of child labor with Bub Mell, a young boy whose family kept him at work, at the expense of even a small amount of public schooling. The boy, ignorant and addicted to tobacco, ultimately died in an industrial accident.

Phelps summed up the problem of class bias, moral indifference, and rationalizations based on political economy, in the confrontation of Perley Kelso with her fiancé, Maverick Hayle, a junior partner in the firm. He barely paid her attention as Perley explained her painful, new awareness of the want of her employees. As the indifferent Maverick continued to ignore her, the exasperated, Perley threatened, "I think you will be sorry if you play with me any longer." Maverick then suggested that she should talk to his father, now the senior partner. Her reply is that she had already talked to his father: "He said something about Political Economy; he said something about Supply and Demand. He said something, too, about the state of the Market. He said, in short, that we cannot afford any more experiments in philanthropy" (Phelps 1871, 134–35).

Maverick acknowledged only an economic nexus with the workers and otherwise was indifferent to them: "They go about their business and I go about mine. Master and man meet on business grounds, and business grounds alone" (Phelps 1871, 136). In short, people relate in one dimension only. The impersonality of the market, which Sumner had lauded, allowed employers like Maverick to avoid confronting issues of responsibility with multidimensional people.

Phelps's morality, portrayed in the book, was a religious morality whose obligations trumped personal gain. Though religious, her ethic did not depend on scriptural legalism, in an age when making a rule of a literal reading of a single Bible verse was common. Like the abolitionists, she looked for broad ethical themes, broad principles, in scripture. Second, she perceived that "Political Economy" was the enemy, for it disputed the very assertion that moral obligation between people exists; indeed, as portrayed by Phelps, business practices emphasized that people in economic relations had the right to be indifferent to anything human about those they dealt with—beyond the economic nexus. Instead, supply and demand dictate what is to be done—any human relatedness, save the economic, disappears. Third, this impersonality of the market was evil, for it abetted persons like Maverick to continue in willful ignorance of, and indifference to, his employees' conditions. Fourth, Phelps's novel, while gaining its power from painting the workers as individuals, never stopped with individual remedies; Perley Kelso did not propose individual "charity," but envisioned the establishment of institutions of benefit to all employees. Finally, the weakest members of the workforce (children) had the greatest moral claim upon others in Phelps's ethic.

An additional component of Phelps's morality was her emphasis on human dignity, especially as it emerged from hardship. In response to a marriage proposal, Sip Garth stated, "I'll never bring children into this world to be factory children . . . and to bear the things I've borne . . . I've heard tell of slaves before the war that would n't [*sic*] be fathers and mothers of children to be slaves like them" (Phelps 1871, 287–88). Sip Garth's message was clear: human dignity is more important than life itself. The book closes with Sip as a street preacher, critiquing the mill owners and assuring workers of God's love.

LIBERAL RELIGION

The Social Gospel and liberal religion viewed scripture as being relevant to contemporary social issues. In America, abolitionists (chapter 7) had abandoned the method of a literal reading of biblical verses (which often seemed to acquiesce to slavery); they sought more general biblical principles (that would oppose slavery). So the spirit of the liberal German "higher criticism," which tried to disentangle enduring meanings from the particular worldview of ancient writers, was already established in America (Stackhouse 1987, 38). Further, Americans studying in Germany had become familiar with this advance in scholarship (including Richard Ely, chapter 9). To the Social Gospel thinkers, the Bible could be about more than personal salvation; they saw a social ethic in the Hebrew prophets' demands for justice and Jesus's special affinity to the poor and outcast.

The American religious liberals were also open to science, including the theory of evolution—despite its polemical uses by their opponents such as William Graham Sumner (chapter 8). From evolution Walter Rauschenbusch would extrapolate to the possibility of ethical progress (Beckley 1992, 47–51). In short, the liberals were open to new ways to understand the American economy.

Social Gospel thinkers shifted from religious individualism to a systemic focus; the social dimensions of life became the context that nurtured virtue and vice. The doctrine of original sin was given a social interpretation with evil being propagated by a culture's institutions. So, too, goodness could be propagated by a culture. This systemic emphasis intertwined with an optimistic view of human nature, which differed from the older evangelical outlook, rooted in Calvinism's doctrine of sin. For the liberals, reform of social evils might well reveal a far better human nature waiting to emerge. The Social Gospel liberals also emphasized the notion of God working in history, and of experiential knowledge over formal doctrine. Conversely, they deemphasized highly private religion and were skeptical of the miraculous (Smucker 1994, 94). Although this outlook had roots in Enlightenment rationalism, Social Gospel thinkers criticized laissez-faire, another product of the Enlightenment.

The clash of this liberal Social Gospel with laissez-faire was obvious. The proponents of evolutionary reform confronted a doctrine based on the premise that economic laws were unchangeable. Liberal ministers, attuned to the needs of their urban parishioners, faced legal and moral doctrines that always trumped the solution of economic ills as understood by those clergymen. Those who sensed the importance of a culture's values to cultivating human goodness or evil confronted an individualistic doctrine that hardly recognized social influences. Religious liberals, who interpreted scripture's central message to be moral obligation toward the weak of society, encountered a doctrine that held any obligations to be unacceptable impingements on self-autonomy ("individual freedom"). These religious liberals adopted an empirical rationality, appealing to social statistics and personal experience, as they confronted the preset axioms, self-contained logic, and casual observation of laissez-faire. Liberals, who saw self-interest as morally dangerous, met a positive assessment of self interest.

WALTER RAUSCHENBUSCH

Walter Rauschenbusch (1861–1918) was a Baptist minister of German heritage who came to the Social Gospel through his experiences in a New York City pastorate that exposed him to the realities of urban poverty and to Henry George's analysis of poverty. In addition to these influences, Rauschenbusch studied at various times in Germany where he encountered European religious liberalism. After his eleven years in New York City, he became a seminary professor in Rochester, New York, where he authored *Christianity and the Social Crisis* (1907), which gained wide attention, and *Christianizing the Social Order* (1912), which was the fullest exposition of the Social Gospel. His books implied an understanding of economics far different from the received theory of laissez-faire.

In *Christianizing the Social Order* Rauschenbusch charged that the self-centered otherworldliness of much Christian thought was unbiblical. "The Church has meant getting to heaven; Jesus meant living the right life with God and man" (Rauschenbusch 1912, 293).[1] Jesus and the Hebrew prophets were preachers of God's kingdom, a reign of social justice on this earth. Rauschenbusch understood the prophets, not as future-tellers or even as proclaimers of religious truths, but as those who exposed "the sins of the ruling classes" (1912, 51). He strongly implied a parallel between class differences in America and the class differences the prophets had challenged.

Rauschenbusch contrasted Jesus's values with what he saw as the misguided values of Jesus's contemporaries:

> The people expected the Kingdom to be set up by force . . . Jesus repudiated the use of force. . . . They connected it with the hope of self-aggrandizement . . . he democratized the idea of the Kingdom and put all who sought it under the law of service. They connected it with ceremonial and ecclesiastical religion; he set it within the domain of secular and ethical relations. To many of them the material benefits were the main thing . . . to Jesus fullness of ethical and religious life for all was the real end and substance of the hope. They expected it by catastrophe; he worked toward the law of gradual growth. (1912, 66)

Jesus's kingdom-of-God ethic embodied these values, Rauschenbusch said, and took them as the authority for his own ethic.[2] In short, the norms he found in the kingdom-of-God ethic were: nonviolence, rejection of class privilege, democracy, and social instead of private morality. He rejected religion that pushed justice off to the millennium and promised personal salvation (e.g., Rauschenbusch 1907, 345).

Rauschenbusch's ethic was simultaneously a religious *and* secular ethic, depending on the characteristics one uses to classify it. He claimed revelation as the source for the kingdom-of-God ethic. But he reckoned the actual content of his ethic could easily be acceptable to non-Christians, or even anti-religious people. Also, Rauschenbusch suggested that the norms of the kingdom of God were universally valid. For example, even socialists grasped the validity of some parts of the kingdom-of-God ethic.

Rauschenbusch claimed a connection between democracy and Christianity. After acknowledging the historic opposition of official Christendom to democracy, he continued that "struggle for political democracy in its infancy was so closely connected to the struggle for religious toleration and freedom that it is impossible to disentangle the two." He added that "the success of political democracy was most early and durable where radical and pure types of Christianity had gained a footing and influence" (1912, 153–54). Democracy, in short, developed in conjunction with the struggle of the churches of the left wing of the Reformation for their freedom of worship against Protestant state churches.

For Rauschenbusch, "Christianizing" the social order did *not* mean granting churchly authorities a say in the counsels of government, or establishing a state religion (1912, 124). A secular state, if it established economic and social justice, would meet his standard of being "Christianized." Over the centuries, four vital sectors of human life had been Christianized—the home, the church, the school, and lately politics. For example, the patriarchal home, in which wife and children were little more than property, had been redeemed under the pressure of Christian values. Even the churches had needed to be Christianized, for they had failed to understand that advancing the kingdom of God was their true work. Politics had been reformed by the infusion of democratic principles. That these institutions had made progress in Christianizing gave hope for reforming the economic order; this reformation would be along the lines of "equality and mutual solidarity."

The middle third of *Christianizing the Social Order* analyzed American business and its value system. American business had led "to injustice, inequality, and to the frustration of the Christian conception of human fellowship" (Rauschenbusch 1912, 163). The drive for profit was the defining element of the system, and "whenever profit has collided with the higher interests of humanity, the latter have hitherto gone down with sickening regularity" (1912, 165). Yet, money issues did not constitute all the problem. Workers could have had real wages doubled and still have been alienated, for "the unrest of our American workingmen is in part at least the unrest of men who know liberty and are forced to live in unfreedom" (1912, 194). Away from the job, people meet others in mutual respect. Management remained undemocratic and disrespectful. A sensitivity to the quality of human interactions marked Rauschenbusch's relational morality.

Rauschenbusch attacked the competitive value system. According to him, competition suppressed cooperation, "represses good will, and calls out selfishness and jealousy" (1912, 172). In the competitive arena, each one "is taught to seek his own advantage, and then we wonder that there is so little public spirit" (1912, 173). Competition evokes "covetousness, cunning, hardness, selfish satisfaction in success, or resentment and despair in failure" (Rauschenbusch 1907, 397; also 265). Competition creates a race for the bottom: "the worst man sets the pace, and good men follow because they are afraid" (1912, 173). The competitive system enmeshed individually "good men" so that they became participants in systemic evil.

Rauschenbusch, however, was relatively generous in his definition of legitimate profit, which he distinguished from "unearned profit." This arose from four causes: employer collusion in the labor market, the transfer of production costs to society, ownership of scarce land (evidence of the Henry George influence), and monopoly in the product markets (1912, 227–33).

According to Rauschenbusch, capitalism is an aggressive moral system as well as a set of economic practices. It never leaves other realms of society alone, undermining the arenas of human life that have previously been Christianized, and vigorously resisting its own reformation. At the time he wrote, industry was fighting passage of a pure food law, and such resistance to change was aided and abetted by conventional economics (1912, 289). In his *Christianity and the Social Crisis*, Rauschenbusch had maintained that American "scientific political economy has long been an oracle of the false god," reversing moral priorities: "political economy will be Christianized when it puts man before wealth" (1907, 371). In the fifth chapter of *Christianity and the Social Crisis*, Rauschenbusch had graphically described poverty, industrial ills, and urban problems, which he attributed to the profit motive.

Self-interest received different treatment from Rauschenbusch than from orthodox economists. He conceded that self-interest is "a necessary part of human nature," and so could be an integral part of human goodness (see Beckley 1992, 72–74). However, self-interest did not necessarily contribute to the good, and in the case of the American system it was aligned *against* the public good. Rauschenbusch wrote that the moral judgment of mankind "has always . . . despised those who sold out the common good for private profit" (1912, 290). In common with Puritan divines, he held that when self-interest finally leads to wealth, the result can be morally disastrous for "wealth emancipates from that sense of dependence" on God and on others, which is the real human condition (1912, 300). The "self-sufficient" believe they are autonomous and so have no obligations to God or others.

The final third of *Christianizing the Social Order* is a survey of what is necessary to Christianize the economy. The fundamental step is "the abolition of unjust privilege" (1912, 337), which derives mainly from various sorts of monopoly power. Departing from the John Locke tradition, Rauschenbusch called somewhat vaguely for a new type of property rights, namely, "a share of and a right in a collective accumulation which belongs to a larger group jointly" (1912, 343). These rights would include entitlements to employment and care in old age.

Rauschenbusch also endorsed economic democracy, which meant "the right of the organized workers to control their own industry . . . the control of the people over their own livelihood . . . the power to cut all monopoly prices . . . the absence of class rule" (1912, 361). Although he gave no details, the purpose for economic democracy was to give to workers a sense of their worth (Beckley 1992, 91–2). Similarly, labor unrest was less about material benefits than "a spiritual demand for a fuller and freer manhood" (Rauschenbusch 1912, 194).

Rauschenbusch was critical of the materialism in socialist doctrine, but thought it was not integral to socialism. In fact, socialism's "fundamental aims are righteous," he wrote (1912, 405). Rauschenbusch believed that the ethic of Jesus was welcomed in some unconscious fashion even by nonreligious socialists. Socialism promoted cooperation, which could regenerate individuals (Beckley 1992, 93).

Finally, Rauschenbusch critiqued the American legal practice of turning economic freedoms into absolutes. The doctrine of freedom of contract must not be used, he said, to legitimate *any* contract, on the grounds that it was signed voluntarily. Necessity causes persons to accept conditions that they ought not to accept. And we "do not allow the workman the freedom to commit sudden suicide; why should be allow him to commit slow suicide" (1912, 413)? In short, individual autonomy should not define right and wrong. Similarly, private property rights are never absolute: "Neither religion, nor ethics, nor law recognizes such a thing as an absolute private property right" (Rauschenbusch 1912, 426). Here, Rauschenbusch was solidly within the tradition of relational morality that always held economic rights to be conditional on their service to a greater good.

Set against these false absolutes, the true standard by which to judge an economy was human dignity—the "personality and manhood of men":

> To break down a man's sense of his own worth murders his power of aspiration. It chokes the god in him just as surely as faith in his higher possibilities awakens the soul. . . . The conservation of life demands the emancipation of the soul. (Rauschenbusch 1912, 418)

Good economics would be "a rounded expression of all sound and wholesome human life" (1912, 400). This vision of human dignity clearly was an individualistic vision. But it recognized that relationships are of central importance to the realization of individual dignity—for bad relationships break down one's sense of worth.

The many elements of Rauschenbusch's ethics added up to a reaction to the American Industrial Revolution, whose outcomes were greatly shaped by economic ideas forged in the Enlightenment. The early political economists had proposed a system of "natural liberty." But, during the nineteenth century, the system of natural liberty seemed to Rauschenbusch to have become a system of oppression. Rights, such as property rights, which had been intended to liberate individuals from the constraints of the old order, had with time become oppressive.

Rauschenbusch's thought also was motivated by Enlightenment impulses. He, like the first economic thinkers, was formed by a rational tradition. However, their rationality amounted to deduction from premises that had seemed self-evident in the eighteenth century; Rauschenbusch's rationality started from empirical observation of what was obvious in America's industrialized cities of the late nineteenth century. As did the Enlightenment thinkers, Rauschenbusch took the betterment of mankind as his goal. But his subject was people he encountered in New York City rather than the eighteenth-century rising industrialists and merchants who served as the model for the early political economists. Rauschenbusch also reflected the Enlightenment tendency to deemphasize the supernatural in religion and to focus on the ethical. When he did, however, he found that his reading of Jesus' kingdom-of-God ethic was at odds with the American economic system.

THE EMERGING ROMAN CATHOLIC
ECONOMIC ETHIC

With the large migrations of the nineteenth century, Catholicism become a major actor in American religion, and ultimately in economic moral thought. At an organizational level, the Roman Catholic Church spent much of the century addressing the economic conditions in which its members found themselves, establishing parochial schools and Catholic charities. However, a papal encyclical of Leo XIII in 1891 addressed economic morality in the industrial era. This was later elaborated in America by Monsignor John Augustine Ryan, whose writings spanned almost the first half of the twentieth century.

POPE LEO XIII: ON THE CONDITION OF LABOR

Pope Leo's encyclical *Rerum Novarum* (in English often rendered *On the Condition of Labor*, 1891) enunciated the official Catholic position. It contained positive moral content, despite its emphasis on refuting European socialism. However, it also refuted the indifference of laissez-faire to poverty and other issues of economic justice, declaring "that some remedy must be found, and quickly found, for the misery and wretchedness which press . . . on the large majority of the very poor" (Leo XIII 1891, paragraph 2).[3]

Rerum Novarum first justified private property (pars. 5–8) using natural-law arguments.[4] The pope asserted several reasons for the validity of private property. However, the primary reason was derived from rational human nature: the human ability to foresee future needs implies the right of private property, said Leo, for property ownership (wealth) is a way of preparing for future uncertainties. Property thus is a logical consequence of rational human nature, and no state may justly extinguish property rights. Yet, in contrast to Enlightenment thought, property rights are not absolute, for there exist "limits of private possession" (par. 7); and "it is one thing to have a right to the possession of money, and another to have a right to use money as one pleases" (par. 19). Property exists to meet real human needs, not unlimited desires.

After several paragraphs aimed at refuting socialism, Leo turned to the labor market and stated that wages cannot simply be set by exploiting the weakness of others: "rich men and masters should remember this—that to exercise pressure for the sake of gain, upon the indigent and destitute, and to make one's profit out of the need of another, is condemned by all laws, human and divine" (par. 17). Making the maximum profit, at the expense of the weak, is not a morally justifiable principle.

When Leo addressed labor relations, he was very protective of the rights of private property. Nevertheless, he eventually advanced a potent basis for worker rights, which was ultimately more important than particular rights themselves: "No man may outrage with impunity the *human dignity* which God Himself treats with reverence, nor stand in the way of that higher life which is the preparation for the eternal life of Heaven" (par. 32—emphasis added). Minimum employment conditions, thus, were mandated by human dignity, which Leo found rooted in the human ability to transcend material existence (i.e., to attain a higher life). Leo continued by denying extreme moral autonomy: "Nay, more: a man has here no power over himself. To consent to any treatment which is calculated to defeat *the end and purpose of his being* is beyond his right; he cannot give up his soul to servitude" (par. 32—emphasis added). A worker is not morally autonomous and so does not have the right to agree to work that thwarts attainment of ultimate human potential. The concept of human dignity provided the foundation for an economic ethic; it also mandated potentially a broader assignment of human rights and duties than Leo chose to discuss. Significantly, Leo did not equate human dignity with self-autonomy; indeed, he said the opposite, that no one has the right to assent to conditions that demean universal human dignity.

The importance of preserving human dignity led Leo to call for working conditions that do not conflict with that norm. He then turned to wages, stating that "remuneration must be enough to support the wage-earner in reasonable and frugal comfort" (par. 34). He then reiterated that the mere agreement of a worker to a contract does not make a wage just: "If through necessity or fear of a worse evil, the workman accepted harder conditions . . . he is the victim of force and injustice" (par. 34). The just wage, as defined, potentially could exceed the competitive wage of unregulated markets. However, human dignity as spelled out by Leo did not demand more, such as universal equality of income.

Leo also addressed child labor, asserting that "great care should be taken not to place [children] in workshops and factories until their bodies and minds are sufficiently mature" (par. 33). Linking this statement to the notion of the right of humans to attain their potential, he added that "too early an experience of life's hard work blights the young promise of a child's powers, and makes any real education impossible." (Indeed, a clear implication of

Horace Mann's crusade in the 1830s and 1840s had been the substitution of education for child labor; on Mann, see chapter 5.) Leo's discussion of the just wage seemed to imply that it should be adequate for a parent to keep his or her children out of the workforce (par. 35).

Even though it mandated a relatively modest wage, Leo's norm of human dignity challenged both the presumed justice of the competitive wage and laissez-faire's doctrine of free contract: "Wages, we are told, are fixed by free consent; and, therefore, the employer when he pays what was agreed upon, has done his part." However, such "reasoning is by no means convincing" (par. 34). In rejecting the unconditional validity of free contracts, Leo might have spelled out a role for the state in defining legitimate contracts. Instead, he was careful to reject "undue interference on the part of the State" and opted for voluntary worker associations, organized along religious lines. Unlike labor unions, these associations would not strike over wages and benefits.

In raising the concept of human dignity, Leo provided a vehicle that American Catholic bishops in 1986 rode to far stronger conclusions (see chapter 15). Human dignity is a fundamental, and potentially elastic, norm, which is applicable to far more than wages and working conditions. Leo knew that real people—not impersonal markets operating outside the realm of conscious moral decision—set wages and should do so justly. Traditional economists take Leo's position to task at this very point: "What was wrong with Roman Catholic social thought in the nineteenth century was . . . its lack of understanding of how the free market can work. . . . [Moral] concern can accomplish little without knowledge of the causes and cures of the disease" (Sadowsky 1986, 21). In this modern economist's view, "understanding of how the free market can work" comes logically prior to morality and so sets constraints around morality by dictating what can and cannot be accomplished given economic laws. Thus, for this critic, writing in the 1980s, the ethical approach of the nineteenth century was still alive: economic inevitabilities made much morality irrelevant because they dictate what simply is not feasible according to the science of economics. Leo seemed to understand very well that free-market principles had been used to restrict morality or even push market behavior entirely outside the realm of ethics. Leo affirmed that economic ethics *starts* with human purposes not with economic laws. (Obviously he relied on expert opinion that was skeptical of the validity of many of the laws of laissez-faire.) Leo did not lack understanding of the free market, as the 1980s economist claimed. He simply disagreed with a particular understanding. In general, Leo's moral principles were far more robust than the policy conclusions he was willing to draw from them.

EXTENDING CATHOLIC THOUGHT: JOHN AUGUSTINE RYAN

John Augustine Ryan (1869–1945), a Minnesotan of Irish-American heritage, articulated Catholic economic morality for forty years, starting with the publication of his doctoral dissertation, *A Living Wage* (1906). Ryan's work was influential especially in promoting the minimum wage. His *Distributive Justice* was issued in a revised edition as late at 1942. Ryan stayed close to policymakers in Washington for much of his long career at Catholic University and as head of the department for social action at the National Catholic Welfare Council. He put the burden of proof on those who would change the status quo, yet was attacked by more conservative Catholics. An editor of Ryan's work stated that Pope Pius XI's promotion of Ryan in 1933 "officially affirmed the orthodoxy of his teaching" (Beckley in Ryan 1996, xi).

Following Pope Leo's teaching closely, Ryan affirmed each person's right to the perfection of human nature. In *A Living Wage*, Ryan affirmed that "every individual is an 'end in himself,' and has a personality of his own to develop through the exercise of his own faculties" (Ryan 1996, 162). The notion of rights was tied directly to that of moral dignity: "the human person is intrinsically sacred and morally independent," in the sense of possessing "inherent prerogatives, immunities and claims we call rights" (113). And among these rights is included "the opportunity of pursuing self-perfection" (115). As with Rauschenbusch's statement on human dignity, this was a distinctly individualistic vision.

Economic rights, for Ryan, were instrumental rights that existed only to advance or preserve human dignity or self-perfection (Beckley in Ryan 1996, xiii). For example, the right to private land ownership exists only because it contributes to the average person's well-being (Ryan 1996, 17). Ryan denied that the status of property depended on "metaphysical and intrinsic conditions" (19). Similarly, Ryan justified interest on loans only if it would advance human welfare, rejecting the idea that interest is the just reward for abstinence (51–52). Ryan's major concern was wages, because it is through labor that most people must meet their needs. A living wage should be paid in order that a worker might pursue self-perfection. While the state was not the source of the right to a living wage, Ryan said, it was "obliged to enact laws which will enable the laborer to obtain a living wage" (116–17).

Ryan attacked alternative definitions of wage justice, particularly those of the orthodox economics of the time. The followers of Adam Smith, according to Ryan's 1942 edition, "tended to convey the thought that competitively fixed wages were more or less in accordance with justice" (Ryan 1996, 103–104). In Ryan's era, some economists emphasized that competition equated marginal product of labor with the wage, imputing to this a kind of justice (see chapter 9). Yet, according to Ryan, the marginal product does not reflect "the laborer's efforts, sacrifices or needs, and that when labor becomes too plentiful, the value of the product may fall below the cost of supporting a decent standard of living" (110). In short, other things besides one's contribution to productivity are relevant in deciding whether a wage is just. This said, Ryan did not claim that productivity was not relevant at all, for productivity could be too low to provide a living wage (Beckley 1992, 134).

In America of Ryan's day, the strongest enemy of the living wage was what he called the "Rule of Free Contract," a legal doctrine that if two free parties voluntarily and rationally contracted to a wage, then such a wage is just. American courts in Ryan's time constantly upheld this doctrine to over-rule statutes dealing with wages, working conditions, child labor, and so on. Like Pope Leo, Ryan held that no man has a right to agree—voluntarily or otherwise—to something that provides less than the "requirements of a reasonable life" (Ryan 1996, 102–103). In sharp contrast to the autonomy ethic, one in not free to waive the right to a wage that meets reasonable needs. When in Franklin Roosevelt's era the Supreme Court finally rejected the free-contract doctrine, Ryan quoted Chief Justice Hughes approvingly in rejecting the notion that liberty is "absolute and uncontrollable" (1996, 143).

In the early decades of his career, Ryan's moral endorsement of the living wage was itself a challenge to the economic status quo. However, beyond this Ryan resisted more radical measures.[5] Except for the living-wage concept, Ryan's moral writings rarely challenged the status quo. Once a living wage had been achieved, traditional standards of distributive justice—such as productivity, sacrifice or effort—could legitimately justify unequal rates of pay (127).

Ryan provisionally supported the larger incomes of capitalists and landowners—provided the living wage was in force. However, for Ryan, capitalists' incomes were *neither* untouchable nor morally wrong. Social changes in the income of capitalists would have to be justified on other than moral grounds—on economic or pragmatic grounds. Lacking clear moral guidance, the burden of proof would fall on those who seek change. On the issue of wealth inequality, Ryan was also morally neutral: limitations on wealth are not necessarily morally wrong, but "the possible, even probable, evil consequences of [such limitations] are so great as to make these measures of very doubtful benefit" (Ryan 1996, 84). Again, Ryan's work demonstrates that it is a gross oversimplification to equate relational morality with radical or socialist morality.

The living wage, of course, was a reform that would remove workers and their families from poverty. However, some poverty would remain, and Ryan simply stated that the poor should receive "surplus wealth" as charity, and also noted the Christian duty of stewardship to the weak (89). He was silent on the question of why human dignity should make the living wage an entitlement of justice for workers, but created no similar claims for nonworking poor.

In his discussion of charity given out of one's surplus, Ryan asked, what is a person's surplus? This became the vehicle for an attack on the Enlightenment understanding of humans as autonomous, self-interest calculators. He stated with certainty that most people would overestimate their "needs" because most have accepted the unchristian model of the insatiable, materialistic "economic man." Ryan attacked the new, twentieth-century version of this: the error that the "worthwhile life must include the continuous and indefinite increase of the number and variety of wants" (94). His reference to "continuous and indefinite" increase in "wants" reveals his perception that no restraint on excess is built into autonomy morality. Ryan's belief in human dignity provided such a restraint, for one's inherent value did not depend on material possession, consumption, or superior status to others.

CONCLUSION

Both Rauschenbusch and Ryan rejected the Enlightenment idea of moral autonomy as it had developed by the late nineteenth century. Both rejected that economic justice was nothing more than the fulfillment of contracts, nominally voluntary in nature. Both held that the fulfillment of humanity required much more than economic self-determination. Both rejected a definition of ethics that left the self as its own moral norm, for both believed in moral standards external to the self. Rauschenbusch invoked a biblical kingdom of God as the standard of conduct, and Ryan invoked the Catholic notion of uniquely human ends. A detailed analysis would show differences between their moralities. However, of more importance, both approaches defined the good by standards external to the self—the good was not merely the fulfillment of self-defined interests.

Despite their different starting points, both Ryan and Rauschenbusch placed human dignity at the center of their moralities, and both affirmed that human dignity creates an entitlement to economic conditions and institutions that uphold such dignity. Ryan focused almost exclusively on the living wage. Rauschenbusch envisaged a greater array of economic rights. But both understood their agendas to serve the cause of human dignity.

There are noticeable differences in style between these moralists. Rauschenbusch painted on a grand canvas, portraying class oppression over the millennia and the grand struggle over time to Christianize the social order. By contrast, Ryan's style was cautious, very detailed, and painted only in shades of gray. His goal was not to Christianize the economy, but to have it meet minimal standards of morality dictated by universal human nature. Given the complexity Ryan insisted on exploring, his statements were highly qualified and he challenged the status quo only when he could meet the burden of proof. When he believed he could not prove the moral need for change, Ryan largely deferred to institutions and practices that already existed—even if they were the result of accidents of history. This is not to imply, in contrast, that Rauschenbush's grand visions were necessarily radical; for example, he was relatively generous in defining what he considered legitimate profits.

Despite Ryan's measured appeal to natural law, presumably open to perception by everyone, his arguments would not necessarily have been persuasive to everyone. To even a friendly reader, natural-law arguments rarely seem as compelling as advocates claim.[6] The same may be said of any particular version of biblical ethics, when scripture lends itself to multiple interpretations.

However, though scripture may have varying interpretations and natural law may be less than fully persuasive, both served as counterweights to the alternatives that existed at the time—either a positivism that put all authority in the state or autonomy morality that placed few limits on economic actions. The consequences of the latter had been exposed by the excesses of the late Industrial Revolution, when accumulated economic power was wielded by men whose moral norm was self-interest. The moralities of Rauschenbusch and Ryan were responses to the way autonomy morality was playing out, a way unforeseen by eighteenth-century founders of autonomy morality.

Despite possible weaknesses, both the natural-law and the kingdom-of-God ethics were at least as morally persuasive as laissez-faire morality, which depended on a blend of state-of-nature arguments (Locke), faith-claims (the invisible hand), and asserted economic or evolutionary laws of arguable validity (indeed, the wages fund had already been overthrown and rising productivity was overwhelming Malthusian ideas). Rauschenbusch and Ryan introduced consistent, alternative moralities to confront the operational orthodoxy of laissez-faire in America. In this sense, "Ryan and Rauschenbusch shared a view of justice" (Beckley 1992, 188).

APPENDIX: DIFFERENT EXPRESSIONS OF HUMAN DIGNITY

Human dignity as an ethical norm did not first appear with Walter Rauschenbusch or Leo XIII. Abolitionists (chapter 7) declared slavery evil because it violated inherent human traits such as love of one's children; these intrinsic traits were understood to be universal and bestowed on all humans the dignity that any would claim for themselves. The possession of a moral character, to know right from wrong, was also highlighted by Francis Wayland in his anti-slavery writings. Closely related to this concept, but more explicitly religious, was that of the Quakers, who understood "that of Christ" to be within all persons. The socialist Moravians found all humans to be elevated by Christ's sharing human existence. Horace Mann implied human dignity to be the end point of human perfectibility—this perfection to be actualized through education. Both Rauschenbusch and Pope Leo associated human dignity with the realization of humanity's highest potential.

The precise nature of human dignity may not be of crucial importance for economic morality. The belief in *some* version of human dignity has implications for the ways in which economic life ought to be carried out. Thus, human dignity could be invoked against slavery—which demeaned humans—as well against markets in vices that demean humans. More affirmatively, dignity can be invoked to mandate social responsibility for certain economic rights: that is, universal education, a universal living wage, or even universal health care.

Although both Rauschenbusch and Ryan focused most clearly on the individual's claim to human dignity, their thought was well within the bounds of relational ethics. Indeed, both thinkers discussed the bad human relationships produced by a failure to respect human dignity. Human dignity was at its core a relational concept, for all humans partook of it and it commanded mutual respect.

This does not deny that a certain notion of human dignity was associated with laissez-faire. Enlightenment thought was in large measure a protest against premodern society's lack of respect for the individual. Premodern constraints on individuals ranged from the economic (mercantilism, restrictions on practicing a trade) to the religious (conformity to state religion) to the political (lack of democracy, royal prerogatives) to the civil (arbitrary detentions). Against this background, classical economics was part of an Enlightenment movement for individual rights; economic freedoms were part of a broader agenda to free the individual from ancient constraints and empower the individual. This implied a notion of human dignity: that average people are competent to define their own welfare and, indeed, are the best judges of their own interests. More comprehensively, Enlightenment human dignity meant self-definition.

Ultimately, however, ideas designed to free the individual from feudal oppression came to exalt the ego, and to deny most moral constraints. While logic implied some moral restraint (Wayland's "reciprocity"), the ability of the egoistic self to rationalize the priority of its own desires overwhelmed mere logic. And in the industrial society, which produced vast differences in economic power, autonomy came together with power to produce excess. By 1900, a context existed in which the Enlightenment's ethic had produced results never contemplated in the eighteenth century.

ELEVEN

The 1920s and 1930s

Depressed Old Values

BY THE 1920s, the older economic theories of the nineteenth century had substantially changed. As noted (chapter 9), marginal theories had replaced old doctrines such as the wages fund; laissez-faire was succeeded by neoclassical economics. And, by the 1920s, the American middle class experienced relative abundance rather than Malthusian scarcity. The story of morality in the 1920s and 1930s is one of efforts to adapt individualistic moralities to a world of abundance and to the massive institutions that produced that abundance.

Even the Great Depression was a testimony to abundance. By plunging the economy into unemployment and poverty after a period of economic growth, the Depression goaded economists and policymakers to explain why such economic hardship was abnormal, not the norm. The Depression also challenged individualistic ethics (especially autonomy ethics). It created widespread economic insecurity that did not spare the economically virtuous. That almost *everyone* faced anxiety underscored shared human experience. According to one historian, during the Depression more of the middle class "came to identify its interests with those of the poor" (McElvaine 1984, 7). In short, the Depression combined with other factors to undermine the most individualistic values, while perhaps giving a relative boost to relational morality, which had always possessed a notion of common experience.

National leaders nevertheless for a long period based public policy on old verities—Franklin Roosevelt's early administration as well as Herbert Hoover's administration. Hoover worried that relief for the unemployed would undermine individual initiative. Compared to political leaders, the economics profession adapted quickly. Many economists by 1930 recommended active government intervention in the economy. The Depression stimulated new economic theories to explain why an economy that could produce more would fall into a state of unemployment and poverty. Turning first to the 1920s, we observe efforts to mesh individualistic values with the new experience of abundance and large-scale firms.

THE 1920s

World War I did much to set the moral climate of the 1920s. According to one commentator, "having at last paid their dues" Americans could with clear conscience turn to more self-oriented behavior (McElvaine 1984, 10). The war had provided precedent for economic activism by government in administering agricultural prices, encouraging unions, and guiding wide sectors of business with a War Industries Board. In the 1920s, the nation retreated from such government activism. The decade witnessed the rise of consumerism, spurred by advertising, as rising productivity created an every-increasing flow of goods (see McElvaine 1984, 17). Consumption on such a scale undercut old individual virtues such as thrift and self-discipline. Another remnant of the Puritan heritage, the duty of productive labor in a calling, lost appeal when compared to the fruits of speculation—largely in the stock market and real estate.[1]

If these were trends among well-off people, what were the values of skilled workers? Labor leader Samuel Gompers perhaps reflected his constituency in accepting the legitimacy of capitalism and business management. Gompers's values blended a small measure of worker solidarity with a larger measure of individualism. Workers' cooperative values were strictly limited to cooperation necessary to get the job done, force a concession from management, or protect each other's jobs. Gompers proclaimed the dignity of the worker, but offered no vision of what dignity meant. Indeed, when asked the goal of the labor movement, Gompers had famously answered with one word—More! This was a vision of at least potential abundance for workers, but implied little beyond ever greater consumption. If Gompers's views were representative, then skilled workers largely accepted the self-defining individualism of American capitalism.

If any segment of society retained the nineteenth-century scarcity mentality, it was less-skilled workers, who concentrated on defending jobs that were being eliminated by technical change. The efficiency expert Frederick Taylor designed ways to rationalize production, introducing a management philosophy centered on "managerial domination, rationality, uniformity, and systematic effort" (Bernstein 1997, 191). Workers resisted Taylorism, which made their limited skills irrelevant, and also made them mere adjuncts to machines. The response to Taylorism showed up as exceptionally high turnover, discipline problems, and "passive resistance" (Bernstein 1997, 192). An implicit worker-ethic of this group defined a fair day's labor and disciplined individual workers who threatened the norm (Bernstein 1997, 205).

During the 1920s, the Social Gospel, which never appealed to the evangelical Protestant majority, was largely eclipsed in everyday churches. The liberal strain did not completely die as the Social Creed of the Churches, adopted in 1908 by then-new Federal Council of Churches, was reaffirmed by various older ("mainline") Protestant denominational bodies. Their statements ran the gamut from declaring that cooperation must replace competition to affirming the need to democratize industry (Miller 1958, 36–38). However, in local congregations of even mainline denominations, the state of economic morality was better represented by a best-selling book.

THE MAN NOBODY KNEW

The effort to adapt popular Protestant individualism to the new era was reflected in Bruce Barton's religious bestseller, *The Man Nobody Knows* (1924). Barton affirmed the old Protestant ethic: there is, he said, no "difference between *work and religious work*" (Barton 1924, 179). This is exactly what a Puritan divine would have said of a vocation. Barton added that "all work is worship; all useful service is prayer," echoing words used by Max Weber in describing the Protestant ethic.

Barton portrayed Jesus of Nazareth as the forerunner of the 1920s American business executive. Different chapters depicted Jesus as executive, advertiser, and founder of modern business. Somewhat like the Puritans, Barton suggested that the key business principle was service to the customer, not personal success (163–64, 177–78). Yet, to Barton, service and success were not really so different. He argued that those who provided great service would also reap great rewards: "let a man start out in life to build something better and sell it cheaper . . . and the money will roll in so fast that it will bury him" (168). This reprised old themes and ignored changes in the American economy: like Benjamin Franklin, Barton gave individual, utilitarian advice that service would yield consequent reward to the individual.

Barton taught an optimistic, liberal religion in which God "seeks to develop perfect human beings, superior to circumstances, victorious over Fate" (179). And he rejected much orthodox doctrine. Barton thus demonstrated that the ethics of a Walter Rauschenbusch (chapter 10) were not necessarily the only logical outcome of religious liberalism. Scripture, he wrote, taught but four lessons: that God was one, just, good, and father of all (95, 96). A fifth was that this father wished "the good things of life" for all (157). In saying this, Barton anticipated "prosperity theology" that would emerge clearly in Pentecostal circles as the century progressed. Perhaps because of America's victory in World War I, Barton happily proclaimed that the world was automatically becoming better and better, "fairer, juster and happier" (157).

The Man Nobody Knows, for all its liberal, humanistic religion and secular optimism, showed continuity with older American morality; clearly it restated parts of the old Puritan ethic (chapter 2). It also appealed to the utilitarian strain in American values dating back at least to Franklin (chapter 3). Like Franklin, the values Barton promoted were relatively wholesome, if narrow, business virtues. Barton did not promote greed—suggesting that success will take care of itself if one but adopted good business principles. Yet, these values were self-oriented.

Barton devoted a whole chapter teaching that Jesus was the forerunner of the twentieth-century advertising executive (one of whom Barton, in fact, became). Barton thus gave assurance to many white-collar workers, who might have felt meaningless as they toiled anonymously in the offices of large-scale businesses, that their personal efforts indeed mattered. Ironically, Barton used Jesus to sanctify the values of individualism for workers in a profession whose object was to use mass communications to induce people, en masse, to consume more of what mass-production industries produced. Thus he restated individualist values for a new era of abundance whose very business methods challenged individualism itself.

Bruce Barton presented a significant contrast to Walter Rauschenbusch (chapter 10). Both shared a religiously liberal outlook, with similar hope for an empowered humanity. Rauschenbusch saw the need for systemic reform because a huge economy created its own values, with which individual morality could not deal. Barton, however, affirmed that individual morality was adequate by equating American business practices with Jesus's teachings. Barton idealized personal business virtues within a system of massive corporations that served their own purposes. Barton was an advertising executive, yet his book did not acknowledge that advertising served its corporate clients, whose purposes might not have been those of Jesus.

Prosperity Theology: Father Divine

Barton's *The Man Nobody Knows* was a favorite of a middle-aged, itinerant preacher, who finally settled in New York during the 1920s. This African-American clergyman (born George Baker) was to become Father Divine, who evolved a prosperity theology. The roots of Father M. J. Divine's ideas have been traced to nineteenth-century New Thought, which advocated that health was a matter of positive thinking. Positive thinking was also believed to be effective in economics (Watts 1992, 22). An experience with Pentecostalism by the young Baker helped unite the ideas of positive thinking with the immediacy of the experience of the divine spirit. As a young itinerant preacher, he confronted the poverty of American blacks well before the rest of the country would encounter poverty in the Depression. His ministry began to "guarantee eternal life, assure salvation, and promise social, economic and political progress" (Watts 1992, 32). He assured congregations that "you can have success and prosperity as individuals and also collectively, if you will but live it" (quoted in Hoshur 1936, 219). Thus, prosperity was an act of individual will.

From these words one could deduce that the prosperity being preached was understood in American, individualist terms. Yet, this was not standard self-contained individualism, for New Thought emphasized the believer harmonizing the self with the divine. Father Divine lived a paradox by combining his affirmation of capitalism and material success with his own *communally* structured organization. Beginning very early in his ministry, Father Divine's closest followers lived together in shared houses, some employed on the outside and contributing their incomes, and other volunteering labor directly to the organization; expenses were tightly controlled (Watts 1992, 44). With this strict regimen, the group quickly accumulated assets. Speeding this process was a puritan moral code (44). Later, his followers often started small businesses, or farms, and typically operated them on a cooperative basis (104–105). These Peace Mission enterprises, as they came to be called, also provided some relief for the poor and unemployed (106).

Despite the communal style of his organization, Father Divine, as noted, expressed more than a tolerance for capitalism. Even in the Depression he refused to see capitalism as the cause of the mass hardship. Instead, "the individual was to blame" for collectively "Americans had created the depression with their negative attitudes and alienation from God's internal presence" (Watts 1992, 88). If this implied that millions of Americans had simultaneously allowed negativity to overwhelm them, this did not deter Father Divine's diagnosis. Further, he held that capitalism was the counterpart to democracy (101). He also opposed the New Deal.

Father Divine's popularity attests that among the African-American community in the 1920s—and even in the Depression—many accepted teachings based on positive-thinking principles that had developed among the relatively affluent white population of the previous century. This phenomenon mixed self-improvement individualism with a notion of harmonizing the self with a being (God) beyond the self.

Like Barton, Father Divine was preaching a version of individualism for a new, prosperous era. This contrasted with the nineteenth century's assumption of scarcity. And so Father Divine's individualism did not need to promote competitiveness; in its own unique ways, his movement even exhibited cooperative tendencies. However, the primary emphasis of Father Divine's teaching was on the abundance an individual could expect, not on that individual's obligations to others. In their own ways, both Barton and Father Divine anticipated the "prosperity gospel" of later twentieth-century Pentecostalism. And both taught an individualism that persisted despite abundance that depended on massive industries.

ECONOMICS: THE LAST DAYS OF SAY'S LAW

The 1920s would be the last decade in which Say's law, a part of laissez-faire doctrine, remained credible to a majority of economists. Sometimes abbreviated as the idea that supply creates its own demand, Say's law held that so long as prices were flexible, the economy "tended automatically to produce full employment" (Hansen 1953, 6). This tendency to full employment did not mean that business cycles could not happen; but cycles were temporary disturbances from which the economy, by itself, would recover. Stated differently, recessions contained within themselves self-correcting tendencies (see, e.g., Hansen 1953, 13–14). Typically it was held that in competitive economies any unemployment merely represented transient lags in adjustments. Many American economists quickly began revising such views after 1929.

Say's law was more than technical; it reinforced the old hands-off doctrines of laissez-faire. Nothing need be done to alleviate depressions beyond what the economy would do on its own. At best, government action would merely hasten what was an inevitable adjustment; at worst, intervention would risk misplaced remedies that caused harm and delayed adjustment.

THE MORAL MEANING OF THE 1920S: AN ASSESSMENT

Although the economic morality of the nineteenth century was framed against the context of scarcity, the 1920s proved that many of the highly individualistic values could be transformed to deal with abundance. Individualistic values could even be restated in ways that gave meaning to those who toiled in massive and bureaucratic institutions. Barton told people that they could be "superior to circumstances" and Father Divine told people with poorer prospects that they could realize prosperity essentially by willing it. A measure of the transformation of individualism is seen in the phasing out of the sterner virtues of unremitting labor, diligence, and self-denial; these could be replaced by the right business principles or simply living as though one were successful. Further, abundance removed the old Puritan suspicion of high levels of consumption. Barton even extolled the advertising industry, whose very purpose was to promote mass consumption.

Both Barton and Father Divine helped relatively benign, yet self-oriented, forms of individualism endure in the new era. However, they did so by ignoring much that contradicted their core messages. Barton's individualism give personal meaning to those who toiled in relatively impersonal, anonymous bureaucracies, which in turn served corporations whose purposes overrode those of individuals. Father Divine preached prosperity based on individual willpower to followers whose actual successes often involved cooperative forms of enterprise. In neither case was individualism equated with competition, as in the nineteenth century; there was enough for all.

THE DEPRESSION: REQUIRING CHANGE

An economic morality gains plausibility if it has many points of contact with a major theory of the economy. As noted previously, competitive self-interest is more easily seen as virtuous, if economic science affirms than an invisible hand reliably turns self-interested actions into the public good. Inaction in a depression, by agencies capable of acting, is less reprehensible if Say's law promises to restore prosperity anyway. However, when the Depression of the 1930s persisted for years, it became difficult to sustain faith in Say's law. Further, the prosperity of the 1920s made it difficult to believe that the hard times imposed by the Depression simply had to be endured (a view more in keeping with the nineteenth century).

When the Depression began in 1929, the administration of Herbert Hoover responded within the framework of orthodox economics and individualist values, a pattern followed in the early years of the Roosevelt administration. Political opinion as late as 1932 favored conventional budget-balancing for the federal government (Davis 1971, 35). Hoover and Roosevelt shared some views that were paradoxical, given the circumstances: for example, they each favored public-works relief projects only if such projects did not unbalance the budget. This was a self-defeating requirement because projects of sufficient size would surely unbalance the budget. However, politics sometimes drove them to go against the economic wisdom of the times: both favored sustaining or increasing the earnings of workers, a prescription that would raise real wages, whereas orthodox economics called for *falling* real wages to aid employment.

American economists' thinking was in advance of either Hoover or Roosevelt, for in significant numbers they advocated more activist relief measures than the presidents were willing to undertake. By early in the Depression, the doctrine that "'natural laws' control the economic universe" was "not widely held" in America (Davis 1971, 9). Thus, economic theory was swinging to a position compatible with an idea of relational morality: that economics is a human invention, subject to human action, and not the inevitable working out of economic laws. Many economists also doubted the idea that price and wage deflation would cure the Depression in a timely manner (Davis 1971, 37). This, to be sure, was a changing consensus on *perspective* rather than any specific theory, but it supported the belief that inaction would be intolerable.

FDR ECONOMIST: REXFORD TUGWELL

Although Roosevelt in 1932 held conventional opinions, he understood the humanitarian (and political) need for action and chose advisers accordingly. Some advisers recognized that the Depression called for new theory as well as policy. Rexford Tugwell was a Columbia University economist who joined Roosevelt's Brains Trust in 1931. His theoretical book, *The Industrial Discipline* (1933), and his published recollections of the first presidential campaign (1968) reveal the developing fusion of his economic theory and morality.

Tugwell's retrospective commentary on Herbert Hoover's 1932 acceptance of his nomination was at heart a moral commentary. He critiqued a president who listed all the conventional moral principles he had honored by refraining from action to help people in need (Tugwell 1968, 387). Hoover's relief programs were carefully crafted so as not to weaken "the enterprise" of citizens, or to "relieve individuals of their responsibilities," Tugwell wrote (388). He also claimed that Hoover thought "individual initiative" would create the recovery (388). Tugwell's personal view was clear: "in hard times welfare must come first" (397). However, Tugwell believed that beyond immediate response to the humanitarian crisis caused by the Depression, theoretical understanding of it was necessary.

Tugwell was to offer an alternative theory, which explained that depression was no longer to be accepted as a natural phenomenon that would eventually cure itself. His theory would build on the very efficiency that produced ever more abundance. He criticized the moral effects of scarcity, which made people "narrow and hard" and grasping, and which turned them into ruthless exploiters of "their employees, their competitors, and the consumers of their goods" (Tugwell 1968, 409). The Depression had brought back scarcity, yet Tugwell professed that scarcity was not the fundamental reality. Tugwell held that recent changes in large-scale, integrated production had made the possibility of abundance the new reality. Abundance could be had, he said, if firms could be large enough and cooperative enough to achieve all the benefits of planning and mechanization.

Tugwell's theory of integrated industries provided one perspective on the Depression. He posited that prices of goods had failed to drop as much as costs in the ever more integrated and more efficient industries; when costs dropped faster than prices, profit's share of national income increased and the share of wage-earners and farmers, who are the high consumers, fell (Tugwell 1968, 42–43, 473–74). Underconsumption resulted from this redistribution toward corporate profits, which almost by definition were not spent in large enough proportion. Efficiency (a good thing) increased too fast to avoid too much profit (and too little wages) being earned and so caused underconsumption. Reapportioning the national income would cause demand by high-consuming sectors to increase; production would follow the increasing demand. The cause of the Depression was "the disparity, the imbalance, the uneven distribution" (Tugwell 1968, 43).

This was a theory of economic deadlock for the maldistribution of income shares was unlikely to resolve itself, especially if efficiency kept lowering costs faster than prices fell or wages rose. The dilemma Tugwell exposed could only be solved with government intervention: consolidated firms were the basis of abundance, but large firms would not set prices and wages in ways that allocated national income correctly to produce enough demand. Thus, industrial consolidation and prosperity would occur together only if government stepped in to adjust prices while preserving consolidated industries. Tugwell made government involvement both feasible and necessary.

Tugwell pointed to economic insecurity as the worst product of American competition. Given that industrial integration made abundance possible, insecurity was a great failure. Average people "do not ask much" other than basic security—"security of access to the goods of simple living, security of employment, security in ill health and old age, security of maintenance and training for their dependents" (Tugwell 1933, 198). He suggested that ability to provide security implied an obligation to do so, for the unemployed were "fellow human beings."

In one way, Tugwell extended a theme of the 1920s—the new reality of abundance. However, for Tugwell, abundance was not something to be viewed as a private reward for those with certain personal virtues or positive attitudes. Abundance was not merely the background setting for individual actors practicing private virtue; rather, it was a central reality, the result of complex technological developments, and subject to human understanding. Tugwell thought that certain American economic values would need to change to accommodate to that new reality. For example, in order to realize the full benefits of large, integrated firms, the American esteem of competition, with its many small firms, would have to be altered.

Small, competitive firms could not provide the technical integration that produced abundance. Government was not a hindrance to production, but crucial to it in setting a distribution of income and coordinating businesses. The self-interested individual was an inessential ingredient in an economy that depended on large, integrated firms and cooperative teams of workers. Tugwell's theory clearly was at odds with many of the values of autonomy morality. Conversely, his theory reinforced many specific aspects of relational ethics: concern for the lower-income sectors of society, an emphasis on the very relatedness of society, an emphasis on the value of government, a call for cooperation and economic security instead of competition. However, in Tugwell's theory such propositions were not derived from a view of human nature, but a view of the nature of technology. Further, although Tugwell was motivated by ethical concern for the economic welfare of individuals, his ideal economy would depend in significant measure on collective decision-making. This was a departure from traditional relational morality.

THE VALUES OF NEW DEAL PROGRAMS

The kind of detailed involvement of government in industry implied by Tugwell's high-order theorizing did not pass view by the Supreme Court. Nevertheless, government policies changed in many other ways. By 1934–35, Roosevelt's administration had endorsed major work-relief legislation, which showed an acceptance of governmental responsibility for unemployment. However, the relief took the form of *work*, not a dole, as the resilient Puritan work ethic persisted. The nature of the work performed was a significant moral statement, too; the workers built social infrastructure (e.g., public build-ings, bridges, parks) that augmented the common life of the nation. In addi-tion, such projects would not compete with services the private sector might have desired to provide.

In 1935, Congress passed the Social Security Act, an umbrella law that not only provided old-age pensions, but included aid to disabled workers and to the survivors of deceased workers, unemployment insurance, and aid for families with dependent children ("welfare"). During hearings, reactions from some quarters reiterated the traditional values as "business leaders predicted the end of initiative, thrift" and other virtues (McElvaine 1984, 256). Although the legislation was limited, for the first time, the nation accepted responsibility for some of its weakest members. There was also a balancing of values: a commitment to the work ethic was preserved, for Social Security pensions were only for those who had paid the wage tax during years of employment. On the other hand, the legislation obviously considered incen-tives to be much less important than traditional autonomy morality had made them out to be.

New Deal legislation also established minimum-wage and overtime-pay laws, as well as a legal framework for labor unions. American law thus shifted from the principle that the doctrine of free contract trumped labor legislation, to the recognition that society may define the boundaries of acceptable labor arrangements. As noted, Msgr. John A. Ryan (chapter 10) rejoiced when this legal pillar of laissez-faire gave way. Union legislation endorsed *bargaining as a shared method* of determining some of the conditions of employment. The timing of these laws suggests that the Depression had caused a major value-shift that permitted their passage. At the highest level of generalization, these laws embodied the relational view that economic life occurs within a human community and that such a community may define the boundaries of eco-nomic activity.

KEYNESIAN MACROECONOMICS

Although many economists abandoned Say's law early in the Depression, the profession did not soon coalesce around an alternative theory (certainly, Tug-well's theory was not widely accepted). But, in the late 1930s, the British economist John Maynard Keynes provided a theory as to why an economy could fail to self-correct and so stagnate in unemployment. In Keynes's the-ory, only a large increase in aggregate demand, which the system by itself could not generate, would reestablish high-employment equilibrium. (Tug-well's theory also pointed to a lack of aggregate demand; however, Tugwell's theory sought to restore it indirectly through elaborate, government controls on industry. Keynes saw that demand could be restored directly.) The policy implication was that government could increase demand through deficit spending, tax policies favoring spenders, and monetary policy. The Keynesian theory pointed to a fundamental cure, and so placed an obligation on government to act. And it did not require government to tamper with the structure of industry, as Tugwell's theory did.

Some commentators, nevertheless, reacted to Keynesian policies as though they amounted to socialism. However, in Keynes's own mind, the theory provided an *alternative* to socialism. In fact, he opposed Marxism both for its economic incompetence and its authoritarianism (Skidelsky 1992, 517–21). Keynes emphasized that government did not need to own or manage businesses to achieve increased aggregate demand. In fact, its first strategy might be to encourage private actors to consume or invest: the state did not have to own "the instruments of production" in order to encourage investment, said Keynes (1936, 378). Aggregate investment spending mattered, Keynes argued, but "there is no more reason to socialize economic life than there was before" (379). Perhaps an unintended effect of the Keynesian emphasis on demand was that it allowed very high levels of consumption to be viewed as a sort of economic patriotism.

Keynes suggested that his theory might actually save neoclassical economics: the new theory could keep the economy at full employment, in which condition the competitive system would prove its own particular virtues (378). Keynes credited conventional markets with efficiency and other positive outcomes. He was "keenly aware of the advantages of individualism and free enterprise—the play of self-interest, the safeguard of personal liberty, the exercise of personal choice" (Hansen 1953, 222). Keynes viewed the conventional economics as valid within the realm of full employment; application of his theory would ensure full employment. In short, Keynes saw himself as a doctor for a sick competitive system that when healthy had its virtues.

It would, however, be a great mistake to view Keynes as a doctor who uncritically thought his sick patient, once healthy, was *wholly* admirable. Keynes scorned the petty traits and minor vices of a competitive system—such as a constant fixation on the bottom line or one's bank balance. He tolerated the petty side of capitalism only because at another level its efficiency would be instrumental in overcoming want (see, e.g., Skidelsky 1992, 237). The end of want (which he believed was feasible with free markets) would eventually render these petty traits extinct. Ironically, Keynes quibbled with petty aspects of capitalism, while proclaiming that as long as his theory could keep the economy healthy, a wide domain existed for the practice of autonomy values.

Keynes did express views on income inequality; however, he gave no explicit ethical reasons for his views. All he did was dismiss reasons traditionally given for inequality. To the traditional argument that inequality is needed to provide necessary incentives, he asserted that the required degree of inequality was debatable. For incentives to exist, it was not necessary that economics "should be played for such high stakes," for, he said, "much lower stakes will serve the purpose" (Keynes 1936, 374). In sum, Keynes discredited one of the usual justifications for great inequality and did not pursue the argument further in his major work. As he stated it, more equality was simply something he preferred.

Keynes's main contribution to economic morality was implicit. That an economy in depression could be cured, as Keynes argued, made the common good a proper public obligation. Perhaps the most significant part of this was that the cure had to be administered by government. In finding such a role for government, Keynes went far beyond the limits that autonomy morality would place on government. In trusting government to regulate aggregate demand, Keynes implicitly accepted the premise that discourse and consensus are possible in human society.

At the level of economics, Keynes divided theory into (his) macroeconomics, and the traditional economics, now called microeconomics. Each had its legitimate domain, although the overall economy had to be kept at full employment for traditional economics to work as it was supposed to. Ethically, too, Keynes seemed to see two ethical domains: an arena for public decisions, which could be justified by relational morality; and a separate arena for individual economic decisions, in which autonomy values retained their worth. The question arises whether such a division of economics and ethics is a stable arrangement. Unfortunately, such efforts to divide the economy into self-contained realms, each with its own values, have proved problematic. Since Keynes wrote, government macroeconomic policies have often been influenced by vigorous private parties, which have sought their own advantage in the way macroeconomic policy was carried out. In short, Keynes's own policy recommendations created opportunities for the private, profit-making sector and government sector to interact, although each was premised on different values.

SOLIDIFYING THE CHANGES:
PAUL SAMUELSON'S *ECONOMICS*

Paul Samuelson's introductory textbook (1958 edition cited) appeared originally in 1948 and presented his version of Keynes's theory; the book dominated the American college market for decades, as had Wayland's text the previous century. The very arrangement of the text defied the older economics by placing the new macroeconomic sections *before* microeconomics, which embodied most of the traditional wisdom. This primacy of place implied that the neoclassical microeconomics must take second place to the common good represented by macroeconomic stability. Early on, Samuelson stated a similar point explicitly: that the economist cares about "the economy *as a whole* rather than in the viewpoint of any one group" (Samuelson 1958, 8). He added that, all too often, "everybody's business is nobody's business" and suggested that that was an intolerable situation (an obvious challenge to the invisible-hand doctrine). Clearly, the common good should take precedence over self-interest.[2]

In his very first chapter, Samuelson emphasized the danger of the *fallacy of composition*: it is false to think that what is "true of a part, on that account alone," is "true of the whole" (11). Here, in the form of a logic lesson, he repudiated the invisible hand, which allowed the good of self-seeking economic actors (the parts), to be equated to the public good (the whole). The fallacy of composition, particularly, could mean that *in depression* "individual virtues may be self-defeating social vices" (12). For example, thrift, which is good for individuals, in a depression may reduce aggregate demand. That the classical ideas worked only under conditions of full employment was essentially Keynes' position (see above).

Samuelson warned against regarding the price system "as perfection itself" (Samuelson 1958, 38). Because of the invisible hand's propensity to make mistakes, the modern economy had evolved into a "mixed" government-private system. In citing this transformation, Samuelson essentially proclaimed that the economy was properly the object of change by humans for the human good, a key element of relational morality.

Before he even turned to economic theory, Samuelson dwelled at length on the basic facts of the American economy and its institutions. This followed the tradition of Richard Ely (chapter 9), who held that economics should start with *description* rather than the *abstractions* of the laissez-faire tradition. Samuelson covered such topics as income distribution and discrimination, the labor movement, the role and governance of corporations, and Social Security. The chapter on income distribution stated that even when competition works perfectly, "many would not consider it ideal" as a way to distribute income (42). The "rich man's dog" may live better than the poor child. As if to show that inequality is not natural, Samuelson noted that income inequality far exceeds inequalities of mental and physical traits (71). Samuelson conceptually distinguished ethics and economics. However, his juxtaposition of the well-being of a dog and a human child left no doubt that moral judgment is relevant. The reader could only conclude that public moral consensus should decide income distribution, for there is nothing "*necessary and inevitable*" about income distribution (72).[3]

Like Ely before him, Samuelson took the position that policy issues of ethical import should be decided by the democratic process. This approach may have avoided his having to defend a particular ethical perspective. However, it still strongly repudiated autonomy ethics, which removed such issues from the realm of public morality entirely. Indeed, Samuelson thought that democratic consensus could not possibly favor laissez-faire (43). A history lesson enumerated the public ills of the nineteenth century and held that remedies were chosen democratically: the United States "would not if it could, turn the clock back" (114).

Toward what goal would democracy be headed? Samuelson's discussion of Social Security gave some idea. He noted that contemporary society no longer blamed economic losers for their misfortunes. Benefits under the Social Security act did not require meeting a humiliating "needs test." He noted that Social Security is even better than private insurance because it "rests on the general tax capacity of the nation." Thus, although inflation (or stock market crashes) could decimate private insurance and savings, the Social Security program would essentially survive unscathed (179). He added, other nations have "gone much further" in providing economic security.

There is considerable moral parallelism between Keynes and Samuelson, which is apparent in the preceding sections. As moralists, both presented economic theories that were compatible with long-standing premises of relational ethics. As evidence of this, parallels in the thought of Richard Ely (chapter 9) and Samuelson have been noted.

CONCLUSION

The 1920s witnessed the shift from people assuming that scarcity was the dominant economic reality, to the assumption of benign economic possibilities—or even of abundance. American economic values remained highly individualistic. However, thinkers such as Bruce Barton ignored that individualistic values had to be lived out in a world of large-scale, impersonal economic institutions that made abundance possible. For example, the advertising executives that Barton admired as followers of Jesus served corporate clients and aimed through mass persuasion to stimulate mass consumption of certain products. Barton promoted individual values to white-collar workers who toiled in an anonymous corporate bureaucracy whose characteristics no longer matched the ethic promoted.

The Great Depression made it impossible to ignore the common experience of participants in the economy. What finally emerged was a theory of the economy *as a system*, in which individuals shared a common economic existence. At a programmatic level, the new focus on a shared economic good appeared in New Deal programs. At the theoretical level, Keynes and Samuelson mandated government involvement in the economy to keep it out of depression. The changes brought about by the Great Depression demonstrated the interdependence of morality and theory, for theory delineates what is supposed to be feasible or not feasible; this, in turn, denotes what is within the realm of ethical choice.

The theoreticians of the Depression emphasized economics more than ethics. However, they discovered and promoted a theory that provided more support to relational morality than had laissez-faire or neoclassical economics. At a minimum, the Depression seemed to demonstrate that individual actions (virtuous or not) had less utilitarian significance than people had thought—for the economically virtuous suffered along with those less virtuous. The

Depression forcefully taught that people shared a common destiny within a huge economic system. On one hand, no one individually caused what the economy did; there were too many interactions. On the other hand, the new macroeconomics did point to key points at which government would have leverage to cure the depressed economy. Theory explained that major policies, requiring government action—and presumably a high degree of democratic consensus—could affect the whole economic system.

Even without specifying the content of a morality, this new theory had some moral implications. First, if government action could reduce human misery, then the mandate for government action was increased. Second, the Depression emphasized the commonality of the human experience. Third, if the government could steer the economic ship, then common values became crucial in deciding the method of steering and the destination. Thus, Samuelson endorsed democracy as the process for discerning social values. All this was compatible with themes in relational morality.

Despite this, Keynes, the theorist of the new macroeconomics, took a dualistic approach. He left room for an ongoing "microeconomic" realm in which competitive markets—and the accompanying autonomy values—could persist. He accepted the welfare economists' result that competitive markets were efficient and so failed to consider how markets might need to be bounded. Although dualistic approaches may have superficial appeal for keeping the best of two approaches, Keynes seemed uneasy with his own dualism. He fully realized that markets produced more than just efficiency and questioned whether the degree of economic inequality created by free markets was necessary. He also scorned the petty behaviors associated with capitalism. Keynes might have foreseen that two realms of economic activity, macroeconomics and microeconomics, operating according to different values, could coexist only imperfectly. Private interests in the competitive economy would attempt to influence government's antidepression policies to advance their own interests, thus moving macroeconomic policy in directions Keynes might never have intended. Later, John Kenneth Galbraith (chapter 14) would criticize Keynes's followers for advocating government spending as macroeconomic stimulus without regard to the impact of such spending at the microeconomic level; some kinds of spending would be better than others, he held. The dualistic approach was never a good solution.

At a certain level, Samuelson followed Keynes: he wrote of the "neoclassical synthesis," in which macroeconomics and microeconomics ruled in distinct realms. However, that said, Samuelson was willing to draw boundaries around the private sector and assign more duties to government than the "neoclassical synthesis" might seem to have implied. His favorable discussion of New Deal innovations made it clear that government was responsible for far more than simply avoiding depressions—in particular, for providing economic security. His sentiments were those of relational ethics, which always saw the need for boundaries to markets.

TWELVE

Too Agnostic, Too Certain

Welfare Economics, Chicago Economics

BY THE TWENTIETH CENTURY, many economists were becoming self-consciously scientific in outlook and desiring a value-free discipline. If economists were to make value judgments, they should at least be based on norms of what constituted economic goodness that were inherent in economics itself. From the late nineteenth century to the mid twentieth, European and American "welfare economists" strove to discover norms embedded in the utilitarian and individualistic presumptions of historic economics. They also sought to be scientific by taking nothing for granted—assuming very little and deducing results from the weakest possible assumptions. Economists had long accepted that self-interested people acted in ways consistent with utilitarianism; the welfare economists kept a generally utilitarian outlook. However, despite a major effort to define the good economy, welfare economists produced very modest and incomplete results. Although there were very good reasons the welfare economists' results were so meager, economists associated with the University of Chicago nevertheless greatly expanded upon them. They proclaimed certain hypotheses to be true and moved ahead, finding new reasons for a free-market vision of the good economy.

WELFARE ECONOMICS

In the 1960s, William Baumol defined welfare economics as the study of the policy statements "that the economist is entitled to make" (Baumol 1965, 355). The economist was *not* entitled to make recommendations based on values imported from outside economics itself. The economist, as economist, should recommend only policies that are consistent with what economics can

147

prove are better than other policies by economic norms. If outside values come into play, as in political environments, they should be explicitly labeled as foreign to economics.

After much literature had been written, welfare economics eventually came to the consensus that *Pareto optimality*—that is, a state of maximum economic efficiency—was the norm by which economies should be judged. Pareto optimality results from having made every possible *Pareto improvement*—that is, every change that improves the subjective welfare of some person(s) while hurting no one's welfare (Baumol 1965, 376). To be better-off was a utilitarian standard of the good, and was based on the affected individual's private, subjective judgment. Once all possible improvements of this type had been made, it would be no longer possible to better anyone except by harming someone else (i.e., taking something away from that person), and Pareto optimality would have been achieved.

Pareto improvement is about efficiency. If resources are being wasted, then greater efficiency in the use of existing resources provides a free benefit so that some people can be made better-off without harm to others (taking away from others). Only when all unrealized efficiency gains have been exhausted are Pareto improvements no longer possible, and the economy is in an optimal position.[1]

A Pareto improvement makes at least some people better-off without harming others. If one accepts the utilitarian view, then a Pareto improvement is a good thing. To avoid what they saw as imposing their own value judgments about the meaning of "better-off," the welfare economists relied on *people's own assessments* of whether they were better-off or not. In this way, economists could remain value-neutral, or agnostic, about the meaning of "better-off." The strategy of using people's subjective assessments of "better-off" may have been successful in keeping out economists' value judgments. However, the price was steep: it resulted in making it *impossible to compare the relative positions of different people*—for purely subjective feelings cannot be compared.

Although welfare economics was generally utilitarian, earlier utilitarian thinkers such as John Stuart Mill had believed that *interpersonal comparisons of utility or welfare were possible* (see appendix, this chapter). That is, people presumably had enough in common that economists could compare different persons' welfare levels. (It could be known, e.g., that a poor person was worse-off than a rich person.) To meet what welfare economists saw as a scientific imperative (i.e., to minimize making their own judgments about other people's subjective welfare) they rejected all possibility of interpersonal comparisons of utility or welfare. Thus they made a major claim about human nature: that people have so little in common—that they are so isolated and autonomous, so disconnected from each other—that their welfares cannot be compared. This agnosticism about people was a deviation from earlier utilitarian thinking.

Leaving aside for the moment this claim (that people have almost nothing in common), we first note that Pareto improvement appeals as a norm for judging an economy. Even nonutilitarian moralists would not object to a chance to make some better-off (without making anyone worse-off), lacking good reason for the objection. In a sense, objection to Pareto improvements amounts to favoring inefficiency or wasted opportunity. Of course, a nonutilitarian moralist might object if an unworthy person were to be the proposed recipient of the efficiency gain. But that labeling of someone as "unworthy" is the just the kind of value judgment the welfare economists wished to strike out of economics. Furthermore, objection to the particular recipients of an efficiency gain is not an objection to efficiency itself.

Welfare economics also tried to show that a *perfectly competitive economy* would allocate resources in a Pareto optimal way (Baumol 1965, 365–66). Samuelson cited Pareto's "strong position that competition produces a *maximum d'utilite collective*" (1947, 212). If competition, therefore, is so good, a very important question arises: are markets truly competitive? If they are not perfectly competitive, then government intervention may be justified to improve efficiency. A major strand of welfare economics was then devoted to the study of cases in which noncompetitive situations or *market failures* could prevent the efficient outcome. Government remedies might be applied to make markets work better to achieve efficiency.

The Pareto standard was not entirely value-free (it accepted an individualistic, utilitarian definition of the good based on people's autonomous assessments of their welfare). However, it did achieve a degree of value-neutrality from the welfare economists' own perspective. First, it did not require the comparison of different persons' subjective welfare; people needed only know if a change improved their own welfare or not. Second, no one was judged by an external morality to be more or less worthy: anyone's deterioration of welfare can signal that a change is not a Pareto improvement. Third, efficiency as a norm by which to rank economies appeared to be consistent with a central concern of economics.

Leaving aside problems already noted, the Pareto standard had other problems of its own. Pareto efficiency does not produce a complete ranking system—a problem long noted by critics of welfare economics. The problem is that multiple states of an economy may all be Pareto-optimal. The welfare economist cannot go any further in ranking economies (or states of a given economy) that are already Pareto-efficient without invoking some other values. While the economist recommends Pareto-optimal economies over those that are not, there is no guidance in recommending one economy over another one if both are Pareto-optimal states. Yet, many people (including economists), for good reasons, might be sure that one of the two economies is morally superior to the other. This means that welfare economics failed to discover some other relevant norms.

Paul Samuelson (1947, 220) suggested a halfway measure to deal with this impasse. A "social welfare function" would weight and combine the welfare of different persons in order to measure which state of the economy produces the highest welfare overall. These "weightings," which may, for example, make a welfare gain by the poor worth more than a similar gain by the rich, would impose some explicit value judgments. Presumably these value judgments would be those of elected officials, who might hold any values. The social welfare function ultimately allowed the ranking of more states of the economy than the Pareto standard alone. However, "weightings" of the social welfare function combine the worst of two worlds: the weightings are treated as arbitrary values, possessing no compelling relation to the good; on the other hand, they represent a retreat from the very value-neutrality the welfare economists were striving for. From a broader moral perspective, the social welfare function only weights individuals' welfare; thus it retains economics' very individualistic bias.

WELFARE ECONOMICS IN A BROADER MORAL CONTEXT

Welfare economics' efficiency norm is important in a world of limited resources. To fail to take all possible efficiency improvements is waste, and few would make the case that waste is in general a good thing. That non-economist moralists have ignored efficiency makes this norm an important addition to economic ethics. Gross inefficiency, resulting in poverty, may well assault other human values, such as human dignity. Thus efficiency would be an instrumental good even from a nonutilitarian perspective.

Competition was esteemed as a means to efficiency by the welfare economists. Yet, for competition actually to lead to efficient outcomes it must satisfy highly stringent conditions. Whether markets in fact fulfill all conditions needed to be truly competitive has long been debated. If markets *are* in fact truly competitive, then government intervention to improve efficiency is unnecessary. Conversely, if markets are not perfectly competitive, the norm of efficiency requires governmental intervention in markets to improve efficiency.

Aside from competition's link to efficiency (the main interest of economists), the moralist must ask if competition is morally attractive in its own right. To economists, the character of competition is a relatively neutral, technical matter. However, more value-laden, negative terms from popular language, such as "cutthroat competition," require consideration. Non-economists often juxtapose "competition" against "cooperation," which by implication is morally more attractive. As conventionally understood in economics, competition is motivated by *self-interested profit-seeking*; a morality that considers intentions might raise objections at this point. Finally, if profit-making is all that guides the competitive firm, profits gained by unfair dealings may be just as appealing as efficiency-generated profits. Welfare economics did not consider these broader implications of competition.

Despite its significance, Pareto efficiency can hardly be the *sole* norm by which to judge the goodness of a society. Many have noted that two efficient economies may have vastly different degrees of economic inequality; surely the degree of inequality is relevant for rating the goodness of any economy. Less frequently noted is that Pareto efficiency is an incomplete moral standard for additional reasons. If efficiency is all that matters, then society should expand competitive markets into all possible arenas, including those previously outside the market. But the Pareto standard is silent on the moral status of certain kinds of markets—some potential markets may be outlawed for good reason. For example, competitive markets in *vice* might produce a Pareto improvement as *measured by market participants themselves* (the only way welfare economists would measure an improvement). Yet, vices may be condemned on moral grounds that many people find compelling—for example, some vices demean human dignity. Similarly, democratic societies typically outlaw or try to restrict buying and selling legislative clout. Yet, the Pareto standard offers no insight into these examples.

The Pareto standard runs into this trouble because it uses self-defined welfare as its norm. A few people might find the marketing of vice to increase their self-defined welfare. Yet, the standard of self-defined welfare may itself be questioned. Why should self-defined welfare trump social norms or values? *Simply assuming the superiority of self-defined welfare over other norms, as the welfare economists did, does not prove it to be so.* As seen by the laws societies make, some market activity may be judged wrong by society *despite* the preferences of participants in those markets. Personal preferences do not validate themselves as moral statements. Earlier utilitarian moralists, such as John Stuart Mill (see appendix), argued that preferences could be ranked objectively—thus rejecting self-defined welfare.

Another problem with preference-based definitions of personal welfare lies in how narrowly preferences must be defined in order for the usual welfare results to be obtained. Welfare economists have insisted on a very narrow and egoistic definition of preferences: "an individual's preference depends only upon the things which he consumes and not upon what others consume" (Samuelson 1947, 224). Welfare economists used egoistic preferences, in part, to solve a theoretical problem: the straightforward connection between competitive markets and increased efficiency exists without qualification only with egoistic preferences.[2] If people's welfare depends on the consumption of others, or their consumption affects the welfare of others, market prices do not reflect the full value of goods to everyone in society; thus unmodified markets cannot achieve efficiency. The conclusion that competition yields efficiency depends on egoistic preferences. Welfare economics thus decreed something about human nature: participants in the market must be thoroughly egoistic—

devoid of benevolence, altruism, and any other-regarding kinds of human goodness (also devoid of envy, malice, etc.). Welfare economics decreed a hardly plausible human psychology in order to prove the efficiency of competitive markets. Thus, welfare economists essentially ruled out moralities that could not conform to their thoroughly one-sided definition of human nature.

Another problem with the notion of preferences in welfare economics is that they must arise entirely from within the individual—that is, preferences must be purely autonomous. If one's preferences can be shaped by others, then they are hardly one's preferences and there is no point defining efficiency in terms of such preferences. In the extreme, a monopolist or central planning board could allocate resources as it desired and then shape preferences until the dictated allocation became the most preferred by the populace. In this example, maximum welfare obviously does not require competition. Also, the autonomous individual loses moral significance. If people's very preferences can be shaped by others, then the meaning of autonomy and individualism itself is challenged—for one's individuality is defined by one's preferences. What does self-interest mean if one's preferences can be manipulated? What is individualism if not one's unique preferences?

The mere fact that egoistic preferences are necessary to the competition-efficiency link does not provide a reason to believe that all real persons' preferences are so self-oriented. As noted, some people may have altruistic preferences—sensing their own welfare to be increased when others do better. But there are other exceptions that break out of utilitarian modes of thought. For example, a devout Christian or Jew may follow certain biblical injunctions, quite apart from personal preferences or effects on personal welfare. Indeed, *doing something other than what one personally prefers* may constitute right action according to some types of morality. Subordinating self's will to the divine will, or to some general moral imperative, in such moralities is the core of right behavior. The right deed might even decrease self-perceived welfare. Is preference-based welfare the proper measure of the good?

In the end, welfare economists admitted that people's preferences actually had at least one thing in common (namely, egoism). But, if egoism can be assumed, what is to stand in the way of admitting that people may have *even more in common*—enough in common to make interpersonal comparisons of welfare? This, alone, would open the door to ethical norms other than efficiency. Further, if people should hold a lot in common, then even nonutilitarian ethics become possible, for moral discussion is feasible.

The welfare economists' agnosticism about people, if it had been tenable, would have been an expression of the ultimate autonomy morality: people are so autonomous as to be psychologically opaque to other people, ruling out ethical discourse based on common humanity. The severe handicap that their assumed agnosticism imposed on welfare economists suggests that alternatives should be considered. The assumption that people have much in common and can engage in meaningful moral discourse might allow for more fruitful economic morality. This is even possible within a utilitarian framework, as Mill argued (appendix). However, it need not be utilitarian.

Despite these major criticisms, maximization of human welfare for judging economies is a conditionally attractive notion (although few moralists would make it the *only* standard). Who would defend the proposition that reducing people's welfare was a morally desirable end (absent some other highly morally compelling reason)? However, as noted, the maximization of welfare cannot be the *sole* norm in judging the goodness of an economic system. Too many other characteristics of an economy are obviously important in rating its goodness.

CHICAGO: THE SCIENCE AND ETHICS OF SELF-INTEREST

Welfare economics was part of the long economic mainstream, with its heavy emphasis on self-interested individualism and competitive behavior. Surprisingly, however, a group of neoclassical economists associated with the University of Chicago in the mid-twentieth century began to assail even the modest deviations of welfare economics from stricter laissez-faire principles. This camp rejected suggestions of welfare economists that unfettered markets might contain a few technical failures to be improved by government actions. And, while the welfare economists accepted egoistic preferences as necessary for their proof of the efficiency of markets, the Chicago economists went further: they named egoism as the key to virtually all human activity. This school defined people as bundles of self-defined (or innate) preferences—with no apologies to other views of human nature. Their hypothetical economic person sought only to maximize the satisfaction of personal preferences; their business firms sought only to maximize profits in a competitive manner. The Chicago economists argued that the economy was actually competitive enough for government to stay out. The absence of government would give maximum freedom to persons and firms to fulfill their self-defined, highest good.

SELF-INTEREST AS SCIENCE

Chicago economists boldly hypothesized exclusively self-interested people and claimed that this hypothesis predicted human behavior better than alternative hypotheses. A reader of Milton Friedman's essay on methodology might have thought that the Chicago economists would be tentative in their use of the universal self-interest hypothesis. According to what seemed a cautious methodology, Friedman taught that theory assumed a "hypothetical and highly simplified world" in which phenomena acted merely "as if" the hypothesized factors were present. He even added that generally "there is more than one way to formulate such a description" (Friedman 1953, 40). This statement would seem to allow room for other "forces," such as morality, outside the "simplified world" of self-interest. Further, even accurate predictions would only mean that people act "as if" self-interest determined their behavior. This led to Friedman's conclusion that "any theory is necessarily provisional" (41).[3] From this, one would expect the self-interest hypothesis would have been held only tentatively.

If Friedman's methodology sounded tentative about claiming too much for a theory, this was not the way things were to occur; to the contrary, claims by the Chicago school of economics became ever more absolute. Prominent Chicago economists clearly took self-interest to be more than merely a scientific hypothesis; it was a highly certain statement about human nature itself. George Stigler (1982, 35), a leading member of the Chicago school, eventually claimed that "Man is eternally a utility-maximizer," and not merely in the economic realm, but "everywhere" in life. Stigler (1975, 140) flatly asserted that it is "essentially inconceivable (but not impossible)" that such a theory could be wrong. Conceding that it was "not impossible" for the theory to be wrong implied an open mind—but that was hardly the message sent.

Converting the self-interest hypothesis into a universal truth, Chicago theorists applied its logic to explaining marriage, child rearing, criminal behavior, and the like—not just run-of-the-mill economic problems. The link of this to morality is very clear when one considers how these economists analyzed crime. A decision to commit a crime or not, they said, depends exclusively on the calculation of probable costs and benefits to self. Costs must be understood to include potential prison time, loss of job, loss of social standing, and so on. Benefits would be any gains from the crime. The potential criminal's belief in the concept of law (or Law), or sense of obligation to the Ten Commandments, or recognition that one's potential victim is just like oneself and deserves not to be violated, are all irrelevant from this perspective. The *only* relevant difference between criminals and law-abiding citizens was that the costs and benefits balanced out differently. The Chicago school's cost-benefit calculation amounted to an essentially amoral calculation of gains and losses to the self, which probably was a good approximation of the way criminals think. However, the Chicago economists applied it to everyone—in effect implying that everyone is a criminal in the orientation of the soul.

As the example of criminal decision-making suggests, this extreme neoclassical interpretation of human nature denies terms like right and wrong any independent meaning, for behavior must be fully predetermined by (1) one's preferences, (2) the conditions or constraints prevailing, and (3) the drive to maximize personal gain given the preferences and conditions. As with all other decisions in the neoclassical framework, the criminal's cost-benefit calculation would always produce the same result, given the same preferences and external conditions—the theory is deterministic.[4] What is fully determined by preferences and constraints leaves no room for moral notions of right or wrong.

If humans are essentially too self-interested for ethics to play a meaningful role, why does the language of morality persist? It may persist as an exercise in group self-interest. George Stigler described a marginal role for ethics in harmonizing plural self-interests: ethics are "rules which in general prohibit behavior which is only myopically self-serving" (Stigler 1982, 35). A collection of self-interested individuals, concerned with nearsighted actions by a few that reduce others' welfare, state rules to avoid the losses. In short, ethics are rules to enforce something like Wayland's principle of reciprocity. Stigler labeled such rules "ethics," but held out little hope that the rules will consistently work. After all, such rules do not appeal to the psyche of the selfish person: why should a selfish person obey rules if disobeying pays off better?

Some neoclassical economists (often textbook writers) have attempted to sugarcoat the Chicago theory. They state, for example, that one of the costs of committing a crime might be the subjective discomfort (guilt) felt from violating personal ethical precepts. Thus, moral values get to the table by entering the self-interested calculation as the cost of guilt feelings. However, behavior motivated by such personal discomfort is not the same as behavior motivated by the belief that something is truly right or wrong. Behavior is still only motivated by a selfish calculation—just one that includes trying to avoid certain psychological states of mind. Besides, this guilt-feeling ethics is illogical if only self-interest matters. If people are exclusively self-interested, why would anyone entertain a set of beliefs whose only result is to prevent the enjoyment of the fruits of selfish deeds? Unless guilt feelings reflect some *independent truth* about right and wrong, an idea that neoclassical economists do not entertain, it is illogical to let such feelings interfere with selfish pleasure. Guilt-feeling morality cannot logically be melded with Chicago morality. The Chicago theory would recommend that anyone deterred from doing something solely by guilt should see a therapist.

PROFIT-MAXIMIZATION AND COMPETITION

Besides asserting the principle of self-interest maximization, Chicago economists asserted the symmetrical principle that businesses are always profit-maximizers. Adopting a Darwinian argument, Friedman said that unless businesses were profit-maximizers they would quickly fail, that profit-maximization "summarizes appropriately the conditions for survival" (Friedman 1953, 22). Another reason for the dogged faith in profit-maximizing is that as a driving force in competition it helps assure efficiency.

There is a moral implication in the profit-maximizing premise. Making maximizing choices, solely dictated by market and technological conditions, allows the running of a firm to be a completely deterministic activity. The necessity of profit-maximization leaves no room for the freedom to make costly moral choices. It is therefore not surprising that Milton Friedman stated that "there is one and only one social responsibility of business," which was to make profits (1962, 133). Friedman's profit-maximization position meant that no such free choice exists; the firm follows the deterministic rules to maximize profit, neglecting all else, or fails as a business.

In contrast to the welfare economists, who had discussed cases where markets were not perfectly competitive, Chicago economists minimized the importance of market failures and of noncompetitive industries. They held that the theory of competition predicted the actual behavior of even highly concentrated industries. As noted, Milton Friedman believed that it was predictions that mattered. And, although some industries did not fit the definition of being competitive, Friedman denied that their behavior showed "any recognized contradiction of predictions" from the competitive theory (Friedman 1953, 15). This meant that concentrated industries or monopolies could be dismissed as concerns for government policy if their behavior fit the predictions of competitive theory. This claim was novel and bold: concentrated industries actually behaved according to competitive theory! If true, it would be a reason for government to take a laissez-faire policy.

Friedman was very assertive that what appeared to be noncompetitive industries actually behaved like competitive industries. He stated how he was "impressed with how wide is the range of problems and industries for which it is appropriate to treat the economy as if it were competitive" (Friedman 1962, 120). He affirmed the "relative unimportance" of monopoly from the perspective of the larger economy (121). Even if one thinks that monopoly exists, one cannot know it, for "it is difficult to cite a satisfactory objective measurement of the extent of monopoly and of competition" (121). He thought the public had a "mistaken impression" that monopoly was significant (122). Another economist made the similar assertion that "even highly imperfect markets may generate results close to the theoretical ideal" (Hirshleifer 1984, xii). Stigler added that in the arena of regulated industries, empirical contradiction of neoclassical theory "simply will not arise." Finally, Stigler simply closed off argument by stating that in any case "there is no alternative hypothesis" to the competitive hypothesis (Stigler 1975, 140).

This dogged defense of the competitiveness of the economy was used to claim that American industry indeed was efficient and, therefore, that unregulated, free markets represented the appropriate economic policy. By implication, the values long associated with laissez-faire and American capitalism were also endorsed (see chapter 13 to see how such neoclassical economic theory closely supported libertarian ethics).

CRITICS AND CRITICISMS OF
CHICAGO ETHICS AND ECONOMICS

The bold assertion of the Chicago economists was that industries indeed behaved as though they were competitive—essentially that industrial concentration, corporate power, or market failures were minor matters that could be ignored for policy purposes. This was paired with the equally strong assertions about the thoroughly self-interested nature of all human behavior. Both welfare economics and Chicago economics were highly congruent with autonomy morality; they have proved controversial among even economists. First, a short recap of logical inconsistencies already discovered is in order.

The Chicago economics was as logically inconsistent on its own terms as was welfare economics. Chicago economics promoted the case for economic freedom from government. Yet, their neoclassical theory was deterministic, given a person's preferences and the market conditions the individual faces. Faced with those "givens," a person's choice is determined—there is only one way to "maximize utility." And, given a firm's technology and market conditions, its profit-maximizing moves are determined, for other decisions will provide suboptimal profits. This is a logical paradox: what does freedom mean in the context of a system that is deterministic? Uriarte (1990, 605–17) notes the "beguiling paradox" of extremely neoclassical economists simultaneously defending individual freedom alongside an economic theory based on deterministic decisions.

FRANK KNIGHT: AN INSIDE CRITIC

Frank Knight (1885–1972) was a leader of the University of Chicago economics department in the generation immediately before the developments previously described. Indeed, some of the central figures in this later Chicago school overlapped with Knight's tenure. Broadly speaking, Knight agreed with laissez-faire because he extremely disliked what he saw as authoritarian social alternatives. However, he was acutely aware of the moral weaknesses of markets, which were simply ignored in the work of the later Chicago economists. In a sense, Knight critiqued the later Chicago economists before they came into prominence.

In a classic essay "The Ethics of Competition" (1923), before he permanently moved to a position at the University of Chicago, Knight enumerated a full dozen "postulates" (along with subconditions) that would have to exist for the competitive system to work as claimed. At the end of rigorous assessment of whether the postulates were fulfilled in reality, Knight drew some conclusions about how actual competitive systems would rate in terms of common ethical and economic norms. His conclusions were: (1) the "theoretical tendencies" of competition are offset in society by "fundamental limitations and counter-tendencies," (2) that, despite their importance in allocating resources, prices in the real world "diverge widely from accepted ethical values" (3) that "untrammeled individualism" in the market would corrupt "popular taste," (4) that in practice the competitive system is "inefficient in using resources," (5) that this system rewards people "on the basis of power, which

is ethical only in so far as might and right are one," (6) that the competitive
system is a "failure in the field of promoting many forms of social progress,"
and (7) that the system "'collapses' at frequent intervals" (Knight 1999, V.1:
74,75). How different this is from the story told by the later generation of
Chicago economists.

When Knight assessed the postulates of competition, he found that they
were rarely met. He noted that markets must be made up of rational participants, who are truly free individuals. At the simplest level, this requires that
people *know* their desires. But, said Knight, "human activity is largely impul-
sive, a relatively unthinking and undetermined response to stimulus and suggestion" (V. 1: 68). This directly challenged the rational, calculating "economic
man" of neoclassical economics. Meaningful individualism also requires that
people's desires must truly be their own. Again, Knight noted a major problem, for the economic actor "is in large measure a product of the economic system, which is a fundamental part of the cultural environment that has formed
his desires and needs" (V.1: 68). Knight here denied the autonomy of individuals. In effect, he asked his future colleagues: what individualistic end does
competition serve if it simply serves wants created by the system?

Perhaps Knight's criticism of the morality that emerged after him at
Chicago is best summarized by his editor. To Knight, "liberalism was fine for a
society that viewed its chief problem as organizational efficiency for the purpose of given wants. But the most important social problems are the decisions
as to what we should want and what rules to use for mutual relationships, not
those of organizational efficiency" (Emmet in Knight 1999 V.1, xix). Knight's
emphasis on the importance of mutual relationships as opposed to efficiency
sounded much like relational morality. The editor goes on to explain why
Knight nevertheless supported the competitive-liberal system, despite his
strong relational views. For him, it seemed the only system that maintained the
possibility of moral discussion without resorting to authority, which Knight
rejected. Unfortunately, the later Chicago economists posited autonomous
people with innate (or self-defined) wants, in isolation from others, who never
considered the possibility of moral discussion. Knight, himself, wrote much
like a relational moralist who lacked one thing: the ability to understand that
individualism could exist without autonomy. He was willing to risk an economic system, whose ills he clearly perceived, to protect his autonomy.

ETZIONI AND OTHERS ON LACK OF EVIDENCE

Despite the strong claims of economists such as George Stigler, that the predictions of the self-interest theory virtually never failed, the actual evidence
was skimpy. Evidence against the self-interest, utility-maximization approach
has been found in recent years by psychological and experimental economists,
who have demonstrated experimentally that people often make intentional

choices that are not in their self-interest. For example, in experimental game situations, people often make choices, against their own self-interest, in order to punish noncooperative and selfish players (Sigmund 2002, 83–87).[5] Outside the realm of competitive games, psychologists also have found evidence that people do not evaluate gains and losses, or the utility-enhancing possibility of a greater range of choices, as neoclassical economic theory posits (Schwartz 2004, 71–75).[6]

One of the most thoroughgoing critics of the neoclassical economists' methods and evidence was Amatai Etzioni in the book *The Moral Dimension: Toward a New Economics* (1988). Etzioni's survey of the evidence concluded that neoclassical "predictions are still rare and frequently invalid" (1988, 19). That is, neoclassical theory failed by its own criterion. He devoted a full chapter to evidence that people act in ways that the self-interest theory cannot explain. For example, the highly neoclassical, public-choice school seems to give the wrong reasons why presumably selfish people bother voting (61–62).

Etzioni noted the close connection of the postulate of autonomous preferences and the value of freedom in Chicago thought. The neoclassical economists must deny any social influences on people, for if "preferences of individuals can be manipulated," then "one undermines the foundation of liberty" (Etzioni 1988, 10). In order to protect their vision of autonomous and free people, neoclassical economists must deny the influence of other humans on people—no matter what common experience says to the contrary. Etzioni argued that in doing this they are wrong about the facts, and also that they were morally wrong, for true liberty is not autonomy, but "requires a viable—albeit not overbearing—community" (10).

Finally, Etzioni attacked the neoclassical camp on grounds of its methodology. Quoting another economist, Etzioni noted that neoclassical theorems "either cannot be falsified or are very difficult to refute," so that they are essentially "complete or near-tautologies" (18). An example of tautological method is the contorted effort to reduce apparently altruistic behavior to some kind of selfish motivation. But, stated Etzioni, appealing to the direct experience of many people, "people do some things because they judge them to be their duty, to be right, whether or not they enjoy these acts" (26).

In the third part of his book Etzioni questioned the neoclassical implication that it is always worth increasing competition and reducing social oversight in the economy. He made some remarkably prescient comments about the effects of market deregulation, noting that "the more unfettered competition becomes, the more keenly one becomes aware of the need to be concerned . . . with the rules of the game" (204). His warning would have been relevant in the case of the deregulation of California electric markets, which opened the door to alleged market manipulation and obvious chaos in 2000 and 2001. Lack of regulation led, in part, to the "subprime" crisis of 2007 as well.

CONCLUSION

Both welfare economics and Chicago economics contained internal contradictions. For example, the welfare economists in the name of science chose to be agnostic about people's preferences, and how they perceived their welfare. However, when it was necessary to prove that competitive markets are efficient, then they lost their agnosticism long enough to declare that preferences are egoistic. And the Chicago economists promoted the autonomy of the individual within a system that was deterministic by nature. Those who attempt to soften the doctrine of extreme self-interest, to make it more palatable, offer up their own contradictions. The same may be said for George Stigler's revised notion of ethics, which, he said, was a set of rules to curtail "myopic" selfish behavior. Given the kind of human nature Stigler proposed, there would be no reason for a person *not* to act in "myopic" ways if it served the self. Indeed, the lack of self-restraint could be expected in any economy populated by the kind of people defined by the Chicago economists.

This critique of the self-interest theory does not require one to accept the opposite view—that self-interest plays no role in human behavior. Few moral systems would deny that some degree of self-interest is a reality, which in many instances serves the good. The objection is to the claim that only self-interest matters and to the determinism that leaves no room for behavior motivated by a morality whose validity is believed to lie outside the self.

One economic moralist has suggested that Chicago economics is a worldview that qualifies as type of "religion"—one that is incompatible with biblical religion (Nelson 1998, 156). The central meaning of this, of course, is that if human life is at heart exclusively self-interested, then an autonomy morality would be the only tenable morality. It is very clear that traditional biblical teachings favor a relational morality. One Christian economic moralist—after completing a long review of welfare economics—also saw this, writing that the extremely neoclassical and Christian views of the good "simply belong to different worlds" (Hay 1989, 140).

APPENDIX: THE UTILITARIANISM
OF JOHN STUART MILL

The radical direction in which utilitarianism was taken by twentieth-century economics is readily apparent by comparing it to the social utilitarianism of the British economist John Stuart Mill (1806–1873). Mill and the twentieth-century economists agree only that good is defined by utility—that unit of measurement of human happiness or welfare. However, here the resemblance ceases. Mill's utilitarianism was neither egoistic, nor agnostic about interpersonal comparisons of utility. Instead of welfare economics' need for a person to consider exclusively his or her own utility, Mill's essay *Utilitarianism* (first appearing in book form in 1863) stated that the utilitarian standard is "not the agent's own greatest happiness, but the greatest amount of happiness altogether" (Mill 1965, 198–99). Indeed, Mill believed that an individual might sacrifice his or her own good for that of others. Mill, therefore, was a social utilitarian, in sharp contrast to the egoistic utilitarianism of more recent economists.

Mill never advanced the notion that utility was such a completely subjective experience that comparisons of utility were impossible. Mill argued vigorously for the objective superiority of certain pleasures over other pleasures. He famously declared that it was "better to be Socrates dissatisfied than a fool satisfied" (197). Mill was sure that a panel of competent judges, having experienced various pleasures, could objectively rank them. In short, Mill believed that humans are similar enough that comparisons among them can meaningfully be made. To Mill, the agnosticism that the welfare economists imposed on themselves would have seemed mystifying. And the sacrifice the welfare economists made in assuming people to be such isolated beings—indeed beings who are essentially aliens to one another—is that no utilitarian ethical judgments can be made about income inequality or a host of other important issues. Mill's brand of utilitarianism never presented such an obstacle.

THIRTEEN

Moralists of
Twentieth-Century Capitalism

THE MID-TWENTIETH CENTURY saw capitalism challenged externally by Soviet communism and internally by Depression. Although New Dealers and Keynesian economists viewed themselves as physicians to an ill capitalism, some were alarmed by their prescription of increased government involvement in the economy; meanwhile, academic literature discussed central planning, and nations in Western Europe had nationalized some industries. It is not surprising, then, that advocates of capitalism had reason to feel threatened and so mounted a defense. This chapter considers Friedrich Hayek's *The Road to Serfdom* (1944) Milton Friedman's *Capitalism and Freedom* (1962) both libertarian defenses of capitalism published in the late-war and cold war years; Michael Novak's *The Spirit of Democratic Capitalism* (1982) offered a theological defense of American capitalism at a later date.

FRIEDRICH HAYEK

A winner of the 1974 Nobel Prize in economics, Hayek (1899–1992) was a significant member of the Austrian School of economics, which emerged in the nineteenth century and had opposed European socialism. Despite roots in central Europe, this school shared many of the conclusions of Anglo-American laissez-faire. Hayek is best known outside the Austrian school for a short essay, *The Road to Serfdom*, which attacked what he saw as the moral failures of socialism. The book was widely read and discussed in the United States. *The Road to Serfdom* was written in wartime England and anticipated by more than a decade Milton Friedman's libertarian defense of free markets.

Hayek hailed the great expansion of the sphere of the individual in recent centuries. Individualism, he stated, is relatively new in history, dating only to the Renaissance (he ignored the Reformation) with a few earlier roots (Hayek 1944, 14). As individualism broke feudal restraints and liberated personal effort, it produced revolutions in science and industry, which—along with a market revolution—dramatically increased the Western standard of living, Hayek argued (15–17). Thus the historic case for individualism cites its material accomplishments.

Despite the benefits of individualism, Hayek argued, Western nations began to move toward collectivism. Once they began to take for granted material progress, Hayek claimed, Western peoples began to find fault with society's remaining imperfections, to extrapolate beyond actual progress to what they wished could be achieved (17). That is, Hayek turned popular dissatisfaction with industrial capitalism into a tribute to its progress (while ignoring other possible reasons for dissatisfaction). In any case, the proposed solution that Hayek attributed to the critics—central economic planning—attacked the very foundation of progress, namely, individual freedom.

Hayek attacked what he saw as the naïve belief that economic planning can be exercised while leaving the non-economic parts of society free. On the contrary, Hayek asserted, control of the economy inevitably leads to control of *everything*—he pointed to the then-recent examples of fascism and communism. His main argument, however, involved more than pointing to history: central planning logically *must* interfere with personal freedoms because planning must produce a particular plan and no particular plan can satisfy everyone (65). Planning's advocates, according to Hayek, naïvely favor *planning in the abstract* as an affirmation of rationality and order, ignoring that the essence of planning is in the details. But, he insisted on asking, whose ends are to be achieved as the details come into focus? The answer was the planner's ends. Other people's ends would not be satisfied. Hayek implied that any person's dislike of the central plan, for whatever reason, was as morally significant as the reasons for the plan.

Particular plans serve the ends favored by some and not others, for free people are diverse individuals and invariably have diverse goals. Even if everyone agreed that democratic voting would validate the plan, it is actually impossible for a democratic majority to exist for every tiny decision that would need to be made (Hayek 1944, 64). Thus, it proves necessary that the preferences of the *planners* should be forced on everyone else, he argued. Ultimately, Hayek suggested, the disparity between planners and citizens may require coercion to implement the plan.

This reasoning was linked to a discussion of morality. Central planners, according to Hayek, need a set of values by which to decide which of many possible outcomes should be actualized by The Plan. Planning requires a "complete ethical code" to rank the social value of virtually everything. But, because *humans are diverse and finite*, a moral code of such detail that everyone would agree to would be impossible. Planning everything would require a vast number of decisions, wrote Hayek, to which "existing morals have no answer" (58). Presumably this moral incompleteness is rooted in human finitude and limitations; in any case, any individual's perspective can encompass "only an infinitesimal fraction of the needs of all men" (59). This incompleteness of any consensus on priorities, and the need of planners for a complete hierarchy of values, guaranteed that arbitrary decisions would be made by the planners if only to fill in the gaps. Hayek left it to reader to draw the chilling implication that the only way everyone would be satisfied by the plan is that everyone should develop identical preferences to those of the planners—that is, surrender all individuality.

Because identical preferences are not attainable, the state may seek public acquiescence to the values embedded in its plan by controlling the factual information on which individuals must make decisions. Hayek argued that propaganda and false information rapidly become a tool of centralized regimes, for "official values" need to be "justified" by the facts (155). With the Soviet and Nazi examples close at hand, Hayek (155) convincingly asserted that propaganda's results "are destructive of all morals" that rely on "respect for truth."

The alternative to central planning is the market system, which, Hayek affirmed, grew as a twin of the Western individualist tradition. He stated that competition is the only way to coordinate economic activity without government planning (36). A competitive market contains information produced by the interacting of the preferences of millions, and the production decisions of millions, not of a few planners. Ultimately, prices in a competitive environment reflect all relevant information. The market's more informed decision-making preserves more freedom than planning does, presumably because it is more informed than planners can be.

Although he gave a strong endorsement of market capitalism, Hayek claimed not to be a disciple of laissez-faire. The state may have a legitimate role in guaranteeing the proper functioning of the market, or in making general environmental regulations, he said. Hayek (37) stated that "an extensive system of social services" could be compatible with market competition; he also noted that security against severe physical deprivation could be provided (120). However, what Hayek conceded in principle, he took back in application. He immediately added that the amount or type of support to the poor was open to debate; even with the principle accepted, social services could have a hard time actually being funded in a nation of libertarians. Hayek allowed for state action against depressions, yet quickly ruled out fiscal policy, which to many economists would be a necessary part of the mix (121). In the fine print, Hayek severely limited any economic safety net or anti-recession policy. To the careful reader, it would have appeared that Hayek deviated from laissez-faire very little despite his protestations to the contrary. Indeed, if citizens are so diverse that they cannot agree with central planners, then why would they find agreement on any government activities?

The case against planning reveals the structure of Hayek's interpretation of morality. His major premises are the finitude of any person's mind and the nearly infinite range of potential economic choices facing a person. Because finite humans necessarily possess only partial "scales of value" it is certain that different people will have different, and even conflicting, values. There is no transcendent position from which one might judge among, or harmonize, individuals' values. This suggests that no person's values should dominate any other person's and leaves only the "individual as the ultimate judge of his ends" (59). Human differences demand individualism, even autonomy, in ethics.

If planning is ruled out, how is it possible to achieve common goals? Hayek (60) allowed that common action may occur when people agree on common ends. However, he wrote ambiguously as to the amount of agreement necessary for a democratic state to act. He seemed to endorse state action at some level of agreement short of unanimity (the extreme libertarian position), but failed to define the level of agreement necessary. The reason not to act when there is too little agreement, of course, is the suppression of "individual freedom." A pure libertarian would require unanimity before a state could act: the imposition by even a supermajority on a single individual would be unacceptable. Hayek, after seeming to accept the democratic principle, remained ambiguous as to the size of the majority he would require for common action. If he was a democrat, in these passages he was not a democrat in the usual sense.

MORALITY AND REASON IN HAYEK

Hayek's book assigned at least three different meanings to morality. First, he wrote of the values by which planners and others rank states of the economy (57–59). That is, the good society is defined by one's values. That these values are fragmentary and differ among people is a key to his antiplanning argument. Hayek also defined morality as the common rules that circumscribe what is otherwise the realm of individual freedom (58). Hayek barely developed this definition and apparently saw is as a vestige of a less-individualistic past. Finally, in his discussion of propaganda, Hayek (155) asserted that respect for truth is a foundation for morality, and used this to condemn socialist propaganda.

Hayek's main discussion was of values as *preferences or tastes* by which one ranks states of the economy. In effect, he argued that planners would produce outcomes that some people *would not like*, because people's preferences (values) inevitably differ. The reasons people would dislike the central plan were never considered by Hayek; indeed, preferences or tastes are essentially innate (or arbitrary) and cannot be discussed. For Hayek, *any* preference disagreeing with the plan was as valid as any other preference. This is, of course, moral relativism. The failure to address better and worse reasons for disliking a central plan is the logical outcome of a position that views values as nothing but subjective tastes or preferences—about which reasoning is impossible. Because preferences are outside rational discourse, no case can be made that any person's tastes should be normative for anyone else.[1] This is as pure an expression as there is of the ethic of autonomy.

The values-as-preference case made against central planning boils down to the assertion that some people will dislike the plan. This highlights a defining feature of this version of libertarian ethics: few other moralities would equate moral values with likes and dislikes. In principle, Hayek's ethic ruled out reason as a way to judge which likes and dislikes might be more significant than others. In short, in promoting likes and dislikes to the status of moral norms, Hayek abolished moral reasoning or discourse.

Another failure of the values-as-preferences view was exposed when Hayek condemned socialist propaganda. Presumably truth was a norm with far stronger moral status than a mere preference for truth. The existence of some rather robust moral norm, such as the one used to condemn propaganda (truthfulness), is inconsistent with the relativistic, values-as-preferences morality Hayek otherwise promoted. And there is more to be learned from Hayek's condemnation of propaganda. Hayek worried that propaganda would present "facts" confirming a socialist worldview. Hayek obviously accepted that values are related to facts by some reasoning process—and thus are more than merely arbitrary preferences.

Given the difficulties with the values-as-preferences argument, perhaps the burden of the argument can be carried by Hayek's assertion that the competitive-market process is superior to the planning process (e.g., markets might use information better than planners do). Yet, if true, such technical superiority is not moral superiority. Further, much of the information processed by markets reflects how consumers with income spend it. Again, Hayek never established the *moral* superiority of such information.

Hayek (204–5) also argued that the market is non-coercive because it operates impersonally, as opposed to the arbitrary intervention into the lives of particular people under planning. But this remained a highly abstract idea, unrelated to everyday people. Hayek did not explain in what sense a citizen denied something by the market because she could not afford it would feel less coerced than when she was denied it because the product simply was not in the government plan. In particular, Hayek ignored those with no access to markets due to lack of income. Thus, reasons to prefer the market process over the planning process are inconclusive.

Finally, and, perhaps most important, ethically, Hayek insisted that the finitude and limitations of the human mind are central to moral analysis. This is an important insight, for which Hayek should be credited; yet, from it, he drew unlikely conclusions. Human limitations, he suggested, will result in people not only holding different values but accepting no compromise in getting what they want. However, finite and limited humans, who know they make mistakes for that very reason, should suspect that their own values just might be wrong, and that there could be room for compromise. In short, for central planning to be oppressive, Hayek's people must be limited so that they hold differing and fragmentary values, but nevertheless individually believe that they hold *ultimate* values that cannot be subject to compromise. If people understand their finitude, then few should be as dogmatic about the superiority of their preferences and desires as Hayek's argument requires. The possibility surely exists that discussion could lead to consensus among people who know they don't know everything.

MILTON FRIEDMAN

Milton Friedman (1912–2006) wedded libertarian values with the neoclassical perspective of Chicago (chapter 12). Neoclassical economics lends itself to a libertarian ethic because it makes self-interested behavior the defining human characteristic. In turn, economic freedom serves self-interested behavior. Libertarians make freedom, often seen as a natural right, an end in itself. But, whether as an instrumental good or as an inherent right, freedom is highly valued to both neoclassical and libertarian outlooks. Neoclassical economics makes a case for the market based on efficiency (chapter 12). Libertarians, without denying the market's efficiency, make the added case for the market as a counterweight to government (which could always threaten individual autonomy), and as a way to organize society that preserves maximum freedom. From both neoclassical and libertarian perspectives, individual autonomy ranks high as a value.

Friedman's *Capitalism and Freedom* (1962) was written when, as the result of the New Deal, World War II, and baby boom, American government (at all levels) had grown to previously unknown proportions. More than size of government, Friedman feared what seemed to be the growing adulation of the state. He scorned John F. Kennedy's famous advice to ask what one could do for one's country, which he interpreted as placing the state "over and above" individuals (Friedman 1962, 1). Governments are but instruments to individuals' ends and should not command respect.

Like Hayek, Friedman asserted that political freedom and market economics tend to accompany each other (9). Markets respect freedom because all transactions in a market are *voluntary*, being undertaken only when both parties benefit from the transaction (13). With this argument, he meshed the concepts of voluntarism (freedom) and efficiency: voluntary exchanges always improve efficiency because they occur only when mutual gains may be realized.

Although the market is the ideal form of organization, governments do have some role. Friedman, like Hayek, stated that libertarians are not anarchists. A chief function of government is, he said, to prevent individuals from coercing one another. Even a morality of individual freedom must impose something akin to what Francis Wayland called the reciprocity condition (26). The other fundamental roles of government are making sure markets can work, enforcing contracts and property rights, providing a stable money supply, promoting competition, and protecting child and "madman" if private efforts fail (27, 34). Friedman agreed in principle that market failures such as monopolies exist, but argued that in practice their behavior is so much like that of competitive firms that they *do not* justify much government intervention (see previous chapter). Friedman, like Hayek, accepted some role for government in principle, but then consistently argued for severely limiting its actual role.

Friedman's book offered several chapters that demonstrated how government programs tended to reduce individual freedom. One of his examples was education. Friedman was an early advocate of governments funding education, without producing it; education vouchers, he argued, could be provided to parents to use as they saw fit. Friedman's core reason for vouchers rested on differences in individual tastes, a fundamental libertarian and neoclassical proposition. Government-administered education provides a uniform experience, ignoring differences in tastes. Conversely, vouchers could be spent on any school and so would satisfy a wide range of parental preferences (Friedman 1962, 91). Compared to the lack of choice among the presumably uniform government-run schools, "a market permits each to satisfy his own taste" (94). Thus, vouchers would improve consumer satisfaction by better matching schools and students. Friedman did not heavily emphasize that vouchers would improve academic performance, a claim made in recent years.

If freedom is the ultimate moral standard, how is freedom defined? For the libertarian, as defined by Friedman, freedom lacks positive content, being defined negatively as the lack of constraint on the will: the moral norm is that "freedom has nothing to say about what an individual does with his freedom" (12). In short, freedom is a space within which the individual will fulfills itself in any way it chooses. Friedman would not discuss the private values that could fill the void. As with Hayek's values-as-preferences, the human would be left morally autonomous, free to choose altruism, stewardship, and benevolence—or selfishness, hedonism, and materialism—with no reason within the libertarian ethic to value one over the other. The major social rule, similar to Wayland's duty of reciprocity, was that individuals should not impinge others' rights to practice whatever values other people favored for whatever reason.

Friedman believed not only that government may be a threat to individual freedom, but that even corporate management may be a threat. He sketched an argument in *Capitalism and Freedom* (1962, 133–36), which he later elaborated, attacking the notion that corporations (and labor unions) have a *social responsibility*—whether to restrain price increases (in an inflationary era) or to do other deeds of good citizenship. His objection was that corporations exist only to serve their owners, the shareholders, and should leave morality to the underlying shareholders.

One of Friedman's arguments was to push moral decisions back on individual shareholders and not leave decisions of social responsibility to corporations. Although Friedman's distinction appears simple and clean, closer examination suggests a more complex reality. It may be that individual shareholders are unable to respond to problems created by their corporation in an effective way, although the corporation itself could respond effectively by not causing the problem in the first place. For example, shareholders may be in no position to ameliorate pollution caused by their corporation after it has happened; however, the firm may be in the position to prevent the pollution in the first place. Sometimes, the institution is forced to be the moral actor if a problem is to be addressed at all.

Friedman's argument against corporate social responsibility may leap beyond libertarian logic entirely. Unlike governments, corporations operate within markets. The virtue of markets, economists such as Friedman usually argue, is that all transactions are voluntary. If shareholders buy, or continue to hold, the stock of a socially responsible corporation, they must do so voluntarily. Thus, Friedman's claim—that socially responsible managements impose decisions on unwilling shareholders—seems inconsistent with claims about the virtue of markets.[2]

A thoroughgoing libertarianism would object to corporations as such and not merely to corporate social responsibility. Corporations are formed because governments charter corporations and assign important privileges to corporations—such as limited liability for the owners and the ability to raise capital by publicly issuing stock. When individuals choose to accept the benefits of the corporate form of association they are not merely covenanting together, but also with society, which charters corporations and grants them privileges. Shareholders are associating in a particular way, sanctioned by society, which would appear to provide a case for imposing social responsibilities on the form of organization itself. In short, the corporation *itself* is a testimony to the social nature of business. As such, a consistent libertarian might object to corporations.

FRIEDMAN IN A BROADER CONTEXT

Friedman, in common with Hayek, treated moral values as personal preferences, rooted in subjectivity and so outside the bounds of rational discussion. Further, in this framework, people are defined by their preferences, which simply exist and are unanchored in any social matrix.[3] That is, people are fundamentally a bundle of innate (autonomous) preferences. Given this, the only value that logically can be defended is freedom, a realm in which these preferences can have full play. The libertarian ethic, then, makes individual freedom *without constraint* into the highest value; all that is required of the individual is to respect others' freedoms. Freedom for humans, who are seen as bundles of innate desires, is the highest value of libertarianism. In common with the ethics of laissez-faire, this morality suffers from the problem of moral limits. It is one thing to propose that people respect others' freedoms (something akin to Wayland's duty of reciprocity). It is another to expect that persons habituated to thinking only about their own interests would actually restrain themselves when their own preferences loomed large enough to eclipse others' claims to respect.

While individual freedom is an important social value, other social values exist, and a tradeoff between these values and individual freedom may be ethically justified. For example, in the years immediately after Friedman proposed education vouchers, private academies sprouted across the southern United States for the primary purpose of avoiding integrated public schools. If education vouchers had existed at that time, they would have financed such schools. Should one value (free choice) trump all others? (Integration affirmed not merely equality, but human dignity by removing the indignity of segregation.) In other words, libertarians fail to answer whether there is ever an occasion when society should uphold values other than individual freedom and in doing so place social constraints on individual freedom.

Not all defenders of competitive capitalism have operated within a libertarian framework. In fact, the following moralist framed his argument in terms of Roman Catholic social thought. Given the different starting premises of the libertarians and the Catholic thinker Michael Novak, the similarity of their positions is surprising.

MICHAEL NOVAK: THE SPIRIT
OF DEMOCRATIC CAPITALISM

Michael Novak (1933–), a self-characterized Catholic lay-theologian, has argued that modern capitalist society rests on three pillars—the economy, the political system, and the religious-moral-cultural sector. These sectors intertwine, reinforce, and correct each other. Thus, capitalist morality need not be perfect, for where it is deficient the other two sectors remedy the deficiency. This argument is presented in his major work *The Spirit of Democratic Capitalism* (1982). On the surface, Novak's approach does not appear to be libertarian because moral norms may emerge from the moral-cultural sector to correct the libertarian tendencies of the economic sector. Ultimately, however, the necessary moral tension between the sectors is diminished by Novak to the point of vanishing. Novak validates capitalist economics with his view of theology.

Repeating a theme of Hayek and Friedman, Novak stated that it is no coincidence that capitalist societies are democratic, and democratic societies are capitalist. Persons who take responsibility for their economic lives develop the habits needed for self-government as well. Further, capitalist institutions, such as private property, check overreaching by governments. Conversely, the individual freedoms of democracy provide the basis for efficient markets, while the individualism of capitalism reinforces the religious individualism of the moral-cultural realm. Similarly, moral-cultural values can infuse participants in the economy with a broader outlook than commerce imparts.

The values of democratic capitalism are necessarily pluralistic, for this must be so whenever the individual is free. No authority imposes a single set of official values upon citizens as in feudal societies or communist societies. Because individuals adopt the values that seem best to them, pluralism is inevitable. There is "no sacred canopy" of officially sanctioned values, said Novak, a position almost identical to Hayek and Friedman. At a capitalist society's center "there is an empty shrine" (Novak 1982, 53). This means that society does not enforce official values; for example, it is indifferent between selflessness and selfishness. The one rule for society is that it must impose no absolutes on citizens. The similarity with secular libertarianism is obvious. Yet, Novak seemed to advocate this "empty shrine" as a pragmatic step, rather than as a libertarian principle.

Novak's analysis was not exactly that of a Hayek or Friedman. Novak avoided their moral relativism by falling back on the threefold nature of capitalist culture; values of a more robust nature may be promoted in the moral-cultural sector. Because people immersed solely in economic life may be morally stunted, "religious (and other) values are indispensable" in a capitalist society (80). Stated more strongly, the economy, in which autonomy values reign, requires "taming" by religious and other values (121). Economic behavior, though exempt from official criticism, is subject to critique by religion—a point on which Friedman and Hayek were silent. Novak thus suggests that a tension between the sectors should exist. However, his subsequent argument reverses course and seems to *harmonize* the morals of the sectors.

The capitalist economy, of course, is built on self-interest. Novak found much good in self-interest broadly understood. Summarizing Smith, Novak noted that material progress may best be obtained in a system that is non-judgmental about self-interested motives. In short, self-interest succeeds as a motivation (79).

Of most interest in our inquiry is Novak's effort to correlate capitalist economics with Christian doctrines. Novak's concept of co-creation generalized John Locke's insight that human labor can multiply nature's productivity. Novak (39) argued that nature is "incomplete," and that "humans are called to be co-creators" with God, essentially to complete what he as started. The stage for co-creation, he said, is the economic realm. In short, economic activity is given religious significance. Here Novak ignored biblical and creedal statements that place humanity firmly *within* creation, whose only special role is that of steward.

Novak (see, e.g., 210) constantly contrasted the optimism and activism of capitalism with the static mentality of noncapitalist societies. Optimism was, of course, related to the creativity of capitalist society. In contrast, noncapitalist societies believed that economics is a zero-sum game, in which the gain of one comes only at the expense of others. Therefore, precapitalist moralists scorned economic success because one's gain was assumed to be another's loss. Socialism strives for equality but destroys the incentives and creativity that make *everyone* better-off.

Continuing his integration of economic and theological ideas, Novak argued that democratic capitalism is well suited to deal with human sinfulness. He found pluralism's tolerance of less than moral perfection to be highly realistic. Socialism hopes to remake human character, but usually produces tyranny instead, he said. Democratic capitalism restrains evil because it possesses a moral-cultural sector that continues to teach virtue. In a pluralistic system, he argued, virtue will struggle with evil, and will often prevail (85–88). This view puts markets and churches together on the side of virtue. Yet this view obviously ignored the long-held Christian idea that sin and self-centeredness are closely bound together. If markets are the playing field for self-interest, there should be a greater tension between economics and theology than Novak seems to perceive.

To avoid what he regarded as the overworked word love, Novak wrote of *caritas*, to express the outgoing compassion of God. The relevant aspect of this doctrine for economics, according to Novak, was that love seeks the good of the other, whom it respects as a person. He claimed to find the pluralistic, capitalist order to be a social approximation of divine *caritas*. It is difficult to understand this attempt to portray the market order as motivated by love. Indeed, one wonders what contact Novak has had with modern economic institutions that would justify this claim. The purpose for markets is that people may relate through self-interested transactions. Transactions may be voluntary (in some sense), but they are not usually understood to be loving. The voluntary nature of transactions depends on the quid pro quo—each side gets something it wants. The self-giving motivation of love differs fundamentally from the motivation of the self-interested transaction. Stated slightly differently, economic transactions always are calculated—whereas a calculating mentality is the last thing to associate with love. Novak's association of economic noncompulsion with *caritas* does not do justice to the concept of love.

Novak addressed economic morality again in a short tract entitled *On Corporate Governance* (1997). Prepared originally as lectures, and more informal in tone than the earlier book, this short piece perhaps shows the logical end point toward which *Spirit of Democratic Capitalism* was headed. Novak perceived the corporation to be in real danger from reformers who would place the firm in a straitjacket. Contrary to the political state, checks and balances are the last thing a corporation needs; its mandate, to create wealth, requires managerial agility, he said. Novak noted that "the standards of accountability to be met by the head of a major corporation are far narrower" than those facing people who govern (1997, 6). Sounding much like Friedman, Novak (1997, 9, 28) exhorted corporations to resist various kinds of reformers. Presumably, this hard line would be justified by the outcome, for only when corporations prosper do more "of the poor rise out of poverty" (31).

Novak (19–24) imputed to corporate critics the motive of envy. This unfortunately ignored the substantive reasons given for reform by drawing attention to imputed intentions of the reformers. The only substantive issue Novak considered that might call for reform was income inequality, but he dismissed this as a problem on the grounds that Americans accept inequality. He also assured his readership that CEO pay is not a real ethical issue. Having left the impression on readers that corporations need no reforms, Novak concluded the essay by attributing major social problems to the state, which, he stated, overpromises and underachieves (30) This essay contains no sense of the valid roles played by the state and the moral-cultural sector that were central in his earlier book. By 1997, Novak was portraying the unbound corporation as an unalloyed blessing, needing no correction from other sectors of society.

NOVAK IN CONTEXT

Novak argued in *The Spirit of Democratic Capitalism* that the moral deficiencies of the economic sector could be checked by the political and moral-cultural sectors. Yet, historically, this claim seems questionable. During the nineteenth century, very little checking occurred; a laissez-faire economy dominated the other sectors—retarding government with its legal doctrines such as the doctrine of free contract, and drawing highly individualistic religion into the service of unimpeded capitalism. Nor, during much of that century, did the political and moral-cultural sectors check economic *practice* to any significant degree. Only with the Depression, and the consequent loss of laissez-faire's credibility, was there created some balance in the three-sectored society.

Novak's writing also stands in the moral tradition of Adam Smith's invisible hand, holding that the market turns self-oriented *motives* into good public *consequences*. An enduring ethical question—especially for a writer coming from a theological tradition—ought to be whether unintended good consequences can justify bad motives. A long scriptural and theological tradition focuses on the moral significance of a good will.

Novak's claim that what is wrong in economic life is corrected by the moral-cultural sector may be naïve. Novak's position depends on a vital moral-cultural sector. Perhaps Adam Smith could count on Protestant-dissenter businessmen to understood moral limits to economic behavior. It is questionable, however, whether such traditional religious constraints are even known, much less respected, in contemporary and thoroughly secular capitalist economies.

Novak was not the first to describe a three-sector society. Kenneth Boulding was a Quaker economist who developed a three-sector model similar to Novak's some decades before Novak. Like Novak, Boulding thought the moral-cultural sector (Boulding's *integrative sector*) would need to check the market sector and remedy its moral deficiencies. But Boulding wasn't sure it always worked that way, and took pity on the person whose moral character was shaped solely by the market system. If life is restricted to economic activity, he stated in a 1962 essay, the "essential virtues" would weaken, for the market does not sustain moral virtue (Boulding 1968, 236). In short, the self-interest of economic life may become the only morality of many participants—a stunting of their moral capacity. Perhaps Kenneth Boulding stated the most balanced summary and assessment of Novak's vision, years *before* Novak wrote. In a 1954 article, Boulding wrote that the market "must be hedged about with other institutions." He named home, school, and church. Only in these institutions, he said, "can the motive of responsibility [the social expression of love] develop. It is only as we are ourselves loved—by our parents, our mentors, and by our God—that we gain the capacity to love" (Boulding 1968, 218). In short, Boulding clearly located moral growth in a relational context—something he found missing in the market. The market must be hedged about because the self-interest of economic life is not self-limiting and the transaction is not the proper model for human relationships. Self-interest is not capable of producing an adequate morality. Instead, morality grows from living relationships, from the love of parents, mentors, and ultimately God; those relationships do not blossom in the market.

CONCLUSION

The libertarian view examined in this chapter was that humans are so dissimilar that moral consensus is impossible and individual freedom is the only social policy consistent with this reality. But social regulation of economic activity may not be an unwarranted intrusion on an essentially private realm that should be left free. If moral values *can* be discussed and reasoned about, then social consensus is possible and social norms for economics may be justified. A major premise of relational moralists has consistently been that humans have enough in common that moral discourse is possible—that consensus can emerge because humans share much. Relational moralists hold that the merits of individuals' desires and preferences must be compared to those of other individuals and to the merits of broader social goals.

The role for a libertarian government might be little more than enforcing something like Wayland's reciprocity condition (chapter 4). This is a logical requirement for a libertarian system to avoid a breakdown, which would occur if each person otherwise infringed the freedoms of others. However, the libertarians of this chapter are caught in an inconsistency. If there is so little commonality among people that personal values cannot converge, then even an agreement on the minimum elements of "reciprocity" may be impossible. Ultimately, libertarian morality represents the breakdown of morality as a human characteristic, the product of human discourse and reason, which are possible because of human commonalities.

Novak's outlook claimed to be different, for he seemed not to be an agnostic about the ability of moral discourse to occur. He seemed to be clear that the political and moral-cultural institutions of the tripartite society exist for such a discourse; in theory, a relational morality might hold forth in the moral-cultural sector. At least implicitly, some economic values could have been judged wrong and subjected to persuasive correction by the moral-cultural sector. This vision permitted economic activity (motivated by autonomy morality) to operate within moral limits imposed by a social consensus forged in the other sectors of society, which would have reflected the insights of relational ethics. Kenneth Boulding was explicit that his "integrative" sector was a realm of relational morality.

Although this was the possibility held out by Novak's three-part society, Novak's other statements seemed to deny the need for relational morality to have a foothold in his system. Novak's claims to find a parallelism between Christian concepts and capitalist practices suggest that he saw little moral tension between the values of the moral-cultural-religious sector and of the economic sector. This is seen, for example, when he conflated the creativity of God with that of markets, discussed sin without noting the traditional Christian link between sin and selfishness, and confused the nature of economic transactions with love. The moral tension in Novak's tripartite social system collapsed into little more than three different ways of stating the *same* economic values. In sum, Novak saw little reason for religious morality, which is typically relational, to check free-market economics; he proclaimed market economics itself to be an expression of Christian doctrines. This would then lead to complacency about what occurred within the marketplace—leading him to the same place the libertarians came out.

FOURTEEN

Unconventional Alternatives
to the Conventional Wisdom

WITH THE DEPRESSION, alternative ideas arose that did not well fit with the conventional economic thought and its coordinate value system. The neoclassical and libertarian descendants of laissez-faire did not accept this shift and forcefully restated in fresh terms the case for capitalism and autonomy morality (chapter 13). This restatement of the traditional economic morality, however, did not go unchallenged. The common theme of economists who found the traditional views wanting was that the utilitarian, self-oriented individual of neoclassical economics was one-dimensional both morally and economically. This chapter begins with John Kenneth Galbraith, who started to write even before the counterattack on Keynesianism had gained momentum.

JOHN KENNETH GALBRAITH

John Kenneth Galbraith (1908–2006) held that the reality of the American economy (which he said was *not* broadly competitive) and its prevailing ideology (which held it to be highly competitive) were at odds. In addition, conventional economics still worried about the nineteenth-century problem of scarcity, whereas the real question of the new era was how abundance was to be managed. The leaders of the private sector benefited from abundance, but gratefully used the ideology of scarcity to the disadvantage of the public sector and the small remnants of the competitive sector.

Galbraith comprehended that the prevailing perception of economics would help reinforce a culture's value system. In his first widely read book, *The Affluent Society* (1958, with subsequent revisions), he challenged what he called the conventional wisdom of traditional economics. The conventional presumption of scarcity had justified the greatest efforts to increase production. In the nineteenth century, a hands-off policy toward enterprise could be justified to favor more production. Scarcity also produced a harsh morality, for the perception was that society could spare little for its weaker members. This morality was no longer appropriate for the newly affluent society.

The mismatch between conventional wisdom and reality caused imbalance in the social order, according to Galbraith. The ancient threat of scarcity justified ever more production, with the result that so much was produced that the incremental private goods were of little social value. However, public goods were underproduced because of the antigovernment biases inherent in scarcity-based thinking. The illusion of scarcity causes people to exaggerate the sacrifice they would make in shifting resources to the public sector. Additionally, producers, needing to sell all the goods they could supply, create demand through advertising, thus creating a false sense of deprivation, stated Galbraith's *New Industrial State* (1967, 219). In denying scarcity, Galbraith rejected an axiom of neoclassical economics: in neoclassical thought, people's innate preferences were presumed to always prefer more to less, thus guaranteeing some sense of scarcity no matter how much a person possessed. Galbraith refused to accept a definition of the human psyche that guaranteed a permanent sense of scarcity.

Although advertising reinforces the sense of scarcity, so long embedded in conventional economics, it actually represents a mortal challenge to orthodoxy. First, orthodox economic theory requires that consumer demand be based on the independent, innate preferences of consumers. The entire elaborate argument that competitive markets produce Pareto efficiency holds without qualifications only if consumers have independent, or autonomous, preferences. But if advertising *creates* wants, consumers' preferences are not independent—for they are created by manipulation. If the consumer of neoclassical theory (and autonomy ethics) is truly sovereign, then advertising must fail, for such an autonomous individual will be unmoved by ads (1967, 214). Yet, as a contradiction to neoclassical theory, advertising is actually a multibillion-dollar industry. Some neoclassical economists simply ignore that advertising even exists.[1] Galbraith in his first major book concluded that ad-driven consumption is not valuable to society (1958, 129).

The power of advertising also was morally relevant, something Galbraith did not elaborate, but which is important to our inquiry. As noted (chapter 12), neoclassical economics held that the autonomous individual possesses his or her own preferences, the satisfaction of which is the "good" for that person. If advertising can manipulate the individual's preferences, the individual clearly does *not* have innate, autonomous preferences. It is a major problem for autonomy ethics if the individual's definition of his or her highest good can be manipulated by advertisers or other outsiders. The collapse of autonomy morality's central assumption—the self-defined individual with innate preferences—was implicit in Galbraith's writings on advertising.

Galbraith was almost as critical of Keynesian macroeconomics as of conventional economics. In his judgment, Keynesians were too willing to limit the role of the government to stimulating the economy. While it was a step beyond laissez-faire, Keynesian theory said nothing about how all the extra production, resulting from depressions avoided, should be allocated.[2] The Keynesian justification of *any* government spending as economic stimulus ran against the grain for Galbraith, who assigned moral value to the kinds of government spending.

Just as the conventional wisdom, forged in the nineteenth century, did not reflect modern affluence, it did not reflect the actual practice of corporations, wrote Galbraith. The conventional wisdom conveniently imposed stringent rules and restraints on the public sector and the economically weak. Meanwhile, corporations controlled demand for their products and their input costs, and so prospered. This was a theme that repeated itself in many of his writings, including the less-read *Liberal Hour*: "But the modern economic society does not conform to the competitive model" (Galbraith 1960, 51). Corporations controlled business risks in various other ways, including aggressive planning, demand manipulation through advertising, and lobbying the government. (By contrast, the Chicago economists were continuing to insist on the predictive accuracy of the competitive model; see chapter 12.) Galbraith sarcastically noted that insecurity, as a wholesome incentive, continued to be advocated only for the poor; and the virtues of price competition were reserved for small, competitive firms.

The only correction to this, he wrote, would be for an emancipated state to revitalize the public sector. However, Galbraith painted a picture of a state that was subservient to the corporate sector (*The New Industrial State*). In *Economics and the Public Purpose* (1973, 250–51), Galbraith made the "massive but central assumption" that the state could be emancipated from subservience and proposed several areas of needed action, including investment in areas such as health and housing, greater income equality, and protection of the environment; he also called for fewer subsidies to corporations.

Although he criticized aspects of Keynesian economics, Galbraith was willing to accept its full-employment policies; however, with full employment, the economy would be subject to inflationary pressures. These pressures he attributed to the noncompetitive corporate sector, and the large unions, which dominated the economy (Galbraith 1967, 256–59). His unconventional advice was to continue aggressive full-employment policies, but to invoke government wage and price controls (1967, 260–64). Galbraith thought inflation was largely characterized by private price-setting and that there was good reason that the public interest be represented in controlling prices.

As Galbraith challenged the premises of neoclassical economics, he implicitly challenged the morality that conformed to that vision. His emphasis on the public sector was meant to uphold the value of social infrastructure over more private spending. His concern for all in society was at odds with neoclassical economics, which never believed enough resources existed for private use—for individual preferences could never be sated. Galbraith knew that the centrality of advertising in the modern economy was totally inconsistent with the neoclassical theory of autonomous "economic man," of consumer sovereignty, and of moral autonomy. An individual shaped by advertising deserves no more moral status than advertising itself.

It has often been observed that Galbraith was a successor to Veblen (chapter 8). In a very broad sense, both developed the same thesis: economic reality outruns ideologies, leaving the ideologies to serve privileged interests. Both saw economics through the lens of the evolution and behavior of economic sectors, rather than the narrow behaviors of individuals and single firms. And both came to the conclusion that the ideology embedded in traditional economics is, in fact, erroneous. Another notion of the good was needed. For Galbraith, the reality of abundance created the moral obligation for collective action to end want and enhance public infrastructure.

JOHN RAWLS ON DISTRIBUTIVE JUSTICE

John B. Rawls (1921–2002) was a political philosopher whose two works (*A Theory of Justice*, 1971, and *Justice as Fairness*, 2000) probed the essentials of a just society. Specifically, he asked whether greater equality should be required to attain justice in the way a pluralistic, modern society would define justice. In effect, he was looking for the economic principles essential to a modern society's constitution. Rawls's notion of society was modern, not only in assuming a pluralistic population, but also in assuming people possessing a modern (i.e., Enlightenment) outlook. Specifically, Rawls accepted the Enlightenment idea of self-interest and argued for principles of justice that individuals would rationally accept on the basis of self-interest. This starting point led Rawls to a strong case for greater equality. This is a significant result because norms favoring economic equality have failed to emerge from traditional political economy, which shares an Enlightenment outlook. In short, Rawls's result, if correct, suggests that that traditional political economy has reached the wrong conclusion, given its own premises.

Rawls used a social-contract argument, much as John Locke did. Locke's state of nature became, for Rawls, an "original position" characterized by a "veil of ignorance." Representatives of a society yet to be formed would meet in a constitutional convention, as it were, behind a veil of ignorance, to agree to the principles of justice to be built into the society. True to Enlightenment-modern ideals, these representatives would be *free and equal* participants, who in turn would represent free and equal citizens of the future. In Enlightenment fashion, their motivation for forming society would be very much self-interest: to *gain from common action while retaining freedom and equality*. By equality, Rawls meant that people possess all the "moral powers necessary to engage in social cooperation . . . and to take part in society as equal citizens" (Rawls 2001, 20). This is strictly moral equality, not economic equality. Moral equality is assumed; any case for economic equality must be demonstrated.

The "veil of ignorance" specifically means that representatives to the constitutional convention do not know the social and economic positions they (or the group they represent) hold or will hold (Rawls 2001, 14–17). They do not know even the probabilities of their holding various positions in society. They are also ignorant of the degree of social and economic difference that exists, or will exist, between groups. The purpose of this ignorance is to promote impartiality: since no one knows his or her position, there are no self-interested reasons to support provisions that unfairly advance or hinder a particular group. Rawls stated it: "accidental influences from the past should not affect an agreement on principles" (16). Ignorance eliminates this problem, wrote Rawls.

Rawls then asked what fundamental principles would be adopted by such a constitutional convention. The first principle, which always would take priority over others, reads that everyone has the same right to "equal basic liberties" such as liberty of conscience and thought; political liberties; rights within the legal system; rights and liberties required for the person to participate in society (42–47). Economic equality is not considered one of the basic equalities.

Of greater interest for economic morality, Rawls argued that a second, dual principle of justice would emerge: (1) any social or economic inequalities must "be attached to offices and positions open to all under conditions of fair equality of opportunity" and (2) any inequalities are to "be to the greatest benefit to the least-advantaged members of society" (42–43). He called this latter principle the "difference principle." It means that inequalities in income may be accepted for the sake of gains to society; however, only the inequality that *leaves the worst-off group in the best position* available from all alternatives is permitted. The magnitude of the inequality is not at issue: a greater inequality than at present that put the worst-off in the best possible position would be acceptable. The difference principle, said Rawls, reflected notions of fairness that representatives operating behind a veil of ignorance would adopt.

Rawls's difference principle may be compared to Pareto efficiency (chapter 12). The difference principle permits ranking all possible Pareto-efficient economies, whereas the Pareto principle cannot rank them. The Pareto criterion considers all efficiency improvements equally desirable. However, by the difference principle, the particular Pareto improvement that bettered the lot of the worst-off the most would be preferred. A Pareto improvement that simply left the worst-off no worse could be acceptable under the difference principle only if there was no alternative that would make them better-off. Thus, the difference principle provides one way to deal with the incompleteness of the Pareto ethical norm.

Rawls, as noted, insisted that the first principle of justice (i.e., equal political liberties) always takes priority over the difference principle. This ruled out
the possibility that the worst-off group would trade way political rights and liberties for the sake of improving their economic status in society. Rights and liberties define the nature of the society being constructed and are nonnegotiable.

A striking feature of Rawls's argument was that society is populated by
humans who are in many ways like the "economic man" of political economy—founding a society only for what it can benefit them or their group.
They are placed behind a veil of ignorance precisely to deny them the information needed to act on their self-interest narrowly understood. What stands
in stark contrast to traditional economics is that Rawls's argument produces
constitutional rules that favor the economically worst-off. Rawls's result differs from that of laissez-faire and welfare economics, which justified whatever
distributive outcome happened to result from a free market.

In conclusion, Rawls's ideas started with the same rational, self-interested
Enlightenment people that orthodox political economy started with. Yet, he
came to the very different conclusion from political economy, which has traditionally found reasons to defend the economic status quo. What, then, led
to this different conclusion? Ultimately, it was that Rawls's humans had
enough in common that rational participants in the "constitutional convention" could know that being worst-off in a society can be intolerable for anyone. And, they assumed that people will have enough in common to apply the
difference principle, which requires some idea of how much people are bene-
fiting from an economic change. This is a conclusion the welfare economists
could never have reached, given their self-imposed psychological agnosticism,
which forbade interpersonal welfare comparisons. Rawls assumed much was
shared by humans—that they had more in common simply as humans—than
neoclassical economists have been willing to admit. Rawls reached conclusions about distributive justice by rejecting the exceptional model of humanity embodied in neoclassical economics as it unfolded in the twentieth century—namely, individuals so self-encapsulated that agnosticism on issues of
distribution would be the only position possible.

ARTHUR OKUN

Arthur Okun (1928–1980) is remembered for a statistical regularity he discovered between unemployment and economic growth; he was an economic
adviser to President Lyndon Johnson in the era that saw the highpoint of Keynesian policies and large increments in social-welfare programs. However,
Okun's essay, *Equality and Efficiency: The Big Tradeoff* (1975), stepped outside
technical research to explore the moral boundary between the realm of the
market and the realm of the community. His book's title suggests that economic efficiency is but one social good among others—human equality being

the major alternative good. The first chapter defines a *domain of rights*, in which all persons receive recognition as full members of the community. The domain of rights contrasts sharply with the market economy in which income inequality and other distinctions differentiate persons. A good society, argued Okun, provides fundamental rights freely and equally to all citizens, regardless of their economic status (here, he had been influenced by John Rawls). Rights affirm "the human dignity of all citizens" and are the signs of membership in the community (Okun 1975, 14). In addition, rights are "part of the checks and balances on the markets designed to preserve values that are not denominated in dollars" (13). Rights start with legal rights, such as the right to vote or to free speech. A society, as it is able, may also guarantee economic entitlements such as a minimum wage, old-age pension, or guaranteed medical care. At the extreme, the realm of rights might vastly expand to mandate income equality. The rationale for all nonmarket rights is human dignity, "the moral worth of every citizen" and "the mutual respect of citizens for one another" (47). However, in contrast to his insistence on political equality, Okun ultimately did not insist on complete income equality. As will be seen, he thought that equality of income would affect the performance of the economy; it therefore required careful consideration.

For Okun, a society organized solely along market lines would be an ethically deficient "vending machine" society in which everything had its price (13). The moral deficiency resides in the fact that some things cannot be marketed without destroying their essential purpose. Nobel prizes, summa cum laude honors, and Olympic medals are marks of personal excellence whose meaning is rendered null if the award can be bought, he noted. Similarly, based on the doctrine of the innate human dignity of all, life and death should not depend on one's financial ability to buy transplant organs. An all-encompassing market also would be deficient for permitting "trades of last resort," bargains made out of desperation that demean the inherent dignity of man and woman.

Okun argued that the boundary between the realm of rights and the realm of the market is fluid and sloppy. The domain of rights guarantees everyone the same vote, yet money allows one person to run political ads while the other cannot. All are guaranteed a fair trial, but one defendant can hire the best attorney and the other cannot. While leveling all incomes might solve these problems, Okun preferred a strategy of dealing with such imbalances in the civic realm through specific regulations (30–31).

As an advocate of innate human dignity, with its nonmarket realm of rights, Okun dissented from the conventional economic tradition, including its usual justifications of market-determined income inequalities (40–47). However, he did not push his dissent to advocating full income equality because this would impose costs of its own. He was not blind to the things a market does well: specifically, increasing efficiency (50–51). He did not

believe that market efficiency required as much inequality as the present system creates, but he would have preserved the current system for what it does
well. Morally, he would have restricted the distribution patterns of markets;
economically, he viewed markets as efficient producers.

He summed this up as the big tradeoff between economic efficiency and
greater income equality. To act on the moral case for greater equality, a society must pay the price of a smaller national income. He used a telling
metaphor: the leaky bucket. A bucket is used to transfer water (income) from
rich to poor, yet it leaks (inefficiency). A gallon, which is taken from the rich,
results in less than a gallon reaching the poor. In effect, the redistribution itself
causes the economy to dry up to a degree. To change the metaphor: the more
evenly the pie is sliced, the smaller the entire pie becomes. In assigning this
much power to incentives, Okun differed from other economic moralists outside the orthodox tradition, who typically minimize incentive effects.

Okun realized that some, for moral reasons, would keep on bailing from
the cisterns of the rich even if nothing reached the poor. For these people,
equality itself is the goal, even if everyone is left impoverished. At the other
extreme, others would favor no distribution at all even if nothing leaked from
the bucket (essentially the result of laissez-faire and neoclassical welfare economics). Okun stated that he would choose a leakage rate somewhere between
the extremes. The acceptable leakage rate would depend on specifics, such as
how rich the rich were, and how poor the poor. The degree of leakage one
would tolerate is an exercise that exposes one's values.

Okun treated the willingness to tolerate leakages essentially as an unex-
plained preference, thus adding little moral insight as to what criteria might
define a just amount of redistribution. Okun, who followed Rawls loosely in
defending a realm of political rights, thus apparently was unwilling to adopt the
difference principle. He believed that a society ought to move toward equality as
an affirmation of innate human dignity, yet he held that the degree of movement
may be restricted by the shrinkage of the economic pie. He was silent about what
moral principle he would juxtapose against dignity to determine when further
shrinkage of the economy morally overwhelmed greater income equality.

Although Okun's own position was silent at a crucial place, he did not
allow the narrow pronouncements of welfare economics to be the last word on
economic morality. He rejected the agnosticism of the welfare economists: his
common humanity told him that those with the least income benefited from
the additional income more than the rich lost from the transfer. Okun did not
reject efficiency; he held it in tension with equality. This meant that a society
would have to be willing to pay for its moral convictions by accepting the
tradeoff between achieving moral goals and lesser economic output. He was
not willing to make morality easy, by claiming it came with no cost.

Okun's essay also dealt with another moral issue: *where does a moral society set the boundaries of markets?* Historically, the issues of equality and of

boundaries have been interrelated: as market boundaries have been narrowed (e.g., health care put outside the realm of the private market in some countries), the result has been more equal access to what used to be rationed by income, thus effectively equalizing standards of living. Okun believed that the market ought to be kept in its place—recognition of the moral need for boundaries. As the alternative to defining how equal rights should be, Okun seemed willing to settle for an uneasy truce along a somewhat porous border between the realm of rights and the realm of market economics. While this answer is not entirely satisfying, it is a move beyond the ethical incompleteness of welfare economics. Okun made progress by adopting components of relational morality—specifically, the norm of human dignity as something to be honored by society.

Okun's essay highlighted several features of relational economic morality. His emphasis on rights as an aspect of human dignity (as opposed to rights to protect individual autonomy) was characteristic of relational ethics. He also recognized that rights were an expression of the human community and guaranteed one's place in community. Okun demanded a place in society for the market, and also that the market be kept in its place. Relational morality has always accepted market economics (consider that Quakers were famous for their commerce); but, in contrast to autonomy morality, it has always recognized the need for boundaries around markets to protect human values. Okun thought explicitly about where to place the boundaries between the market sector and the rest of society.

AMARTYA SEN

Amartya Sen (1933–), a Nobel winner in economics (1998), has consistently criticized economics for its deficient moral posture. His thoughts were concisely expressed in three lectures published as *On Ethics and Economics* (1987). Sen's first lecture noted that the ancient connection between economics and ethics has become weaker and weaker—to the detriment of both disciplines. His lecture highlighted the growing gap between ethics' and economics' definitions of rationality. Economic theory assumes that humans behave according to a very particular kind of rationality—"that of self-interest maximization." Economics would call someone "rational" simply for taking action based on a cost-benefit calculation of its impact on his or her personal welfare. Wrote Sen (1987, 15), such a view of rationality "has become one of the central features of mainline economic theorizing for several centuries." He noted that ethics recognizes various rational paths for human action.

Sen (15) asked rhetorically why should it "be *uniquely* rational to pursue one's own self-interest to the exclusion of everything else"? Many actions are rational without being purely self-interested, he noted. The notion that humans are solely self-interested is not even good science for it fails to describe actual economic behavior very well. Perhaps with George Stigler (chapter 12) in mind, he stated that "claims that the self-interest theory 'will win' [in explaining behavior] have typically been based on some special theorizing rather than on empirical verification" (18). Sen was careful not to argue that people are always selfless. Yet, humans are motivated by a variety of things other than self-interest that can hardly be called irrational. He cited none other than Adam Smith who ascribed many motives to man in his *Theory of Moral Sentiments*.[3]

In the second lecture, Sen dissected the welfare economists' criterion of Pareto optimality (chapter 12), showing how small a moral accomplishment it was. Sen (32) reminded the reader of the ethical incompleteness of Pareto optimality: an efficient economy can exist "with some people in extreme misery and others rolling in luxury." That is, welfare economics produced no theory of distributive justice or fairness.

This point, however, has been made by many. Sen continued lecture two with a more penetrating critique. He noted conventional economics' utilitarian assumption that "the goodness of a state of affairs [is] a function only of the utility information regarding that state" (39). But, asserted Sen, moral human beings do not restrict their notion of goodness to assessments of their utility (or well-being) alone. The ethical person also understands himself or herself in terms of "goals, commitments, values," what Sen called a person's "agency." Sen (41) continued that someone's agency can include "considerations not covered—or at least not *fully* covered—by his or her own well-being." This observation strikes at the core of economics' traditional self-interested and utilitarian understanding of humans. Yet it merely affirms what is commonly acknowledged by the deepest expressions of literature, religion, and arts, as to what it means to be a human.

Sen made another fundamental critique of the use of subjective well-being as the sole ethical norm. He observed that persons suffering miserable lives may well adjust expectations. Thus, the sense of well-being that those greatly deprived derive from "small mercies" may be great; they may have so suppressed any desire for hopelessly unattainable goods that "their deprivations are muted and deadened" (46). An ethically adequate assessment of the state of such people would show them to be far worse off than an assessment based on their subjective "utility"—the only norm of neoclassical economics. Sen's point was that even if economists overcame the agnosticism of welfare economics and actually used an individual's subjective utility as a measure of welfare, this norm would still ignore people's ability to bias their perceptions of their own welfare. Sen appealed to common humanity as a source for understanding when he stated that it is possible to judge people to be far worse-off than even their own deadened self-perceptions recognize. In short, Sen was working from the proposition that people share a common humanity and so can say morally meaningful things about each other. That is, a proper judgment about someone's welfare may even differ from the person's own assessment.

Sen returned to neoclassical economics' dictum that humans are self-interested maximizers of personal well-being. This is really a compound claim with three parts, he said. First is the assumption of egoism (see chapter 12). Second is the dictum that the rational goal is utility or welfare maximization. Third is that every choice "is guided immediately by the pursuit of one's own goal" (80). Thus economic orthodoxy requires the improbable: that *three* stringent conditions be simultaneously met.

Sen closed with an extensive analysis of the third condition—that each person is guided immediately by pursuit of his or her personal goal. Experiments show that people actually behave far more cooperatively than this condition allows. Citing certain game simulations, in which self-interest always seeks to exploit a partner rather than cooperate with the partner, Sen (84) noted that in fact "cooperation does seem to emerge in these games." Thus, said Sen, the evidence is weak for the existence of the utility-maximizing "economic man" of neoclassical economic theory.

Amartya Sen lends the authority of a Nobel-prize holder to the proposition that conventional economics has promoted an inadequate morality. His argument is that the utility-maximization assumptions not only produce a deficient morality but that they provide a poor basis for the scientific study of economic behavior. It should be clear that Sen, and other critics, do not claim that self-interest has no place in understanding human behavior, or that any self-interest is morally wrong. They object to orthodoxy's insistence that self-interest is the *exclusive* driving force of human behavior. And they object to the inescapable conclusion, based on that premise, that morality is at most an expression of self-interest. While Sen's essay was largely a critique of the morality of neoclassical economics, one should not overlook that his notion of human "agency" embodied some of the core premises of relational ethics.

A SUMMARY AND SHORT CONCLUSION

The common element in each of these writings is the challenge to major premises of conventional economics and the suggestion of better premises. Galbraith recognized that the "conventional wisdom" (i.e., scarcity and competition) justified the economic status quo, at the very time that abundance and planning had replaced scarcity and competition. The result was a social imbalance between the private sector and the public, with the victims of the imbalance being the most disadvantaged. A consistent question of economic morality has been where the boundaries of the market should be drawn. Galbraith's answer was that human welfare would be greatly improved by an expanded public sector and greater constraints on the corporate sector. He treated this conclusion as the natural outcome of removing the false perceptions of the conventional wisdom, although he did not theorize about alternative moral premises.

In some ways, John Rawls's challenge to the orthodox economics is the most fundamental. Starting with the same self-interested, utilitarian people posited by political economy, he arrived at very different definition of a just distribution of income. This suggests that the long tradition of laissez-faire and neoclassical economics has perhaps reasoned incorrectly, or inserted some hidden assumptions, to reach its hands-off policies toward the status quo of income distribution. A likely candidate is the insistence in the conventional economics that humans are so self-encapsulated that they share nothing, that they are alien to each other. Thus, no shared judgments can be made about the welfare of others or about a good society. As far as such agnostic people know, the status quo may be as good as any other situation. Rawls challenged this with the sensible proposition that representatives to an original constitutional convention could understand what poverty might mean to each other and to future generations. Indeed, their consensus would mean that human commonalities dominated differences.

Arthur Okun believed that markets, in their realm, were highly productive and therefore necessary; nor did he strongly challenge neoclassical economics as such. (In this sense, he was somewhat like Keynes and Samuelson; see chapter 11.) Yet, unlike the most orthodox economists, he never believed that the norm of efficiency was the most that economists should say about the nature of the good society. He insisted that efficiency could not be the sole moral norm. Although Okun did not elaborate his reasons for acknowledging a realm of rights, he seemed to reflect the influence of John Rawls. The closest Okun came to justifying his position was a negative argument; he refuted various reasons typically advanced for the justice of the prevailing (highly unequal) distribution of incomes. Having removed such reasons to keep the status quo, Okun was open to the possibility of greater equality. For Okun, efficiency was a genuine norm, but he never considered it the sole basis of an ethic.

Sen's greatest contribution is a sense of alternative philosophical and ethical traditions. He marvels at the extraordinarily narrow meaning that the word "rational" takes within traditional economics—to calculate one's own advantage—and he protests at the hijacking of the meaning of the word. In so doing, Sen objects to the extraordinary claim of neoclassical economics that moral commitments that require sacrifice are not "rational."

Although these moralists addressed various issues, a theme connected their statements. In one way or another, each held that economics should be designed to serve a higher notion of human dignity than that recognized in neoclassical economics. Galbraith said little explicitly about dignity, but his argument amounted to destroying the traditional argument that society was too poor to afford to care about the weakest of its members. Rawls and Okun explicitly focused on rights, which are recognitions of the dignity that all would claim for themselves. Sen critiqued the one-dimensional vision of humans incorporated in neoclassical economics. Ultimately, such a one-dimensional version of humanity demeaned human dignity.

All these authors emphasized one or more aspects of relational morality and critiqued one or more aspects of autonomy morality. All but Rawls were economists and all appreciated the market economy and the contributions of traditional economics; none was a socialist. However, the significant difference between Galbraith, Okun, Rawls, and the neoclassical economists is that they recognized the need for boundaries to the market—the classic tendency of relational moralists to limit markets to their significant moral functions. Okun and Galbraith disagreed on where the boundaries might be set (Galbraith would have restricted the private sector far more than Okun). However, relational morality has never advocated a rigid formula for the placement of boundaries; the tendency has been to set bounds to protect human relationships and fulfill the obligations of a society to its members when markets threaten those relationships and obligations. This is surely an evolving norm. Rawls showed that utilitarian thinking can benefit from a major premise of relational morality: that humans can understand each other, have common concerns, and therefore can reach consensus on limits to market outcomes (at least when they are freed from their vested interests by the "veil of ignorance"). Sen concentrated more on the one-dimensional understanding of human nature embedded in neoclassical economics. He understood people to live in many dimensions, including the dimension of their commitments to other humans.

FIFTEEN

An Ecumenical Consensus
on Economic Ethics

DESPITE GROWING CRITICISM within the discipline (chapter 14), the mainstream neoclassical economics in the late twentieth century continued to understand humans primarily in terms consistent with autonomy morality. As well, economists were prominent among extremely libertarian moralists. Although there have been religious writers whose ethic was compatible with that of traditional economics (e.g., Paley, Wayland, Bruce Barton, Novak), many religious thinkers across three major Western traditions have articulated a relational moral vision. As early as the 1960s, the Jewish teacher Abraham Heschel labeled the self-interested, modern life (largely shaped by economics) as devoid of moral content. In a 1986 pastoral letter, U.S. Roman Catholic bishops stated that economic institutions should be judged by the standard of their contribution to the greater human community. About the same time, a team of sociologists with a distinctly theological orientation, headed by Robert Bellah, documented the deficiencies of autonomous individualism in modern Americans' everyday lives. The Protestant ethicist Philip Wogaman directly confronted the neoconservative defense of free-market ethics, primarily critiquing its failure to understand humans as social beings. In the mid-1990s, the Friends Committee on National Legislation restated the Quaker vision of economic morality, affirming principles stated as early as William Penn and John Woolman (chapter 2). At the turn of the millennium, Protestant theologian Sallie McFague produced a postmodern critique of the autonomy values that underlie the American economic culture; she used contemporary ecology to argue for a relational economic ethic. This ecumenical group is united in critiquing the neoclassical economic morality by insisting that life in inherently relational.

ABRAHAM HESCHEL ON MORAL AUTONOMY

Abraham Heschel did not explicitly engage economics. Nevertheless, he summed up the biblical critique of the utilitarian and self-oriented thinking that encapsulates the moral values of modern economics. He was forced to address the issue because this is the moral posture generally of modern persons. The modern person "feels, acts, and thinks as if the sole purpose of the universe were to satisfy his needs" (Heschel 1955, 34–35). Heschel protested the modern's tendency to be guided by amoral calculations of benefits and costs weighed on the scale of self-interest.

Such utilitarianism denies the very essence of human nature, which is *not* fulfilled by gratifying the ego, said Heschel. The truth is the opposite, for the essence of the human is "in his ability to stand above his ego" and to make the holy more important than the self (117). Heschel's point applies to modern economic thought perfectly: a moral being's nature lies in transcending the very self-orientation that defines the person of neoclassical economic theory. Heschel (169) did not deny the reality of self-interest or even condemn it indiscriminately, but warned that it easily transforms into a "suffocating selfishness."

The twin of self-interest is an extreme sense of personal autonomy, or freedom, as libertarians emphasize. Heschel's biblical sensibilities, however, immediately saw the emptiness of a freedom whose content is defined only by personal desire: "Is liberty alone, regardless of what we do with it," he asked, "the highest good" (170)? He suggested that the meaning of liberty depended on its righteous use. This pointed to the emptiness and relativism of libertarian ethics and economics.

Although Heschel was not singling out economics, his writings came close to the target. The autonomy ethic and related neoclassical economics have asserted that morality must conform to a reality defined by exclusively self-interested persons. Conversely, Heschel (374) restated the biblical tradition, pointing out that the self can become "rival of the good" and of God. He concurred that ego is indeed a powerful reality, but, unlike the political economists, did not exult in this fact; nor, like the libertarians, did he ever consider that freeing the ego from all possible constraints was the sum of morality. Indeed, the unbridled self is prone to excess. Conversely, Heschel affirmed that "virtue demands self-restraint, self-denial" (374). Self-restraint, as noted, is an unfailing theme of relational morality.

The mere existence of self-interest is not evil. Rather, Heschel said (400) that evil lies in the inability of a self—detached from others—to restrain itself. Ultimately it sets up itself "as the ultimate goal." This is, of course, a spiritual evil as well as a moral evil—for an inflated Self may become one's god. In contrast to autonomy ethics, he said (399) the biblical insight is that the good "is the attachment of the soul to a goal that lies beyond the self."

Rabbi Heschel said little explicitly about economics. And yet his religious insights directly challenged the core assumptions of autonomous individualism—which had been restated in ever more stringent terms by the twentieth-century neoclassical school.

THE U.S. CATHOLIC BISHOPS ON ECONOMIC LIFE

In 1986, the Catholic bishops of the United States published a pastoral letter entitled *Economic Justice for All*. Their starting point was scripture and Catholic teaching (see also chapter 10), not a preconceived theory of how the economy works. Thus they avoided starting with economic theory, which has a history of declaring many moral reforms to be scientifically unfeasible. By beginning with religious teaching, the bishops avoided having their moral thought censored in this way by traditional economics.

The ethic of the pastoral letter embodied three principles. First, social duties and rights are directed toward enhancing human dignity (National Conference 1986, pars. 69, 70; all references to document paragraphs). Second, human dignity depends on participation in community (pars. 63–65, 77–79). And, finally, the economic order exists to serve the life of the community, particularly its weakest members (pars. 38, 66, 70, 71). However, the bishops resisted deriving a set of economic prescriptions or policies from these principles. Rather, they recommended incremental, trial-and-error changes whose direction is informed by the moral principles.

In contrast to the tradition of political economy, the bishops did not censor moral ideas that did not easily accommodate to hypothesized economic laws. In fact, the bishops (par. 92) rejected the notion of "inexorable laws" of economics. By this they did not mean that any economic arrangement would work as well as the next—that moral principles alone may dictate the design of an economy. They seem to have meant that any economic regularities are far less restrictive than traditional economic theory would have it. The bishops took the pragmatic position of trying morally acceptable plans to see what would work. Economic morality "must interact with empirical data," they declared (par. 134). In short, the interaction of morality with economics must reveal itself through experimentation with policies rather than adherence to a priori economic doctrine.

Perhaps as a passing reference to the work of Michael Novak (chapter 13), the pastoral letter disavowed the libertarian notion that the free market "provides the greatest possible liberty, material welfare, and equity" (par.128), or "automatically produces justice" (par. 115).[1] Instead, the bishops (pars. 128, 129) placed themselves in the tradition of relational morality that "the economy has been created by human beings and can be changed by them." In short, ethics, not economic theory, should lead in thinking about economic morality.

The bishops' central norm was *human dignity in community*, and those on the margin of community require special attention, they said. All institutions of the society, from government to business firms to volunteer organizations, are morally responsible to integrate the weak into the economic community. According to the bishops (par. 189), voluntary charity cannot produce the results that are required, "private charity and voluntary action are not sufficient." The society is morally required to preserve a place for the weak in community; this obligation cannot be delegated to optional charitable activity. The value of community is so great in the pastoral letter that the bishops even favored some uneconomic policies, such as subsidizing functioning agricultural communities, to assure the vitality of communities. Although the bishops recognized the efficiency of very large farms, they expressed concern over the loss of small farms because this loss undermines viable rural communities (par. 226).

The importance of community is seen in the bishops' discussion of business. They sounded the familiar theological note that ownership of property never conveys absolute authority to do as one wills. Businesses have benefited from their communities, and so are accountable to them (par. 113). In direct contrast to the libertarian assertion that firms owe nothing to society except profitability (chapter 13), the bishops affirmed (par. 111) that the true calling of business managers is to the public good.

A moral society may be structured in many ways. Human dignity, not the particular shape of an economic system, is what counts. The bishops recommended an incremental approach. Start with the actual economy and if economic practices do not meet the norm of "human dignity lived in community, they must be questioned and transformed" (par. 28). Presumably a number of potential reforms could be undertaken, and there is no unique blueprint of the just society.

In another break with neoclassical economic doctrine, the bishops rejected the notion that moral reform imposes a tradeoff of reduced economic efficiency or reduced growth. They suggested that practices that enhance human dignity could actually improve economic performance. For example, greater corporate democracy "can enhance productivity" (par. 300). This possibility runs directly counter to Darwinian arguments of conventional economists that in the competitive struggle for survival any changes that enhanced efficiency already would have been discovered. The bishops imply that the Darwinian drive for efficiency takes place in one dimension, while totally ignoring possibilities that do not fit the neoclassical model.

The pastoral letter (par. 5) contended that markets shape human moral character. The bishops expressed dismay at the materialistic expressions of self-interest promoted by advertising (par. 345). And they warned that people may define themselves only with respect to their own position and goals instead of the fuller human community (par. 22).

When the bishops' pastoral letter is compared to the earlier teachings of Pope Leo and Monsignor Ryan (chapter 10), the comparison reveals that the bishops have continued the emphasis on human dignity. The notion of human dignity has been somewhat reshaped as well: there is less emphasis on a natural-law notion of dignity; now dignity is defined as *dignity-in-community*—an even clearer expression of the intertwining of dignity and human relationship.

ROBERT BELLAH: HABITS OF THE HEART

The thesis of Robert Bellah and colleagues' widely read *Habits of the Heart* (1986) was outlined by him several years earlier in a short article. In it he argued that Enlightenment social philosophy had decisively shaped modern values, so that modern persons understand themselves to be highly individualistic selves with no fundamental connections to others or a larger community. The starting point for such radical individualism, according to Bellah, was Thomas Hobbes who "portrays precisely an atomistic man rent from God and from all other men, who loves and seeks himself only" (Bellah 1981, 12). In describing Hobbes's ideas, Bellah echoed Puritan John Winthrop's description of fallen human nature—apart from God and out of fellowship with other humans. Bellah's assessment of Enlightenment social philosophy was comprehensive enough to apply to classical political economy.

Bellah elaborated the characteristics of "mainstream social science," which has grown from the Enlightenment. Social science is *positivistic*, the belief that "the methods of natural science are the only approach to valid knowledge" (Bellah 1981, 10). Second, it is *reductionist*, explaining the complex in simple, usually materialistic, terms. It is *relativistic*, never judging values to be right or wrong, instead arguing that individuals or cultures simply have different preferences. Finally, social science is *deterministic*, for it explains human actions only by resort to measurable causes. Bellah argued that these four characteristics have not remained confined to social science, but have diffused throughout society.[2]

And what is the outcome of this ideology? Community dies, for our cultural ideology informs us "that we are alone, that we are here to pursue our own interests" (Bellah 1981, 19). Without using the term, Bellah (20) perfectly describes "economic man," that amoral calculator of benefits and costs, for whom even "intimate relations grow more and more calculating." The outcome of measuring everything against the self is ultimately a private moral relativism, for we "maximize individual choice . . . then we deny all objective standards of choice" (21). Bellah perfectly described the relativism of autonomy morality of libertarian and orthodox economics.

The later work, *Habits of the Heart*, filled in this thesis with human details. Bellah and colleagues interviewed numerous modern Americans and discovered lives oriented entirely to satisfying the self. Even when one interviewee discovered that material success was empty, his new passion turned out to be just as self-centered—*emotional self-absorption*. Bellah and colleagues call this "expressive" individualism, in which the self-centered focus shifts to the world of private feelings. The later work also dealt at length with the importance of "therapy" in modern America. According to Bellah and his colleagues, psychological therapy is predicated on essentially the same Enlightenment values that neoclassical economics is: people are assumed to have self-defined goals and values, and interactions with others are modeled as transactions intended to satisfy the self. Most "commitments" are viewed essentially as short-term contracts (Bellah 1986, 128–30).

Even community involvement in modern America, Bellah argued, is really a denial of human interrelatedness. All too often, involvement in governance occurs only when individuals perceive a threat to their isolation. What motivates such activism is not a vision of community, but the NIMBY (not in my back yard) syndrome, which really declares the desire to be left alone. The NIMBY reaction is the wish for autonomy when reality threatens that wish. A related phenomenon is the "life-style" community (sometimes symbolically gated against the rest of the world), an enclave where residents live among neighbors who are essentially copies of themselves in terms of age, wealth, hobbies, and so on.

Bellah and colleagues did not pretend that the modern culture is monolithic. Here and there they discovered genuine communities, often religious communities, in which people found reasons to care for each other and in which people defined their orientation by reference to an embracing community of faith extending into the past and future. And here and there they found true citizens, rather than disconnected individuals. Bellah and colleagues described one such citizen using terminology reminiscent of that of Horace Mann (chapter 5). Their true citizen had "a sense that the public good is based on the responsibility of one generation to the next" (Bellah 1986, 193). Responsibility of one for others, within a true community, which includes its historic dimension, is at the heart of Bellah's relational morality.

PHILIP WOGAMAN: A LIBERAL
PROTESTANT VIEW ON ECONOMICS

J. Philip Wogaman was a professor of ethics at a Methodist seminary when he wrote *Economics and Ethics: A Christian Inquiry* (1986), an ethical critique of economic ethics. He was later better known as pastor of the church attended by Bill Clinton during his terms as president. Wogaman's book was a reaction to the outspoken libertarians and neoconservatives of the 1980s. He pointed out that both groups followed Adam Smith in allowing the invisible hand of the market to decide economic outcomes. They also portray the free market as a great boon to humanity (Wogaman 1986, 17). Proponents of markets value the market as the institutional framework most consistent with individualism, whose virtues they celebrate. That the impersonal market leaves persons to live with the consequences of their choices shows a very profound respect for their "moral dignity," they say (according to Wogaman). These market advocates also place high value on property rights. Wogaman (18) concluded that their concern for personal autonomy and property endorse "the view that people should be left alone."

Wogaman singled out a new element introduced by neoconservatives to the moral assessment of markets. Instead of resting with Adam Smith's judgment that economics is driven by self-interest, some writers find the "exchange relationship to be an expression of love, not self-centered greed" (17). Michael Novak (chapter 13) had developed a similar argument, and Wogaman may have been referring to him.

Wogaman's critique began with historical observation. Looking back at two centuries of capitalism, he stated that people concluded that free-market capitalism "was devastating human society" (20). The New Deal and other reform legislation were direct responses to the actual workings of market economies, according to Wogaman.

Although the market advocates hold a truth that people are creative and free, they neglect that people are also social beings. When the neoconservative writers must explain social interaction, it is in terms of exchange, in which each individual gains something. But Wogaman was emphatic that "society is not just the sum of individual transactions" (21). He added "Human life is *shared* life." The failure of free-market enthusiasts to recognize this leads to "a kind of principled selfishness" (21).

Wogaman made the case for social control of markets, for many problems emerge when society does not put limits on markets. Profit maximization and self-interest never find reasons to constrain their own behavior. Wogaman concluded that some decisions are intrinsically social in nature—that some cannot effectively be made in a purely individualistic framework. Further, Wogaman was skeptical of the non-egalitarian character of the marketplace, where the economic weight of some far exceeds that of others.

Wogaman next considered the theological principles that would be needed to inform an economic ethic. A central premise is a theological version of human dignity. He stated that God's grace "confers ultimate meaning" on people. He added, "We matter because we matter to God" and that this creates relationship, for we become "the family of God" (34). The metaphor of kinship, of course, has appeared regularly in the thinking of relational moralists; it is a natural extension of biblical thought, though not limited to biblical sources. He made the strengthening of community a norm for defining economic justice: the distribution of goods should judged by its impact on community (35). Specifically, economic incentives should not operate on people's insecurities, but economic policy should provide "security in the conditions of life and livelihood" (42). Incentives may be useful, but they should never threaten a person's social existence.

Wogaman considered stewardship among his core theological principles. This meant that "everything belongs to God." The direct implication is one seen regularly in relational, religious ethics: that property rights are not absolute (37). Rather, property rights are defined by society—a clear rejection of John Locke and his modern followers. Of course this view echoed statements of relational moralists as far back as the Puritan William Ames. Wogaman expanded the coverage of stewardship to include respect for other "sentient beings and future generations."

Wogaman's final theological touchstone was the doctrine of sin, which, he said, warned of the moral danger of self-centeredness. Systems that are too optimistic about self-interest will fail to protect themselves against the excess that it produces (37–38). This, of course, directly conflicts with Michael Novak's (chapter 13) optimistic view of self-interest. In stating this, Wogaman was consistent with relational moralists' warnings that self-interest is not self-limiting, and even with the tacit recognition of this problem by some autonomy moralists such as Adam Smith (who, unfortunately, did nothing with his insight).

In sum, Wogaman did not fully dismiss what he called the neoconservative, market morality. But his emphasis was on the elements lacking from that morality. By ignoring the social nature of humans, this morality reduced ethics to the right to be left alone, he noted. What is striking is the fact that Wogaman could have been reacting to nineteenth-century laissez-faire. The libertarian-neoconservative arguments of the late twentieth century, to be sure, did not invoke Malthusian scarcity or the wages fund. But although a few points of theory have changed, the picture of free markets remains congruent with a morality of individual autonomy. In fact, in the late twentieth century, autonomy was defined in far more extreme terms than typically encountered in the nineteenth century. By contrast, Wogaman's ethics bear great similarity to the relational individualism articulated in America as early as the colonial Puritans and Quakers—a relational individualism that is fulfilled in the human community.

FRIENDS COMMITTEE ON NATIONAL LEGISLATION

The Friends Committee on National Legislation (FCNL) has existed for over fifty years to articulate a Quaker witness on public issues. The guiding principles of FCNL are periodically updated in a Statement of Legislative Policy (1994 revision referenced here). The FCNL has historically emphasized traditional Quaker issues such as peace, conscientious objection to military service, and treatment of prisoners. However, its outlook has been broad, linking issues such as economic justice with issues of peace; in addition, concern for the broader human and natural communities is evident in the statement.

The prologue to the 1994 Statement of Legislative Policy elaborates fundamental ethical principles. Policies grow "out of our basic belief in that of God in every human being and that God's love endows all creation with worth and dignity" (Friends Committee 1994, 1). Thus, FCNL's principles are based on a doctrine of divine love that bestows human dignity; this vision of dignity and worth is extended to "all creation." In the tradition of John Woolman, the statement affirmed the relational aspects of human existence. The statement went beyond human relationships and advocated a "right relationship with the earth."

The FCNL emphasized the importance of specific communities, not merely of the idea of community in the abstract. "Supportive and economically viable communities" were seen as the very basis of the nation's future (10). Urban and rural communities were singled out as especially needing strengthening through public policy. In each case, the connection between federal policies and the health of local communities was emphasized. The affirmation that "all persons should contribute . . . according to their ability" means that even the weakest members of community have their worth affirmed by making their contribution; this is similar to the affirmation of the Catholic bishops on this point.

The Quaker organization understood government to be a potentially very positive instrument for the human good, a sentiment echoing that of William Penn, centuries before—and dramatically at odds with the portrayal of government by the libertarian in economics. Government is essential "in safeguarding the integrity of our society and the essential dignity of all human beings as children of God" (6). Indeed, as a lobbying organization, FCNL listed several areas in which it sought more activist government—areas such as guaranteeing work opportunities, equalizing incomes, strengthening communities, protecting the environment. Despite this potential, the government that is portrayed in the Statement of Principles has substantial faults: it trusts too much in armaments and too little in international cooperation; it does too little for less developed nations; it administers justice with an uneven and punitive hand; it has been less than honorable dealing with Native Americans; it has done too little to equalize opportunity and wealth; and has been too passive as rural and urban communities succumb to market forces. That the FCNL can enumerate such a list of faults while maintaining a very positive view of government recalls Quaker beginnings. In the Quaker view, government, like individuals, was redeemable and had a positive function to serve.

The final part of the FCNL Statement began with an affirmation of the natural order: "We recognize the intrinsic value of the natural world as God's creation, beyond its use by humankind." It continued, "We belong to the intricate web connecting all that is natural. Therefore we are bound at times to respect purposes that are not our own" (14). A relational ethic, rooted in theological conviction, is expressed in these words. And the relationship extends to nature, which has an intrinsic value as part of God's creation and does not exist merely as a means to human ends. The FCNL document praises efforts to reduce high-level consumption and reduce pollution and resource depletion.

In sum, as judged by this statement, contemporary Quaker thought is remarkably similar to that of the colonial Quaker moralists as we remember them today (chapter 2). Their emphasis remains on universal human dignity, derived from God's love of humans and all creation. Such humans live related to others and within the web of nature, which also deserves respect in its own right. Of great significance for understanding relational morality correctly, the Friends' relational ethic was articulated first by people whose individualism in matters of faith was great and whose commercial spirit was legendary.

A POSTMODERN THEOLOGIAN: SALLIE MCFAGUE

In their own ways, the religious thinkers of this chapter critique the failure of two centuries' worth of economic thought to relate the individual to the wider human and natural community, other than by means of economic transactions. Sallie McFague's self-described postmodern perspective holds that such economics is the product to an outdated worldview—one formed by the convergence of Reformation and Enlightenment. Its enduring (and valuable) legacy was "the importance of the individual" (McFague 2001, 78). However, that legacy was intertwined with some questionable ideas of the eighteenth century, primarily the notion of the "world as a machine," the product of an aloof and detached Deist god (78). This led to a reductionist outlook that focused on the parts of the world-machine and the social-machine: in this view humans related merely "as a collection of individuals, all operating separately from self-interest" (79). According to McFague, a corollary of this worldview was the notion of ongoing economic growth. From this emerged the "neoclassical" value system that can be summarized in a single phrase: "the satisfaction of the desires of individuals through the means of constant growth" (81).[3] While McFague does not take individualism and economic growth lightly, she holds them to be negative values in the contemporary era.

McFague argued that early in the history of this worldview, its extremely individualistic tendencies were counterbalanced by residual, community-affirming habits of the older, pre-Enlightenment culture (81–83). She cites Robert Bellah (see earlier) on the biblical and republican traditions that sustained an overarching sense of community in the earlier years of the American republic. However, the older traditions of community and mutual responsibility have been lost as individualism has triumphed (83).

As the sense of interrelatedness has declined in modern culture, what has come to provide meaning to the isolated individual? The answer is that consumption has come to provide the meaning of life (84). Consumption is the only general answer that the modern economic value system can give to the core Enlightenment question: what provides individual happiness? McFague argued that consumerism has become a total way of life—in fact, an encompassing religion; but she doubted that high consumption could deliver what it promises, namely, happiness (86–87). More to the heart of the issue, she asked whether "happiness" is even the true end or purpose of life (87). McFague critiqued consumerism as the substitute for human fulfillment in relation to others. The reduction of humanity implicit in American consumerism is clear, for now people are merely "consumers—not citizens, or children of God, or lovers of the world, but *consumers*" (96). Besides the theological and existential implications, there is also an ethical consequence, for if Americans understood themselves as part of a larger human community, they would ask whether they are "under obligation to share" with the rest of the human family (89). However, neoclassical autonomy doctrine teaches that "as insatiable individuals we have no obligation to share." This ethic's barren message is merely that one's fulfillment or meaning in life depends on what one can buy.

Consumerism is an inadequate ethic for relating to the broader human family, and a dangerous ethic for relating to the planet earth, according to McFague. She rests her case on evidence often provided by environmentalists, concluding that the rate of consumption is so high that the resources of the earth are being severely compromised (89–93). The interrelatedness of earth's components is the key concept from which McFague works to develop a new ethic. She argues that it is imperative to replace the Enlightenment-individualistic worldview with an "ecological economic" worldview, which means the use of resources "so as to keep [the planetary] community working indefinitely" (99). The focus would be on the *entire* planetary system, not just humans. The sustainability of the system is at issue—not short-run gain.

McFague did not choose this overview arbitrarily, of course, for she believes it to be consistent with "postmodern science," and also that it provides a necessary mirror image of the Enlightenment model. The primary proposition of this model is that humans are not fundamentally autonomous beings, but are "relational beings" (99). This leads to an economic ethic that is almost opposite that of neoclassical economics, putting sustainability and equity first, before addressing individualistic wants (100). This represents an explicit value judgment favoring the total community, as opposed to the individualistic values of neoclassical thought.

For McFague, individualism is understood as a relational and interdependent individualism, in distinction from the autonomous individualism of neoclassical economics (101–105). The individual and the whole social-environmental system are interrelated. The sustainability of the ecological system must come first; only after that is assured would individual needs be considered in McFague's moral system. Finally, the decisions on sustainability require community involvement (107).

McFague suggested that distributive justice (i.e., more equal incomes) should be approached as part of the question of environmental sustainability.

Without greater equality, the only way to increase the incomes of the poorest of the earth would be rates of economic growth that would be destructive over the long run. This emphasis on limits to economic growth is not a return to Malthusianism, for McFague does not suggest that environmental limits doom humanity—or some major part of it—to poverty. There is enough for all to live well in a sustained way, provided sharing occurs. Without sharing, even unlimited growth—if it were possible—would fail to cure poverty, and indeed has failed. To McFague, as to moralists such as William Penn, economic limits do not imply hardship if sharing is the norm.

The approach offered by McFague differs in one major way from the other thinkers considered in this chapter. The others found the resources within their respective traditions to critique the autonomy morality of mainstream modern economic thought. McFague, instead, used an ecological-scientific outlook as her reference point and from it critiqued *both* the traditional economic morality and theology. McFague's quarrel with Reformation theology is not of primary interest here. However, one wonders if hers is a necessary quarrel, since the other moralists found the resources within their traditions (including the Protestant tradition) to render very similar critiques of the modern economic outlook.

E. F. Schumaker, an economist with strong ecological convictions, gained much attention with his *Small Is Beautiful* (1973), which anticipated many points made by McFague. The book did not suggest that a new theology had to be invented to fit the ecological worldview. To the contrary, Schumaker assumed that an ecological ethic was deep within traditional Christianity: "In ethics, as in so many other fields, we have recklessly and willfully abandoned our great classical-Christian heritage. We have even degraded the very words without which ethical discourse cannot carry on, words like virtue, love, temperance" (Schumaker 1973, 91).

Schumaker (239) did not fault Reformation theology, but condemned the "soul- and life-destroying metaphysics" of the nineteenth century, which he ultimately equated with the reductionism found in nineteenth-century science. In economics, this reductionism occurs when profitability becomes the single measure of success and all broader considerations are lost, he wrote (238). In short, McFague may be overly complicating the issue by seeking a reconstituted theology whereas others—including environmentalists such as Schumaker—find an adequate environmental critique in the legacy of existing religious traditions.

CONCLUSION

This ecumenical selection of economic moralists sharing the biblical tradition reached astonishing agreement on the necessity of a relational economic morality. As examples such as Michael Novak (chapter 13) make clear, religious thinkers are hardly monolithic in their adopting a relational ethic. That said, the message of this chapter is that the themes of relational morality are widely affirmed across a spectrum of religious traditions. All surveyed in this chapter have sharply critiqued ideas and practices that took their initial form in the secular Enlightenment.

All these moralists wrote in the late twentieth, or early twenty-first, century, when the modern economy and its practices dominated the lives of many and indeed taught the values that underlie the market. What perhaps raises the concern of these diverse religious thinkers is that they have seen the values of large numbers of people whose moral frame of reference has been set by economic forces and practices. They have observed the extremes to which autonomy morality, given the possibilities of a modern productive system, leads. McFague caught the urgency these religious thinkers felt when she pointed with distress to a society in which people define themselves as consumers—not by their membership in the human community or even *a* human community. Such an extreme was latent in autonomy morality from the first, but only of late have conditions permitted the results to be seen on a mass scale.

SIXTEEN

Summary, Assessments, and a Projection

AMERICA'S ECONOMIC MORALISTS have divided historically into two discernible schools of individualism. One morality benchmarks values in terms of the autonomous individual; the other defines values in terms of the quality of relationships that shape and sustain individuals. Both autonomous individualism and relational individualism have been presented in this book as loose sets of consistent precepts that are interwoven with supporting beliefs about economic theory. While developments of each ethic have occurred over time, each morality has retained its distinctive characteristics.

These characteristics are best seen in the ways each ethic has responded to several major questions of economic morality. The following section is devoted to recapping these responses. The section after that addresses the question of compromise between the rival ethics: whether relational and autonomy moralities might be combined in some manner. After problems with that approach have been exposed, two later sections assess the roles of the rival ethics in the contemporary American culture. A final section projects ethical trends in contemporary American economic life, and finds in them support for relational ethics.

RESPONDING TO CORE QUESTIONS

The opening chapter set out several fundamental questions, to which relational and autonomy moralists respond in characteristic ways. Although no single moralist would have answered each of these questions in exactly the same way (and some moralists addressed only some of the questions), a consensus framework emerges for each morality.

Self-Interest. Autonomy morality has, from its Enlightenment beginnings, made the freedom of the individual to pursue the self's interests the touchstone of its morality. From the first, incentives that appeal to self-interest have been viewed as the motives for economically beneficial actions. Commonsense notions of self-interest used by the early economists have evolved into the twentieth century as ever-stricter, narrower definitions of self-interest and even of the self itself. The end result has been the neoclassical economists' insistence that the individual is truly an autonomous person with innate preferences—immune to education, advertising, or other humans' pleadings. Welfare economics reached the extreme of the self-contained individual, literally incapable of understanding others' economic needs or welfare. Moral discourse among such people, from which a social consensus could emerge, would be impossible. The primary principle of social morality would be that such individuals should leave each other alone—Wayland's duty of reciprocity. Otherwise, individuals would define their own values; personal morality therefore would be relativistic.

In contrast, relational morality has defined the self and the self's good with reference to a wider human community. Maximizing self-interest, or economic "utility," never was accepted as an adequate notion of the good in relational morality, for the individual's good has been understood to be linked to the good of others. In relational ethics, the good of the individual has never been defined purely by the individual. Rather, an individual's good has been understood against norms that apply to all, for humans are assumed to be kin and so to have much in common. Although human relationships could be construed in terms of inherently unequal relationships (as in feudal societies), or in terms of exclusive relationships (as in tribal societies), the American relational moralists have historically affirmed equality and universality in relationships. Such relationships give rise logically to concepts of universal human dignity and social or economic rights to preserve dignity. For the individual, relational morality does not rule out considerations of personal welfare; however, the individual would define the good against a broader context than just the self.

Rights, Obligations, and Government. True to its name, autonomy morality understands economic rights as protections of individual autonomy against impingements by others. This has been consistently asserted at different times by laissez-faire, Social Darwinist, and libertarian moralists. They placed a very high burden of proof on any proposal to impose involuntary obligations on individuals (in the economic realm, taxes). Autonomy morality understands that individuals sometimes must cooperate, and its preferred mechanism is the market—for economic transactions impose only minimal obligations and avoid the risks to individual freedom of creating a government. When government must exist, it is understood in terms set by John Locke: a voluntary covenant among individuals seeking to benefit personally through concerted action. The main legitimate role of government in autonomy ethics is to protect individual rights. Rights and obligations, in this view, are different sides of a single coin: the central right in autonomy ethics is freedom from imposed obligations; conversely, the main obligation is to respect others' right to this freedom. Commentators have defined this as negative freedom, a "freedom-*from*," which articulates no goal greater than the individual's own preferences.

Human interrelatedness is an alternative foundation for obligations and rights. In the historic case of abolition, relational moralists constantly pointed to the violation of the family relationships of slaves, and the slave's courageous efforts to save their families and communities, as evidence that slavery violated fundamental human rights. This approach appealed to common humanity, for the abolitionists' audiences understood the violation of the slaves at a fundamental human level. Further, the sacrifices of slaves to preserve relationships, as best they could, implied a moral dignity; such dignity called for social recognition and protection. The presumption of a common human dignity implied obligations for society, for universal rights based on common humanity require guarantees that make those rights effective. That relationships persist over long periods requires sets of obligations and rights that guarantee that persistence; persistence over time also enriches relationships with layers of meaning. A doctrine of shared humanity also means that agreement is possible on what constitutes the good—for a common humanity allows people to understand each other. Thus moral dialogue is possible. Government plays a positive role as an instrument to act on consensus reached through moral dialogue. However, all is not left to government, for the individual also has responsibility, including in economic life, for taking actions that support the wider community.

Economic Virtue. Autonomy morality has a strong utilitarian bent: virtue is that which leads to the higher welfare of the individual (or, in the case of social utilitarians, the higher aggregate welfare). This, of course, would make work, thrift, and other ascetic virtues important as means to higher welfare. Little virtue is assigned to pure intentions, for it is consequences (increased utility or welfare) that matter. With each individual focused on the self's welfare, autonomy morality is relativistic. Such relativism implies tolerance; virtue is defined by one's own preferences and so no one can judge another's virtue. If one may say that autonomy morality promotes a social virtue, it is behavior that allows the system of autonomy itself to continue to exist; that is, respecting the same freedom or autonomy for others that one expects for oneself (reciprocity). Autonomy moralists have tended to see markets operating in a virtuous manner because economic transactions are voluntary and impersonal—both characteristics that preserve autonomy.

The virtues of relational moralists tend to have a familiar ring because they echo traditional, often religious, values: pure intentions toward others, respect for the "image of God" in others, love of neighbor, compassion for the weak. All these strengthen or are logical extensions of human relatedness and respect for human dignity. A recurring virtue in the writings of relational moralists is self-restraint—knowing when enough is enough; excess tends to harm relationships or deprive others to whom one is related in some fundamental way. The ethic of human relatedness easily extends itself to a concept of the relatedness of *all* members of the natural order, finding ecological virtues compatible with relational virtues. Relational morality also sees virtue in social processes, such as democratic discourse, from which common values may emerge. At the individual level, economic virtue would reside in actions that affirm the worth of the wider community and its values.

Inequality and Poverty. Autonomy morality justifies economic inequality as the result of individual differences in both abilities and preferences (some individuals may care less about income). In addition, differences in incomes have an important, positive economic role as material incentives. The burden of proof would fall on anyone defending the proposition that actual economic inequality exceeds that caused by individual differences. Poverty is a related, though distinct, issue. Poverty, of course, may be a case of extreme preferences—for leisure over income; no remedy need be applied in this case. Or, poverty may be due to overall scarcity. One response to such poverty is that of modern economics: economic growth, as promoted by free markets, can reduce absolute scarcity. However, mechanisms to share to some degree the benefits of growth are incompatible with the individualism of autonomy ethics; thus, even high rates of economic growth may not be distributed in a way that is guaranteed to end poverty.

In relational ethics, poverty and inequality have not usually been imputed to natural scarcity, but to injustice in the division of adequate resources. If the metaphor of kinship is central to moral thought, then the only inequality should be that found in a well-functioning family. In general, great disparities among close kin are not permitted except when a family member's needs are exceptional and extra resources are assigned to that member; the extra resources are to help keep him or her as far as possible a participating member of the family. As well, because people share a common humanity, they can readily understand the hardships imposed by poverty or extreme inequality. Similarly, poverty is understood as a demeaning of inherent human dignity. Thus relational ethics accepts the legitimacy of economic rights that guarantee basic economic subsistence to all and access to free public goods. In relational morality, individuals value work, not merely as a means to obtaining income, but as participation in the greater community. Because of this connection of work to one's standing in the community, relational moralists do not believe that large material inequality is needed to induce people to work.

Human Dignity as Moral Norm. In autonomy morality, the capability of the individual to define his or her own ends is in itself considered dignity. Freedom to pursue one's ends makes that dignity effective. Stated differently, one earns one's dignity in one's own esteem: the autonomous person defines his or her own dignity.

Relational moralists tend to find human dignity intertwined with human connectedness. Relational moralists within the biblical tradition find a basis for human dignity in the teaching that humanity was made in the image of God and redeemed by God. Harriet Beecher Stowe's abolitionist novel pointed to the sacrifices made by the slaves to preserve their family relationships against all odds as a mark of their intrinsic human dignity. Some moralists, including those in a natural-law tradition, have found human dignity in the fullness of rational human development. Significantly the American Catholic bishops have recently reaffirmed what was in Harriet Beecher Stowe's argument: that dignity is truly fulfilled in community with others.

Moral Boundaries. The two moralities disagree about boundaries around the realm of the market. Autonomy ethics understands markets as the playing field on which individual interests are pursued; thus a greater variety of markets, and hence of choices, always allows an increased range of individual satisfaction. When individuals define their own preferences, there is no limit to the kinds of markets, and of economic activity, that someone might desire. Autonomy morality has had difficulty defining boundaries for market activity, for such boundaries might infringe someone's freedom to engage in desired transactions. At root, autonomy has problems defining limits, for self-interest rarely finds reasons to limit itself. Even Adam Smith suggested that external limits might need to be imposed on self-interested people. Despite Smith's insight, autonomy thinkers have been slow to impose limits on markets or economic behavior: the result has been that excess often appears in such unbounded market economies. Autonomy moralists also tend to emphasize differences among individuals; as differences have been exaggerated, and commonalities minimized, the basis for consensus on limits to markets has also disappeared. Thus, autonomy morality had tended not to set boundaries.

Relational morality recognizes that market transactions are but one kind of human interaction and that sometimes the transaction represents the wrong kind of relationship. Thus, it draws tighter boundaries around the realm of the market than does autonomy morality. Relational morality asks "When is enough, enough?" because excesses harm relationships or demean human dignity. Relational morality can make the case for society limiting market activity; it also creates an outlook in which individuals choose voluntary personal limits.

Limits to economic actions are hard to set when the world is seen in terms of scarcity: for life is always insecure, and "more" always seems useful.

Typically, relational moralists have discounted the central place that traditional economics has given to scarcity. This is not because the rival moralists see natural and technological limits to economics that differently. Rather, relational moralists are willing to measure economic potential against agreed-on limits, against notions of "enough" and of just distribution. Conversely, autonomy moralists have measured economic capacity against individuals' potentially unlimited desires, making it impossible to produce enough to eliminate the sense of scarcity. In this sense, moral limits to excessive consumption render irrelevant the limits imposed by absolute natural scarcity. Conversely, autonomy morality takes as a fundamental reality the insatiable wants of autonomous selves—guaranteeing an ongoing perception of scarcity. With this perception, opportunities to produce more should rarely be limited.

COMPROMISING BETWEEN THE
RIVAL ETHICS, OR COMPROMISED ETHICS?

When sharp alternatives are set out, some people almost instinctively seek a middle position. The idea of compromise may be especially strong if someone mistakenly thinks relational morality requires some form of socialism or communalism. However, the fundamental premise that humans are related as kin does not logically imply socialist ethics; starting with the Puritans and Quakers, the relational morality described in this volume has been *relational individualism*. And relational morality has been advocated by those who participated in market economies. Although the Moravians stretched relational values to include religious socialism, individualism has been the classic expression of relational ethics. *Thus, relational individualism actually is a mediating alternative between socialist (or collective) values and autonomy morality.*

Among the moralists we have covered in this volume, there have been a few who seemed to accept pieces from the rival moralities, typically without success. One approach has been to designate domains into which the rival moralities could be segregated. Andrew Carnegie tried this: he thought productive effort should be ruled by Social Darwinism (autonomy ethics) and personal life by philanthropy (a truncated version of relational ethics). The inherent inconsistency of this approach was graphically demonstrated when Carnegie's corporation engaged in violent strike-breaking activity, while Carnegie, who preferred to consider himself a friend of the worker, absented himself to Scotland. The actions of the corporation he controlled belied his personal morality. Michael Novak theoretically assigned autonomy morality to the economic sector, but allowed his "moral-cultural sector" to promote relational ethics. However, Novak's interpretation of the theology of the moral-cultural sector simply turned Christian doctrines into analogues of concepts found in market economics. Novak had room for the two moralities because they really weren't two: he transformed one into the image of the other. Francis Wayland also tried to mix moralities. He did abandon the utilitarianism of autonomy ethics and relied on biblical injunctions for moral precepts. However, even though he was a clergyman, Wayland never seemed to grasp the relational meaning of biblical ideas. Even when he invoked the supremely relational text "love thy neighbor," he interpreted it simply to mean to leave the neighbor alone, not to infringe his or her autonomy. Wayland could not escape biblical injunctions to be charitable, but, aside from his duty as a clergyman to repeat these injunctions, he seemed to have no sense that these biblical injunctions spoke broadly to the intrinsic human condition. He walled religious obligation off from economic life and saw no obligation toward others (except not to actually harm them). In sum, these cases do not exhibit a successful dualism of relational thought and autonomy thought.

In the cases of Carnegie, Wayland, and Novak, autonomy morality subordinated the relational ideas that had been introduced. Conversely, predominantly relational moralists have seemed uneasy about leaving too much room for autonomy. Macroeconomists, including Keynes, Samuelson, Galbraith, and Okun, all left considerable room for private, market economics (indeed, in principle, relational ethics leaves room for markets). But each was uncomfortable with the tendencies of market economies—the largest source of discomfort being economic inequality and insecurity. Consequently, each (except possibly Keynes) expressed the need for society to set bounds that limit the excesses of market activity and to create institutions that deal with such market outcomes as income insecurity. Relational morality accepts market activity, but its ideal is that the market be bounded by norms set by society (and that the moral individual should set personal boundaries when engaging the market). Again, it appears that when moralists see domains for two ethics, one ethic must dominate the other. And this is surely a logical necessity, for the two moralities conflict in crucial ways.

AN ASSESSMENT OF AUTONOMY ETHICS

The early twenty-first century produced rapidly rising economic output in the United States, a strong argument for market economics (and the autonomy values that usually predominate in markets). It also produced corporate scandals, speculative booms and crashes, increased dispersion of income and wealth, and unrestrained consumption (as the personal savings rate in America reached zero). These events forcefully raised the question that had dogged self-interest ethics for over two centuries: whether an ethic centered on autonomy of the individual (or corporation) is capable of producing moral bounds to self-interested behavior. Can autonomy morality tell the autonomous person when to stop? Though he treated it as an afterthought, even Adam Smith had recognized the problem of the lack of limits in self-interest morality. Events of the present era seem to confirm Smith's worry, for—except when laws restrain it—

excess has become common in economic life. When guided by autonomy ethics, economic life lacks internalized moral boundaries. When the inevitable excesses become politically intolerable, laws are imposed to set limits.

At the end of the twentieth century, an increasingly pluralistic American society has both benefited and suffered from autonomy ethics. Autonomy ethics is inherently tolerant, for it keeps people focused on themselves and consequently relatively indifferent to what others do. Autonomy morality demands little that would drive people apart—though it gives no reasons to create real community. Thus, it is a well-fitting ethic for an impersonal and pluralistic business world. At the economic level, where people interact continuously in their own interests, a least common denominator of tolerance is possible based on autonomy ethics. In a pluralistic economy, the toleration necessary to function may be found in autonomy morality; other moralities, which may prove divisive and harm business, are pushed into irrelevance. Toleration, the ability to function without moral friction in a pluralistic economy, recommends autonomy ethics

One negative side of this is that autonomy ethics, and related economic practice, may become the norm for understanding *all* human interactions; this would turn them into transactions, the standard type of interaction in commercial life. A moral posture, which may be acceptable in economics, threatens to become the model for all relationships—thus reducing the richness of all human relationships. Through the lens of autonomy morality, actions motivated by reasons other than self-interest would become incomprehensible. Love, service to one's community, obedience to law simply out of respect for law, voting as a civic duty, or environmental concern—all lack meaning in this perspective. When all relationships are understood as utilitarian transactions, the observer is blinded to deeper meanings. Thus, the desired tolerance of an autonomy morality could come at a high price: a progressive degradation of human relationships.

A world dominated by autonomy ethics would abound in paradoxes. Individuals who define their happiness as ever-greater consumption have allowed themselves to be defined by those who promote things to consume. But in what sense is someone autonomous if he or she is manipulated by advertising? Autonomy morality's utilitarian outlook historically promoted the ascetic virtues—as means to enhanced future welfare. In the present, autonomy ethics produces the opposite behavior, undisciplined consumption, as a way to gratify present desires. A related paradox—noted long ago by Galbraith—is that even in the midst of per capita output that exceeds anything in the past, the sense of scarcity persists; defining their welfare by their possessions, and lacking a moral reason to say "enough," consuming households always feel deprived. Winners in economic competition may lose all restraint in pushing their advantage, for more is *always* better. The problem of economic inequality (and poverty) is never solved, despite a GDP per capita that grows ever larger; a cultural self-interest ethic makes it politically impossible to consider even a small degree of redistribution as a solution to inequality. Any such plan is viewed as an immoral attack on individual rights or incentives. Thus, inequality persists no matter how adequate the available resources.

Yet another paradox of autonomy morality needs special attention. Autonomy morality closely links its notion of human dignity to individual freedom of choice. However, this means that poverty, and other human failures, must be interpreted as the free choices of the victims. Thus a doctrine, once intended to dignify people, results in the poor being manipulated with incentives designed to make poverty a less desirable choice.

Autonomy morality produces paradoxes of logic as well as of behavior. The self-interested individual of neoclassical economics has been credited with the genius to understand personal preferences and to maximize personal welfare. Yet, this individual was decreed by the welfare economists to be totally incapable of understanding how *other* humans view their welfare. Autonomy logic decrees individuals to be all-knowing in some areas and thoroughly agnostic in closely related areas. And the last logical paradox may be the greatest: the highly valued freedom to pursue self-interest is merely the freedom to follow a course predetermined by material incentives laid down by impersonal market mechanisms. Ultimately, the freedom of autonomy morality has been reduced to determinism.

ASSESSMENT OF RELATIONAL MORALITY

While autonomy morality offers a tolerant moral relativism that complements the pluralistic contemporary economy, that may be its only strength. Otherwise, this morality can give no reasons to curb excess, and excess has become a dominant feature of contemporary American economic life (other features may dominate at other times). In contrast, the great strength of relational morality is that moral boundaries are inherent in the maintenance of relationships. Within relationships, the dignity of the other is recognized, and respect, not excess, is the normal response. The kinship metaphor also implies a moral psychology whereby people understand others and so automatically take account of the impact of their actions on their relationship with others; this implies limits. Limits are also generated by the historical dimension of relationships; relationships persist, and limits that strengthen them through time become norms. The kinship metaphor emphasizes that which is universal: if people are related, then they must have much in common. This premise makes it very difficult to rationalize excessive disparities in the economic condition of people, or disparities in essentials such as health care or education. Finally, a relational ethic has automatic safeguards against runaway materialism. One must be blind to human relationships if one values only material consumption.

Historically, relational morality has drawn its inspiration from humanistic traditions. Yet, relational morality may have stronger connections to contemporary science than it did to eighteenth- and nineteenth-century science. Environmental and ecological concerns have obvious connections with relational morality, for these sciences concentrate on the web of relationships sustaining physical existence. Conversely, the inability of autonomy morality to curb excesses in production and consumption leads to the degradation of earth's environment. That relational morality understands limits, and also understands that relationships may extend beyond humanity to the rest of creation, makes it compatible with environmental outlooks.

The nature of the relationships can make a crucial difference in the suitability of relational morality to the contemporary economic world. Certain types of relational morality would be a threat to global economics if, for example, they construed relationships in tribal terms, which would be unsuited to a pluralistic economy. Yet, tribal values have never been part of America's relational individualism. From the first, kinship has served as an open metaphor for *all* humanity (e.g., the universality of human dignity was a central premise of the abolitionists). The relational moralists considered in this volume have consistently thought of human relationships as being symmetrical between people; that is, they imply universal equality.

Finally, relational morality implies human dignity at the very places that autonomy ethics threatens to demean it. Autonomy morality creates one-dimensional persons, who, for example, may understand all relationships as transactions. Relational ethics rejects this one-dimensional focus, for relationships always create obligations that take precedence over any one goal of the ego. Humans develop as moral beings in community with others; as such, dignity grows in community.

PROJECTIONS OF VALUES AND TRENDS

Autonomy morality proves convenient for business in a global and pluralistic economy, for it is relativistic and therefore tolerant; it understands human interactions primarily as transactions, a standard compatible with business. However, this is a morality that can offer no cogent reason for self-restraint (or, by implication, corporate restraint); therefore, one may project that many new business laws and regulations will be necessary to control what is not self-restrained. Whether this actually occurs will depend on the political power of business to resist increased legal oversight. However, if corporate self-restraint diminishes further, efforts to create legislation and regulations—whether successful or not—are bound to increase. (At this writing, the lack of restraint, or even of self-interested prudence, in marketing "subprime" loans offers the latest example of excess in the modern economy.)

This culture of nonrestraint has so far manifested itself in two general ways. First, exploitative behavior may occur within the firm. An example would be executives who better themselves at the expense of the corporations for which they work, which is obvious in the case of vast increases in CEO compensation unrelated to performance. Unless curbed by external restraints (government or victimized shareholders), excesses within business are likely to continue into the future, given the reigning autonomy values of business.

Second, economic actors may take a predatory posture toward society. For example, the alleged role of energy traders in manipulating the then-newly deregulated California electric market in 2000–2001 was predation by virtually any standard. At this writing, it would be premature to conclude that the great rise in commodity prices in 2008 was the result of speculation; however, autonomy values certainly would not provide the rationale for self-restraint among commodity speculators, and might even be construed to justify the behavior, despite apparent hardships caused to others by rising commodity prices. Another form of a predatory posture toward society occurs when producers view it outside their moral mandate to consider the good of their customers. For instance, video games based on the player taking on the role of a criminal have already been widely marketed. Thus, business may become aggressive in undermining cultural and legal restraints. Assuming society does not acquiesce in this, its answer would be legal restrictions on such products. However, when producers, immersed in the values of free autonomy, literally comprehend no wrong in what they do, compliance will continue to be incomplete and grudging. Such behavior is not limited to the most obvious case of the entertainment industry. The financial industry, for example, often produces products of great potential harm to the users, such as offering credit that tempts susceptible borrowers into excessive debt.

These practices will not easily be abandoned, and protracted battles will occur if society attempts to restrict them. For example, the tobacco industry long ago pioneered a tactic of casting (unwarranted) doubt on well-supported scientific findings that were unfavorable to its product. This tactic is now apparently widely exploited by other industries that produce dangerous products (Michaels 2005, 96). What this makes clear is that, lacking self-restraint, some businesses will also resist well-justified external restraints on their products or practices. Autonomy ethics gives no reason to believe one is wrong in resisting laws to protect the vulnerable. More, the ethic promotes the view that social pressures on businesses are unwarranted infringements on their right to conduct their business as they will.

The dominance of autonomy ethics in the business culture actually creates a need for relational morality. Relational morality will play its most obvious role in defining a rationale for responses to the excesses of the business world. Initiatives to expose products that take advantage of vulnerable consumers represent the kinds of actions that fit a relational framework. Political campaigns to increase the minimum wage, or to mandate a living wage, also represent actions that tend to affirm the common needs of all humans. Shareholder campaigns across an array of corporate-governance issues typically express the idea that there are limits to what corporations may do—and that there are limits to how little a corporation may do as a corporate citizen. Generally, movements to integrate corporate interests with those of their stakeholders—workers, communities, customers, as well as shareholders—represent an affirmation of relationships that transcend what are typically accepted as the responsibilities of business.

Relational morality may also be called on to provide the ethical rationale for preservation of governmental programs that embody concepts of social cohesiveness. The national administration in recent years has made serious attempts to redesign social programs dating to the New Deal, such as Social Security. In 2005, George W. Bush proposed redesigning Social Security to eliminate the common trust fund and replace it with individual accounts. In effect, this proposal would have eliminated the social component in Social Security. Strictly private accounts would have eliminated cross-generational and cross-income financial responsibility. The new private accounts would have been compatible with a sense of autonomy, for each participant would be on his or her own. This proposal exhibited the classic intertwining of values with supporting economic theory. Accompanying the proposal were economic projections that showed the current Social Security system facing a crisis. Yet, the funding crisis existed only by assuming scarcity, which put sufficient sources of funding out of reach. While the 2005 privatization effort failed, it is clear that future attempts are likely to deemphasize the social nature of government programs. When such programs are attacked—in order to promote the greater autonomy of individuals—their defenders need relational values to provide a comprehensive framework for the defense. And relational values are intertwined with their own economic perspective, which is more attuned to abundance. Supporters of Social Security can note that continuing economic growth is sufficient over the long run to provide more resources for Social Security a well as more resources for every other sector of the economy.

Relational morality need not forever be limited to critiquing an expansive autonomy morality. Sociologists in recent years have discovered that "social capital" is important for social existence. Social capital is defined as human relationships and networks that facilitate the work of a society. Other trends in science reinforce the relational outlook as biological and environmental sciences concentrate on the web of relationships sustaining physical existence. Connections of moral beings with other creatures, and ultimately the inanimate world, are implied by ecological sciences. That self-oriented humans should define their own good without regard to the rest of the world has come to be an untenable position.

Notes

CHAPTER TWO. COLONIAL FAITH:
WORK, WEALTH, AND THE WIDER WELFARE

1. Max Weber's thesis held that the Calvinist doctrine of election, which left one's salvation purely up to God, resulted in the average Puritan being uncertain and anxious about his or her salvation. To calm such anxiety, Weber held, Puritans would seek evidence they were among the elect. Because success in one's vocation might be a mark of God's favor, and thus also of election, such economic success gained spiritual importance. This, Weber said, drove Puritans to single-minded economic striving. Contemporary commentators have often followed Weber without question, or even embellished his views (e.g., Nelson 1991, 148). Yet, the idea that Puritans focused narrowly on economic success, without placing economics in a larger moral context, is incorrect. Puritan moralists consistently placed economic activity in the context of service to a common good (Frey 1998, 1573–80).

2. This thesis has been developed in Frey (1998, 1574–78).

CHAPTER FOUR. LAISSEZ-FAIRE FOR AMERICANS

1. See the essay by Daniel Howe (in Noll 2002) for an analysis of frontier evangelical reaction to emerging capitalist culture. The analysis of this chapter focuses on the reaction of more urban evangelicals, such as Francis Wayland, whose ideas endured over the long run.

2. Contrast this with the Puritan William Perkins's condemnation of a popular saying "Every man for himself, and God for us all," which advocated individuals' abdicating any responsibility for the common good and leaving that up to God. Smith reversed Perkins's condemnation, praising the idea of every man for himself, and substituting an invisible hand for God.

3. See Viner (1972, 86–113) on the transformation of divine providence in traditional religious thought into a conservative social construct over many years.

4. A far more detailed discussion of the philosophical and theological aspects of Wayland's argument is presented in Frey (2002).

5. Is it possible to reconcile inevitable poverty with moral free choice as joint causes of poverty? One potential tack would be to distinguish aggregate from individual results: poverty in the aggregate is inevitable, but no individual needs to choose to be among the poor. However, if some poverty in the aggregate is truly inevitable, then even if all the poor chose economic virtue, some must fail to advance. This attempt to reconcile the two claims fails. Alternatively, one could argue that if all the poor become virtuous, then poverty indeed would be eliminated in the aggregate. This opens the door to blaming the poor, but does so by admitting that poverty is not really inevitable.

CHAPTER SIX. RELIGIOUS SOCIALISM: THE COMMUNAL MORAVIANS

1. Thorp (1989, 46–47) argues that Bethania was started to keep Bethabara from becoming too large, not as an outlet for individualists. It was not communal because some of its settlers were not full members of the Moravian brotherhood; they were needed to obtain a large enough population to provide security. Thorp (71) also cites a case of the officials sending a family to Bethania because conditions for children were better there.

2. *Brotherly Agreement for Salem, NC.* 1773. Trans. F. Cumnock, 1992. Winston-Salem, NC: Archives of the Southern Province of the Moravian Church. All references are by permission.

3. Sensbach (1998, 80) notes that the Moravian acceptance of the converted slaves as spiritual equals "varied sharply" from the practice of English-speaking slave-owners whose rationalization for slavery required them to view slaves as different and not equal.

CHAPTER SEVEN. ABOLITION: HUMAN DIGNITY AS A BOUNDARY TO MARKETS

1. For example, Arthur Okun (1975, 9) points out that a democracy is not operating on market logic when it rules out buying and selling votes.

2. Supporters of slavery typically quoted Bible texts pertaining specifically to slavery. Opponents such as Wayland, on the contrary, quoted broad biblical principles such as "love thy neighbor," from which they inferred moral conflicts with slavery. The former approach relied on proof-texts and literalism, while the latter required the interpretation of the meaning of broad principles—such as "love thy neighbor"—when confronted with particular circumstances. In his *Moral Science*, Wayland made these kinds of arguments. Noll (2006) points out that Wayland offered one argument against slavery that might have been unique—for it met the pro-slavery literalists on their own ground and still reached antislavery conclusions. According to Noll, Wayland worked through all the Bible verses describing bondage in ancient Israel. Then he concluded that because slavery in the American South failed to meet all the requirements imposed by the Jewish law, it was not biblically justified.

3. Joseph Dorfman (1946, Vol. 2: 760), who apparently considered only Wayland's text on political economy, incorrectly represents Wayland's overall position on this

issue. He states that Wayland's words on the subject of slavery were to admonish submission to masters on biblical grounds. As shown, Wayland in his *Moral Science* argued in principle that slavery was wrong and that morality required the end of this wrong.

4. Most American relational moralists, such as the abolitionists, emphasized human commonality, which is an affirmation of fundamental equality; rights held by some are held by all. However, a few pro-slavery writers were "relational" thinkers of a different sort. They portrayed slavery as a relationship between naturally *unequal beings* (as a parent–child relationship). Henry Hughes and George Fitzhugh envisioned "society as an organic, familial whole" (Sklansky 2002, 73). Hughes and Fitzhugh used (unequal) relationships in a patriarchal family to support slavery. The member of a naturally superior class (which they took a slave-owner to be) acted as "a trustee of society and a warden of his extended family" including slaves (Sklansky 2002, 100). In short, human relationships were asymmetric; this justified slavery and a system of unequal rights. Whereas Hughes and Fitzhugh used relational language to preach inequality, abolitionists and most relational moralists consistently held that human relationship expressed the likeness and oneness of all humans. In the religious idiom, *all* possessed the image of God, and the love of Christ was for the sake of all. The language of brotherhood and sisterhood implied close kinship—so close that whatever dignity one would assign to oneself was due to all. Instead of the language of brotherhood, Fitzhugh and Hughes invoked the language of hierarchy, paternalism, and feudalism.

CHAPTER EIGHT. SOCIAL DARWINISTS OF DIFFERENT SPECIES

1. When Spencer spoke of economic fitness, he had in mind behaviors that can be learned. When behaviors are learned behaviors, not inherited, policies of "survival of the fittest" would make no sense—for almost anyone can learn. Henry George (chapter 9) criticized Social Darwinists at precisely this point.

CHAPTER NINE. NEW INFLUENCES IN ECONOMICS

1. Output per worker, and living standard, have risen consistently in the last two hundred years in developed nations; the same trend has begun more recently in less developed nations (Easterlin 1996).

2. Marginal product refers to the output of an additional (or "marginal") worker. The worker is not "marginal" in the sense of being inferior, but only in being an increment to a crew already at work. In Clark's theory, the law of diminishing returns meant that the marginal product fell as more and more workers were added to a crew. Provided the marginal product is higher than the prevailing wage, profit-maximizing theory says that a firm will keep hiring workers until marginal product is driven down to equality with the wage; it is profitable to employ workers who produce a value of goods greater than their wage.

3. In laissez-faire, the justice of wages was based on the workers and employers having agreed to a contract. For Clark, the competitive wage was just if it was equal to

what the representative (marginal) worker produced. Clark argued that the worker had a right to what he produced, and this was defined by the marginal product. In Clark's theory, the marginal worker is the representative worker and all workers receive that wage.

4. Richard Ely stated that the marginal-product wage "has no ethical significance, and should not be interpreted as a justification of the present economic order" (Ely 1916, 403). Perhaps his most telling critique: "We can imagine an economic order very different from the present one in which it would still be true that income would tend to equal products" (Ely 1916, 404). Ely's point was that it is possible for wages to equal marginal products in two very different societies. Yet, the wages could be very different in those two societies (say, more equal in one of them). Presumably one of the wage structures would be viewed as more just, or better, than the other by most people with a moral perspective. This demonstrates that marginal product, at best, is *not the only criterion of justice that most people would use*. Years later, Paul Samuelson (1947, 225) said approximately the same thing: "A change in the technological situation [which altered marginal products and wages] will alter individuals' fortunes so that the final result cannot be optimal if the first one was." Again, the conclusion is that people must use other criteria than marginal-product wages to judge the goodness of a society's wage distribution.

CHAPTER TEN. THE SOCIAL GOSPEL AND CATHOLIC THOUGHT AROUND 1900

1. Rauschenbusch's characterization of the church's focus on "getting to heaven" made it as utilitarian as economics is—motivating people by promised rewards. Conversely, Rauschenbusch claimed that Jesus imposes a deontological, or obligation-based, ethic: right living, with or without reward.

2. D. E. Smucker (1994, 83–84) traces various philosophic and theological influences on Rauschenbusch's ethic, finding Kantian influences on his exposition of Jesus's teaching. Yet, Rauschenbusch attributed the ethic to revelation (i.e., to Jesus's life and words), and did not attempt to deduce the ethic logically.

3 It is customary to refer to encyclicals by paragraph number. Different copies may vary slightly in numbering. Paragraph numbers follow Leo XIII (1891; 1963 edition by James P. Sweeney).

4. The key aspect of Leo's natural-law argumentation is the claim that reason can discover the good as that which fulfills true human nature. Because reason is common to all, the ethics of natural law can be agreed to by all.

5. Beckley (in Ryan 1996, xvii, xviii) points out that during the Depression, Ryan advocated additional policies that challenged the *status quo*. However, he states that these were "warranted by economic expediency, not by a principle of equality or a new moral rights claim."

6. For example, Henry George (chapter 9) broadly agreed with Leo XIII's natural-law defense of property. However, in his "Open Letter to Leo XIII" (1891), he argued that Leo's own logic ruled out property in land (George 1898, 28–32). In short, even those favorable to natural-law arguments are often not wholly convinced.

CHAPTER ELEVEN. THE 1920s AND 1930s: DEPRESSED OLD VALUES

1. Of course, speculation in the American economy was not new. Economic historians have studied various episodes of speculative bubbles, but economic moralists have had relatively little to say explicitly about the morality of speculation. By emphasizing a divine calling to productive labor, the Protestant ethic had implicitly ruled against obvious types of speculation for being unproductive activity, in which one's gain was another's loss. On the other hand, autonomy moralists would rarely limit the freedom of individuals to speculate, supporting this permissive view with economic examples in which speculation might actually benefit society (e.g., if a speculator accurately foresaw a shortage of something, bought it when abundant, stored it, and sold it when scarce, this speculator would actually increase supplies of the item when it was most needed). A more relational morality was evident in Mark Twain's novel, *The Gilded Age*, in which speculation was portrayed as ruining lives.

2. A literal reading of this passage would be that Samuelson expected only *economists* to care for the common good (e.g., Nelson 2001, 99–100). This is a strained reading, for Samuelson's textbook audience was beginning economics *students*, whom he clearly wanted to enlist as voting citizens to support the common good. Samuelson consistently affirmed that social decisions are democratic decisions.

3. Given Samuelson's attacks on the "necessary and inevitable" laws of the old political economy, and by his emphasis on the power of the democratic will to change economic institutions, we reject one scholar's classification of Samuelson as part of a natural-law tradition (Nelson 2001, 102). Samuelson's text consistently promoted democratic control of economic arrangements.

CHAPTER TWELVE. TOO AGNOSTIC, TOO CERTAIN: WELFARE ECONOMICS, CHICAGO ECONOMICS

1. Three types of efficiency improvements exist. The first is allocation efficiency, the movement of inputs and outputs to those uses that are of the highest value to society; competitive markets fulfill the technical rules for achieving this type of efficiency and prices guide the movements of resources. A second type of efficiency is increased utilization of unemployed resources. Finally, the exploitation of previously ignored knowledge or technique (sometimes called X-efficiency) also matters. The most orthodox of the neoclassical economists deny the possibility of the second and third types of efficiency.

2. If preferences are intertwined (as with altruism or envy), the competitive price of something will not equal the sum of its values to consumers and so will not lead to allocation efficiency. When one person's consumption changes the welfare of other people, the technical conditions for market efficiency will not be fulfilled. Thus, welfare economists solved a problem by deciding that people must be egoistic.

3. This is strikingly similar to the philosophical Pragmatists' view of theories. Consider William James (1975, 103) on particle physics: "It is, as I have said, *as if* reality were made of ether, atoms, or electrons, but we mustn't think so literally."

4. In only one sense is self-interested economic man "free." Although totally destined to do exactly what he does (given preferences and constraints, etc.), economic man *feels* free because he acts according to his own preferences.

5. Karl Sigmund and others (2002, 83–87) review results from experimental economics; these results contradict the neoclassical assumption of self interest. In the "ultimatum" game, one player has a sum of money and must propose a split with the other player. The second player may accept or reject the proposal, with rejection meaning that the money is lost to both. The neoclassical theory of self-interest implies that the first player will offer as little as possible because the second player knows that anything is better than nothing and so will accept. According to the researchers, two-thirds of offers are close to fifty percent and low offers of less than twenty percent are rejected more than half the time. Low offers are rejected for being "unfair"—an ethical norm. Sigmund also reports that "real people" in other game situations cooperate for mutual gains, and punish free riders who join in the collective reward without contributing; again, such behavior does not fit the self-interest theory.

6. Neoclassical theory implies that more choices increase individual welfare because one can more closely match what is available to one's preferences. Yet, Schwartz (2004, 71–75) reports that "maximizers"—people with personalities most like that posited in neoclassical theory—report less happiness than nonmaximizers, who mostly ignore the extra choice, when confronted with a large number of choices. Schwartz reviews several possible psychological explanations for the unhappiness of "maximizer" personalities. An economic explanation for the lesser happiness is that maximizers continue to sort through choices when the expected benefit of further search is less than the expected cost or bother. This does not help the neoclassical theory, because failing to stop soon enough is in itself nonmaximizing behavior.

CHAPTER THIRTEEN. MORALISTS OF TWENTIETH-CENTURY CAPITALISM

1. The alternative view is that morality surely *can* be reasoned about. Moral values imply some notion of the good, of rights, and of obligations; these are tied together in ways about which it is possible to reason. Rights and obligations are exercised by humans in relation to other humans; they certainly have to make sense as ways humans interact with each other. If humans have much in common, then surely people can understand each other enough for reasonable moral discussion to occur.

2. Friedman might have replied that the ability of dissenting shareholders to get out of the stock of a socially responsible company unscathed is imperfect. Perhaps, but in the years since Friedman wrote, mutual funds that explicitly invest in socially responsible companies have sprung up. Ironically, alternative investment vehicles, which ignore libertarian strictures, survive the test of the market.

3. Neoclassical economics gives operational meaning to this view of humanity. Its theory involves maximizing the "utility" of a person who is defined exclusively by the particular preferences he or she has. The *source* of the preferences is never an issue—if the question is raised, it is said to fall outside the domain of economics. Given preferences, relative prices, and one's budget, the solution to a neoclassical problem shows

what one should consume to obtain the greatest utility (sense of welfare). The point is that in neoclassical theory a person *is* his or her particular preferences and *nothing else*. If one thinks of preferences as desires, a person is exclusively an autonomous ego.

CHAPTER FOURTEEN. UNCONVENTIONAL ALTERNATIVES TO THE CONVENTIONAL WISDOM

1. For example, the text by Jack Hirshleifer (1984) does not even list the word advertising in its index. As for preference formation: "The economist regards the process whereby individuals somehow become pointed toward particular desired ends as outside his sphere of competence. . . . [Tastes and preferences] are, from his point of view, arbitrary" (Hirschleifter 1984, 9). This assertion means that the economic actor is a completely autonomous agent—wrapped up within his or her private preference system.

2. There is a rejoinder: if Keynesian policies reduce unemployment, this reduces poverty and thus serves the common good. But a Galbraithian reply would be that income security for the poor easily could be provided in an affluent society without exclusive reliance on high-employment policy, which is a blunt instrument. Keynesian policies potentially could result in the production of more and more, perhaps to extremes, without necessarily ever ending poverty.

3. It is understandable that Sen wishes to deny the authority of Adam Smith to the self-interest school. However, in his later book, *The Wealth of Nations*, Smith did make self-interest the relevant motive in economic life

CHAPTER FIFTEEN. AN ECUMENICAL CONSENSUS ON ECONOMIC ETHICS

1. Michael Novak was the vice-chairman of a "commission" of prominent, conservative, lay Catholics who in 1984 published a preemptive "lay letter" on "Catholic Social Thought and the U.S. Economy." This document anticipated the bishops' pastoral letter by two years and implicitly criticized it. Drafts of the bishops' letter had circulated in advance.

2. The four characteristics of social science as outlined by Bellah also describe economics as a discipline. The utility-maximizing model purports to explain "rational" behavior. It simultaneously reduces the meaning of "rationality" to little more than self-interested calculations. It is relativistic, for the utility model takes "preferences" as arbitrary "givens" of individuals. This means they are outside the realm of moral discourse and no preferences are better than any other preferences. There are only preferences—no norms. And, finally, economic thought is deterministic, for the calculating utility-maximizer will predictably adjust his or her movements in the direction dictated by relative prices, income, and other constraints.

3. McFague too easily blends classical and neoclassical economics, although her main point is well taken. Neoclassical economics emerged in the later part of the nineteenth century as the successor to the classical economics of Smith, Ricardo, and Malthus and laissez-faire. Although economic growth is arguably an intrinsic goal of

modern economics, as MacFague claims, this was not the view of the earlier classical economists. In their view, population would grow, but other resources would not. Thus, life for most would be miserable: hence political economy was dubbed the "dismal science" (see chapter 4). A thoroughgoing integration of ideas of technical change, productivity measurement, and economic growth occurred only well into the twentieth century and was indeed advanced by neoclassical economists. Even so, neoclassical economics, as theory, has not made growth a central focus. However, it may be argued that the utility-maximizing individual, for whom desires are in principle insatiable, equates economic growth with the highest good.

Works Cited

Ahlstrom, Sydney E. 1972. *A Religious History of the American People*. New Haven, CT: Yale University Press.

Ames, William. 1643. *Conscience with the Power and Cases Thereof*. Microtext. N.p.

Atwood, Craig D. 2004. *Community of the Cross: Moravian Piety in Colonial Bethlehem*. University Park: Pennsylvania State University Press.

Bainton, Roland. 1952. *The Reformation of the Sixteenth Century*. Boston: Beacon Press.

Barton, Bruce. 1924. *The Man Nobody Knows: A Discovery of the Real Jesus*. Indianapolis: Bobbs-Merrill.

Bateman, Bradley, and Ethan B. Kapstein.1999. "Between God and the Market: The Religious Roots of the American Economic Association." *Journal of Economic Perspectives* 14.4: 249–58.

Baumol, William J. 1965. *Economic Theory and Operations Analysis*. 2nd ed. Englewood Cliffs, NJ: Prentice-Hall.

Beckley, Harlan. 1992. *Passion for Justice*. Louisville, KY: Westminster/John Knox Press.

Bellah, Robert. 1981. "Biblical Religion and Social Science in the Modern World." *National Institute for Campus Ministries Journal* 6. 3: 8–22.

Bellah, Robert, Richard Madsen, William M. Sullivan, Ann Swidler, and Steven M. Tipton. 1985. *Habits of the Heart: Individualism and Commitment in American Life*. New York: Harper and Row.

Bellamy Edward. 1888. *Looking Backward*. New York: NAL Penguin, 1960.

Bernstein, Paul. 1997. *American Work Values: Their Origin and Development*. Albany: State University of New York Press.

Boulding, Kenneth. 1968. *Beyond Economics: Essays on Society, Religion and Ethics*. Ann Arbor: University of Michigan Press, 1970.

Brotherly Agreement and Contract of the Evangelische Brüder-Gemeine at Salem, in North Carolina. 1773. F. Cumnock trans., 1992. Digital file. Winston-Salem, NC: Archives of the Moravian Church, Southern Province.

Carnegie, Andrew. 1889. *The Gospel of Wealth and Other Timely Essays*. Garden City, NY: Doubleday, 1933.

Clark, John Bates. 1886. *The Philosophy of Wealth: Economic Principles Newly Formulated*. Reprint. New York: Augustus M. Kelley, 1967.

———. 1899. *The Distribution of Wealth: A Theory of Wages, Interest and Profits*. Reprint. New York: Augustus M. Kelley, 1965.

Constantine, J. Robert. 1991. "Eugene V. Debs: An American Paradox." *Monthly Labor Review* 114.8: 30–33.

Cotton, John. 1641. *The Way of Life*. Microfiche. London: n. p. (Library Resources).

Crews, C. Daniel, and R. W. Starbuck. 2002. *With Courage for the Future: The Story of the Moravian Church, Southern Province*. Winston-Salem, NC: Moravian Church in America, Southern Province.

Crowley, J. E. 1974. *This Sheba, SELF: The Conceptualization of Economic Life in Eighteenth Century America*. Baltimore: Johns Hopkins Press.

Davis, J. Ronnie. 1971. *The New Economics and the Old Economics*. Ames: Iowa State University Press.

Debs, Eugene. 1908. *Debs: His Life, Writings and Speeches* (including biography by Stephen M. Reynolds). Girard, KS: The Appeal to Reason.

Dorfman, Joseph. 1946. *The Economic Mind in American Civilization, 1606–1865*, Vols. 1–2. New York: Viking Press.

Easterlin, Richard. 1996. *Growth Triumphant*. Ann Arbor: University of Michigan Press.

Edgell, Stephen. 2001. *Veblen in Perspective: His Life and Thought*. Armonk, NY: M.E. Sharpe.

Ely, Richard T. 1886. *The Labor Movement in America*. New York: Crowell.

———. 1889. *Social Aspects of Christianity and Other Essays*. New and enlarged edition. Microfiche. New York: Crowell (Library Resources).

———. 1916. *Outlines of Economics*. 3rd ed., rev. New York: Macmillan.

———. 1938. *Ground under Our Feet: An Autobiography*. New York: Macmillan.

Etzioni, Amitai. 1988. *The Moral Dimension: Toward a New Economics*. New York: Free Press.

Fogel, Robert, and Stanley Engerman. 1974. *Time on the Cross: The Economics of American Negro Slavery*. Boston: Little, Brown.

Franklin, Benjamin. 1987. *Benjamin Franklin: Writings*. Ed. J. A. L. Lemay. New York: Library Classics.

Frey, Donald E. 1988. "High Prices and Bad Money: How Salem Coped During the Revolution." *The Three Forks of Muddy Creek*, Vol. XIII. Ed. Frances Griffin. Winston-Salem, NC: Old Salem Inc.

———. 1998. "Individualist Economic Values and Self Interest: The Problem in the Puritan Ethic." *Journal of Business Ethics* 17.14: 1573–80.

———. 2000. "The Puritan Roots of Daniel Raymond's Economics." *History of Political Economy* 32. 3: 607–629.

———. 2002. "Francis Wayland's 1830s Textbooks: Evangelical Ethics and Political Economy." *Journal of History of Economic Thought* 24.2: 215–31.

Friedman, Milton. 1953. *Essays in Positive Economics*. Chicago: University of Chicago Press.

———. 1962. *Capitalism and Freedom*. Chicago: University of Chicago Press.

Friends Committee on National Legislation. 1994. "Statement of Legislative Policy." *Washington Newsletter, 582* (December).

Galbraith, John Kenneth. 1958. *The Affluent Society*. 40th anniversary ed. Boston: Houghton Mifflin, 1998.

———. 1960. *The Liberal Hour*. New York: New American Library, 1964.

———. 1967. *The New Industrial State*. Boston: Houghton Mifflin.

———. 1973. *Economics and the Public Purpose*. Boston: Houghton Mifflin.

Garrison, William Lloyd. 1966. *Documents of Upheaval: Selections from William Lloyd Garrison's The Liberator, 1831–1865*. Ed. Truman Nelson. New York: Hill and Wang.

George, Henry. 1879. *Progress and Poverty*. New York: Schalkenback Foundation, 1936.

———. 1898. *The Land Question, Etc.* New York: Doubleday & McClure.

Hamilton, Alexander. 1956. *The Basic Ideas of Alexander Hamilton*. Ed. Richard B. Morris. New York: Washington Square Press

———. 1966. *The Papers of Alexander Hamilton*, Vol. X. Ed. Harold C. Syrett. New York: Columbia University Press.

Hamilton, Alexander, James Madison, and John Jay. 1787–88. *The Federalist Papers*. New York: New American Library, 1961.

Hansen, Alvin H. 1953. *A Guide to Keynes*. New York: McGraw-Hill.

Harrison, Peter. 1998. *The Bible, Protestantism, and the Rise of Natural Science*. Cambridge, UK: Cambridge University Press.

Hay, Donald. 1989. *Economics Today: A Christian Critique*. Grand Rapids, MI: Eerdmans.

Hayek, Friedrich A. 1944. *The Road to Serfdom*. Chicago: University of Chicago Press.

Heilbronner, Robert. 1972. *The Worldly Philosophers*. 4th ed. New York: Simon and Schuster.

Herbst, Jurgen. 1965. *The German Historical School in American Scholarship*. Ithaca, NY: Cornell University Press.

Heschel, Abraham Joshua. 1955. *God in Search of Man: A Philosophy of Judaism*. New York: Harper and Row, 1966.

Hirschleifer, Jack. 1984. *Price Theory and Applications*. 3rd ed. Englewood Cliffs, NJ: Prentice-Hall.

Hofstadter, Richard. 1955. *Social Darwinism in American Thought*. Rev. ed. Boston: Beacon Press.

Hoshor, John. 1936. *God in a Rolls Royce*. New York: Hillman-Curl.

James, William. 1975. *The Works of William James: Pragmatism*. Cambridge: Harvard University Press.

Keynes, John Maynard. 1936. *The General Theory of Employment, Interest, and Money*. San Diego, NY, London: Harcourt Brace Jovanovich, 1964.

Knight, Frank H. 1999. *Selected Essays*, Vols. 1–2. Ed. Ross B. Emmett. Chicago: University of Chicago Press.

Laurent, John. 2005. "Henry George: Evolutionary Economist"? In John Laurent, ed., *Henry George's Legacy in Economic Thought*. Cheltenham, UK: Edward Elgar.

Leo XIII (Pope). 1891. *On the Condition of Labor*. In James P. Sweeney, S.J., ed., *Seven Great Encyclicals*. New York: Paulist Press, 1963.

Malthus, Thomas Robert. 1798. *An Essay on the Principle of Population*. Ed. Antony Flew. Harmondsworth: Penguin, 1970.

Mann, Horace. 1957. *The Republic and the School: Horace Mann on the Education of Free Men*. Ed. Lawrence A. Cremin. New York: Teachers College, Columbia University.

Marcet, Jane. 1827. *Conversations on Political Economy*. 6th ed. London: Longman.

Mather, Cotton. 1710. *Essays to Do Good*. New York: American Tract Society, n.d. (1840 estimated).

May, Henry. 1967. *Protestant Churches and Industrial America*. New York: Harper and Row.

McElvaine, Robert S. 1984. *The Great Depression: America, 1929–1941*. New York: Times Books.

McFague, Sallie. 2001. *Life Abundant: Rethinking Theology and Economy for a Planet in Peril*. Minneapolis: Fortress Press

McLaughlin-Jenkins, Erin. 2005. "Henry George and Darwin's Dragon: Thomas Huxley's Response to *Progress and Poverty*." In John Laurent, ed., *Henry George's Legacy in Economic Thought*. Cheltenham, UK: Edward Elgar.

Merton, Robert. 1938. *Science, Technology & Society in Seventeenth Century England*. Reprint. New York: Howard Fertig, 1970.

Michaels, David. 2005. "Doubt Is Their Product." *Scientific American* 292. 6 (June): 96–101.

Mill, John Stuart. 1965. *Essential Works of John Stuart Mill*. Ed. Max Lerner. New York: Bantam Books.

Miller, Perry. 1953. *The New England Mind*, Vol. 2. Boston: Beacon Press, 1961.

———. 1956. *Errand into the Wilderness*. Cambridge: Harvard University Press (Belknap).

Miller, Robert Moats. 1958. *American Protestantism and Social Issues, 1919–1939*. Chapel Hill: University of North Carolina Press.

Morgan, E. S., ed. 1965. *Puritan Political Ideas, 1558–1794.* Indianapolis: Bobbs-Merrill.

Myers, Milton L. 1983. *The Soul of Modern Economic Man.* Chicago: University of Chicago Press.

National Conference of Catholic Bishops. 1986. *Economic Justice for All: Pastoral Letter on Catholic Social Teaching and the U.S. Economy.* Washington, DC: National Conference of Catholic Bishops.

Nelson, Robert H. 1991. *Reaching for Heaven on Earth: The Theological Meaning of Economics.* Savage, MD: Rowman and Littlefield.

———. 1998. "Economic Religion Versus Christian Values." *Journal of Markets and Morality* 1.2: 142–57.

———. 2001. *Economics as Religion: from Samuelson to Chicago and Beyond.* University Park: Pennsylvania State University Press.

Noll, Mark A. 2002. *God and Mammon: Protestants, Money, and the Market, 1790–1860.* New York and Oxford: Oxford University Press.

———. 2006. "Impasse over Slavery: Battle for the Bible." *Christian Century* 123.9 (May 2): 20–25.

Novak, Michael. 1982 . *The Spirit of Democratic Capitalism.* London: IEA Health and Welfare Unit, 1991.

———. 1997. *On Corporate Governance: The Corporation as it Ought to Be.* Washington, DC: AEI Press.

Okun, Arthur. 1975. *Equality and Efficiency: The Big Tradeoff.* Washington, DC: Brookings.

Paley, William. 1790. *The Principles of Moral and Political Philosophy,* Vol. 1. 7th ed. (corrected). London: Faulder.

Penn, William. 1957. *The Witness of William Penn.* Ed. F. T. Tolles and E. G. Alderfer. New York: Macmillan.

Phelps, Elizabeth S. 1871. *The Silent Partner.* Reprint. Wesbury, CT: Feminist Press, 1983.

Rauschenbusch, Walter. 1907. *Christianity and the Social Crisis.* New York: Macmillan.

———. 1912. *Christianizing the Social Order.* New York: Macmillan.

Rawls, John B. 2001. *Justice as Fairness: A Restatement.* Cambridge: Harvard University Press (Belknap).

Raymond, Daniel. 1823. *The Elements of Political Economy Vols. 1, 2.* 2nd ed. Reprint. New York: Augustus M. Kelly, 1964.

Robinson, Joan. 1962. *Economic Philosophy: An Essay on the Progress of Economic Thought.* Garden City, NY: Doubleday.

Ryan, John A. 1996. *Economic Justice: Selections from Distributive Justice and A Living Wage.* Ed. Harlan R. Beckley. Louisville, KY: Westminster/John Knox.

Sadowsky, James W. 1986. "Classical Social Doctrine in the Roman Catholic Church." In Walter Block and Irving Hexham, eds., *Religion, Economics and Social Thought: Proceedings of an International Symposium.* Vancouver, BC: Fraser Institute.

Samuels, Warren J., Kirk D. Johnson, and Marianne F. Johnson. 2005. "The Duke of Argyll and Henry George: Land Ownership and Governance." In John Laurent, ed., *Henry George's Legacy in Economic Thought.* Cheltenham, UK: Edward Elgar.

Samuelson, Paul A. 1947. *Foundations of Economic Analysis.* New York: Atheneum, 1970.

———. 1958. *Economics: An Introductory Analysis.* 4th ed. New York: McGraw-Hill.

Sandoz, Ellis, ed. 1991. *Political Sermons of the American Founding Era: 1730–1805.* Indianapolis: Liberty Press.

Schumaker, E. F. 1973. *Small Is Beautiful, A Study of Economics as if People Mattered.* London: Blond & Briggs.

Schwartz, Barry. 2004. "The Tyranny of Choice." *Scientific American* 291 (April): 71–75.

Sen, Amartya. 1987. *On Ethics and Economics.* Oxford and New York: Blackwell, 1988.

Sensbach, Jon. F. 1998. *A Separate Canaan: The Making of an Afro-Moravian World in N.C, 1763–1840.* Chapel Hill: University of North Carolina Press.

Sessler, Jacob John. 1933. *Communal Pietism Among Early American Moravians.* AMS edition. New York: Henry Holt, 1971.

Sigmund, Karl, Ernst Fehr, and Martin A. Nowak. 2002. "The Economics of Fair Play." *Scientific American* 285 (January): 83–87.

Skidelsky, Robert. 1992. *John Maynard Keynes: The Economist as Saviour, 1920–1937.* London: Macmillan.

Sklansky, Jeffrey. 2002. *The Soul's Economy: Market Society and Selfhood in American Thought, 1820–1920.* Chapel Hill: University of North Carolina Press.

Smith, Adam. 1776. *An Inquiry into the Nature and Causes of the Wealth of Nations.* Modern Library edition. New York: Random House, 1937.

———. 1759. *The Theory of Moral Sentiments.* Ed. D. D. Raphael and A. L. Macfie. Reprint of Oxford University Press edition of 1976. Indianapolis: Liberty Fund, 1982.

Smith, Wilson. 1954. "William Paley's Theological Utilitarianism in America." *William and Mary Quarterly* 11.3 (July): 402–24.

Smucker, Donovan. E. 1994. *The Origins of Walter Rauschenbusch's Social Ethics.* Montreal & Kingston: McGill-Queen's University Press.

Spencer, Herbert. 1884. *The Man Versus the State with Six Essays on Government, Society, Freedom.* Indianapolis: Liberty Fund, 1982.

Stabile, Donald R. 2000. "Unions and the Natural Standard of Wages: Another Look at the 'J. B. Clark Problem'." *History of Political Economy* 32.3: 585–606.

Stackhouse, Max L. 1987. *Public Theology and Political Economy: Christian Stewardship in Modern Society.* Grand Rapids, MI: Eerdmans.

Stigler, George J. 1975. *The Citizen and the State: Essays on Regulation.* Chicago: University of Chicago Press.

———. 1982. *The Economist as Preacher and Other Essays* (Tanner Lectures). Chicago: University of Chicago Press

Stowe, Harriet Beecher. 1852. *Uncle Tom's Cabin.* New York: NAL, 1998.

Sumner, William Graham. 1883. *What the Social Classes Owe to Each Other.* New York: Harper and Brothers, 1920.

———. 1963. *Social Darwinism, Selected Essays.* Ed. William Leuchtenburg and Bernard Wishy. Englewood Cliffs, NJ: Prentice-Hall.

Thorp, Daniel B. 1989. *The Moravian Community in Colonial North Carolina.* Knoxville: University of Tennessee Press.

Tocqueville, Alexis (de). 1835. *Democracy in America*, Vol. II. New York: Knopf, 1945.

Tugwell, Rexford G. 1933. *The Industrial Discipline and the Governmental Arts.* New York: Columbia University Press.

———. 1968. *The Brains Trust.* New York: Viking.

Uriarte, Brian (de). 1990. "On the Free Will of Rational Agents in Neoclassical Theory." *Journal of Post Keynesian Economics* 12.4 (Summer): 605–17.

Veblen, Thorstein. 1899. *Theory of the Leisure Class.* Reprint. Fairfield, NJ: Augustus M. Kelley, 1991.

———. 1904. *The Theory of Business Enterprise.* New York: Scribner's, 1927.

Viner, Jacob. 1972. *The Role of Providence in the Social Order.* Philadelphia: American Philosophical Society.

Watts, Jill. 1992. *God, Harlem U.S.A: The Father Divine Story.* Berkeley and Los Angles: University of California Press.

Wayland, Francis. 1837a. *The Elements of Moral Science.* 2nd ed. Ed. J. L. Blau. Cambridge: Belknap Press, 1963.

———. 1837b. *The Elements of Political Economy.* Microfiche. New York: Leavitt, Lord and Co. (Library Resources, 1970).

Weber, Max. 1930. *The Protestant Ethic and the Spirit of Capitalism.* New York: Scribner's, 1958.

Weld, Theodore Dwight, ed. 1839. *American Slavery and It Is: The Testimony of a Thousand Witnesses.* Reprint. Ed. William Katz. New York: Arno Press and New York Times, 1968.

Wogaman, Philip. 1986. *Economics and Ethics: A Christian Inquiry.* Philadelphia: Fortress Press.

Woolman, John. 1971. *The Journal and Major Essays of John Woolman.* Ed. Phillip Moulton. New York: Oxford University Press.

Wright, Conrad, E. 1992. *The Transformation of Charity in Postrevolutionary New England.* Boston: Northeastern University Press.

Index